# The Opioid Crisis

Books in the **Contemporary World Issues** series address vital issues in today's society such as genetic engineering, pollution, and biodiversity. Written by professional writers, scholars, and nonacademic experts, these books are authoritative, clearly written, up-to-date, and objective. They provide a good starting point for research by high school and college students, scholars, and general readers as well as by legislators, businesspeople, activists, and others.

Each book, carefully organized and easy to use, contains an overview of the subject, a detailed chronology, biographical sketches, facts and data and/or documents and other primary source material, a forum of authoritative perspective essays, annotated lists of print and nonprint resources, and an index.

Readers of books in the Contemporary World Issues series will find the information they need in order to have a better understanding of the social, political, environmental, and economic issues facing the world today.

# The Opioid Crisis

## A REFERENCE HANDBOOK

David E. Newton

 ABC-CLIO™

An Imprint of ABC-CLIO, LLC
Santa Barbara, California • Denver, Colorado

**Library of Congress Cataloging-in-Publication Data**

Names: Newton, David E., author.
Title: The opioid crisis : a reference handbook / David E. Newton.
Description: Santa Barbara, California : ABC-CLIO, [2018] | Series: Contemporary world issues | Includes bibliographical references and index.
Identifiers: LCCN 2018014178 (print) | LCCN 2018014619 (ebook) | ISBN 9781440864360 (ebook) | ISBN 9781440864353 (alk. paper)
Subjects: | MESH: Opioid-Related Disorders—prevention & control | Opioid-Related Disorders—history | Analgesics, Opioid—adverse effects | United States
Classification: LCC RC568.O45 (ebook) | LCC RC568.O45 (print) | NLM WM 284 | DDC 615.7/822—dc23
LC record available at https://lccn.loc.gov/2018014178

ISBN: 978-1-4408-6435-3 (print)
        978-1-4408-6436-0 (ebook)

22  21  20  19  18      1  2  3  4  5

This book is also available as an eBook.

ABC-CLIO
An Imprint of ABC-CLIO, LLC

ABC-CLIO, LLC
130 Cremona Drive, P.O. Box 1911
Santa Barbara, California 93116-1911
www.abc-clio.com

This book is printed on acid-free paper ∞

Manufactured in the United States of America

# Preface

Sam Banting was feeling a different kind of "high" on this day. After a very long struggle with opioids, he thought his life was going to turn around. He had been accepted for admission to a well-known treatment center just over 100 miles from his home. He would be starting treatment the next morning and would be on the road to recovery. His wife kissed him goodbye, knowing in her heart that the next time she would see Sam, he would be "clean," or at least making good progress in that direction. The next day she got a phone call from the treatment center. Sam was dead.

The names are fictitious, but the story line is not. In fact, Sam's tale is not at all that dissimilar from thousands of men and women in the United States whose lives have been, at the least, disrupted and, at worst, brought to an end by the nation's opioid epidemic.

The facts used to describe this epidemic are now well known to almost anyone who reads the newspapers or watches news reports on television or the Internet. In 2015 (the last year for which data are available), some 12.5 million Americans misused legal prescription opioids. Just over 2 million of those individuals misused prescription opioids for the first time. Of those numbers, 33,091 users died of an opioid overdose, an average of 90 people every day of the year. In the same year, 828,000 individuals used heroin on a regular basis, leading to 12,989 deaths in the year. Overall, the epidemic was thought to have cost the nation an estimated \$78.5 billion in one year. (All data are from the U.S. Department of Health and Human Services; https://www.hhs.gov/opioids/about-the-epidemic/index.html. Accessed on January 2, 2018.)

Opioids are the most powerful of analgesics, compounds that relieve pain. Their use for this purpose dates back thousands of years, providing the medical profession with one of the most effective of all healing tools in its arsenal. At the same time, opioids have been used for nonmedical purposes as well, purposes that arise out of their tendency to produce feelings of euphoria in a user. Through all these centuries, then, opioids have been a true double-edged sword, with both highly effective medical applications and pleasant but potentially harmful side effects.

If opioids have been around for thousands of years, why are they suddenly responsible for a crisis in the United States and other parts of the world? An important element in that story has been the discovery and synthesis of a whole class of new drugs derived from or based on the oldest of all opiates (opium-related drugs). These compounds are known as *opioids*, a term that originally was meant to distinguish between naturally occurring or semisynthetic derivatives of opium (opiates) and compounds that are totally synthetic, but that work in largely the same way as those substances (opioids). Today, the latter term has been adopted for any compound whose neurophysiological effects are the same as or like those of morphine, the primary analgesic compound in opium.

Cultural attitudes about the opioids have changed significantly over the years. At one time, they were regarded as useful medical products which a few individuals used for recreational purposes, a trend that most societies regarded as sometimes unfortunate but not a major issue to be dealt with through legislation or other forms of opprobrium. In some places at some times in history, opioids actually became quite popular among selected groups of individuals, soldiers returning from the Civil War, women hoping to escape the humdrum of their daily lives, or Victorian artists looking for a "new and different" reality, for example.

Largely through the efforts of pharmaceutical companies, opioids have come to play yet another new role in society. They have become the last therapeutic resort for millions of Americans who suffer from chronic pain, offering a solution that makes life livable for those individuals. But it has also made possible a flood of substances—opioids—for drug abusers who are unaware of or unable to deal with the terrible consequences of dependence and/or addiction to the compounds.

Within the past decade, the opioid crisis has taken another turn, with some abusers moving away from synthetic opioids, such as oxycodone and hydromorphone, to an "old familiar" drug, morphine, or to even more powerful synthetic opioids, such as fentanyl and carfentanil. Designed originally as an analgesic for large animals, such as elephants, the latter compound is said to be 10,000 times as potent as morphine, providing a "high" unmatched by any other opioid with, however, potentially deadly effects.

Therefore, what is to be done about the opioid epidemic in the United States? One part of the answer to that question is that whatever steps are taken, the bill will be high. In the 2017 tax reform bill adopted by the Republican Party in the U.S. Congress, $45 billion was set aside for state grants to deal with the crisis over the next decade. That may seem like a very large amount of money, but many experts argue that is not nearly adequate to meet the problem. Richard Frank, a health economist at the Harvard Medical School, estimated that the crisis would cost the U.S. economy about $14 billion in 2018 and more than $183 billion over the next decade.

Complicating the challenge for health care workers in dealing with the opioid crisis are questions about the best possible way of preventing and treating the epidemic. A number of options have been proposed for helping individuals dealing with opioid dependence and addiction, but no single approach appears to be the best method for dealing with the issue.

This book attempts to provide readers with a history and background of the opioid crises worldwide and throughout the ages (Chapter 1), with special emphasis on current issues and problems and their proposed solutions (Chapter 2). Chapter 3 provides nine contributors to write about their personal experience with the crisis and about other, more detailed, aspects of the epidemic. Chapter 4 includes short biographical and descriptive sections of individuals and organizations that have played a role in opioid issues throughout history, and Chapter 5 is a collection of current data and relevant documents dealing with the issue. Chapter 6 provides an annotated bibliography of important books, articles, reports, and Internet resources on the opioid epidemic, while Chapter 7 consists of a collection of important events in the history of opioid use. The book concludes with a glossary of important terms in the field.

# The Opioid Crisis

Oh, just, subtle, and mighty opium! that to the hearts of poor and rich alike, for the wounds that will never heal, and for "the pangs that tempt the spirit to rebel," bringest an assuaging balm; eloquent opium! that with thy potent rhetoric stealest away the purposes of wrath; and to the guilty man for one night givest back the hopes of his youth, and hands washed pure from blood; and to the proud man a brief oblivion for Wrongs undress'd and insults unavenged.

—De Quincey (1821)

Any number of famous individuals throughout history have experimented with, or become addicted to, opium. Those with a literary bent have tried to express the attraction of the drug as a release from the problems or boredom of everyday life. Thomas De Quincey, in one of the most famous works on opium ever published, is one of the best-known advocates for the use of opium as a way of escaping the real world.

Similar sentiments, although probably in not quite so elegant language, are heard from individuals who use opium and opium products in today's world. In a personal story about

---

An image from the 1674 text, *Opiologia*, depicting a man in Eastern garb slicing an opium bud in a garden. (National Library of Medicine)

opium addiction from less than a decade ago, author Steve Martin writes of the pleasures he had from smoking the drug:

> Closing my eyes for a moment I savored a miracle: the total banishment of pain. The vacuum was instantly replaced by a deliciously tingling wave that crept up the base of my neck and caressed my head with something akin to a divine massage. Whereas moments before my muscles had felt like they were being pinched by countless angry crabs, there now was a soothing sensation of calm and well-being. (Martin 2012, 12)

It probably goes without saying that opium has effects on the human body other than those experienced in the first hours after use, effects such as relief from pain, a sense of relaxation, reduced feelings of anxiety, and a general sense at being "at peace with the world." Those later effects can be so serious as to be life threatening. Indeed, deaths from opioid overdose have increased dramatically in the past few decades. (The term *opioid* is used to describe opium and all its natural and synthetic derivatives.) In 1999, 4,040 deaths due to opioid overdose were recorded in the United States, a rate of about 1.4 deaths per 100,000 Americans. That number began to increase slowly over the next decade, reaching 10,928 in 2005 (3.7 deaths per 100,000). But the number and rate of opioid-related deaths then began to rise dramatically, reaching 20,101 (10.4 per 100,000) in 2015. The number of deaths from opioid poisoning has, therefore, increased almost 400 percent in about 15 years ("Data Brief 166: Drug-Poisoning Deaths Involving Opioid Analgesics: United States, 1999–2011" 2016; Rudd et al. 2016). The magnitude of these numbers prompted President Donald Trump in 2017 to declare the nation's current opioid epidemic as "a national health emergency" ("Remarks by President Trump on Combatting [*sic*] Drug Demand and the Opioid Crisis" 2017). Experts are not optimistic about improvement in the current opioid epidemic. According to one estimate, the number of opioid-related deaths could increase to 93,613 in 2027, an increase of 183 percent over the 2015 figure (Blau 2017). Particularly troubling is the fact that the abuse rate and death rate from opioids among young adults are the highest among any age group. In 2014, for example, a total of 1,741 young men and women between the ages of 18 and 25 died from opioid overdose. That comes out to five individuals per day throughout the year. And those numbers are only a hint of the extent of the epidemic. For every 1 overdose fatality, there were 119 emergency department visits and 22 admissions for treatment ("Abuse of Prescription (Rx) Drugs Affects Young Adults Most" 2016).

## The Opium Plant: An Introduction

In its pure form, opium is a white, crystalline powder. It is obtained from the poppy plant (*Papaver somniferum*) that is familiar to many home gardeners. The plant is a showy annual with conspicuous white, pink, red, or purple flowers. The opium is extracted from the unripe seed pods, by lightly cutting the skin of the pods and allowing a white milky fluid (latex) to seep out. (An illustration of this process is available at Bushak 2016.) The fluid is then dried to form crystalline opium. The poppy plant is also used for the production of other, legal, culinary products, the most common of which is poppy seeds. Poppy seeds contain very small amounts of opium and codeine, another product of the poppy plant.

Opium destined for illegal use is generally processed before shipment to users. It is treated chemically to remove the most psychoactive part of the plant, morphine. A single pound of opium yields about two ounces of morphine. The morphine is then converted chemically to heroin, which is more potent than morphine itself. The resultant heroin, which weighs only about 10 percent the weight of the morphine from which it comes, is then formed into bricks that can be transported more easily than either opium or morphine. Its compact form makes it relatively easy to smuggle across borders and into users' hands.

Opium is also produced for legal purposes, primarily in the medical field. This opium is produced under tightly controlled licenses issued by the United States and other governmental agencies. Currently, most legal opium is produced in Turkey, India, Tasmania, France, Japan, and Great Britain. The illegal opium economy is a much different story, with Afghanistan the world's leading producer of the substance. An estimated 3,300 tons of oven-dry opium was produced in that country in 2015 (the most recent year for which data are available), about 70 percent of all illegal opium produced worldwide in that year. Other major producers were Myanmar (647 tons), Mexico (475 tons), and Laos (92 tons in 2014) ("World Drug Report 2016" 2016, Annex, ix–x). By comparison, the total amount of legal opium produced in 2015 was about 661 tons, of which the largest quantities came from France (204 tons), Turkey (113 tons), and Australia (112 tons) ("Supply of Opiate Raw Materials and Demand for Opiates for Medical and Scientific Purposes" 2015, Table 2, 103).

## The History of Opium to 1800

The origins of opium use in human civilizations have been the subject of extensive research by archaeologists, ethnobotanists, historians of drug use, and other academics interested in the topic. One of the earliest dates mentioned by some authorities is about 30,000 years ago, based on the discovery of fossilized poppy seeds in Neanderthal settlements (see, e.g., "Origins and History of Opium" 1994). Even if this date is correct, there is no way of determining if these were accidental remains of a wild plant or whether they came from cultivated plants used for reasons that can probably never be determined by researchers.

A more common attribution gives sometime in the sixth millennium for the period in which human societies were definitely using opium plants. This claim is based on the discovery of fossilized opium seeds, made in the early 1990s by a team of Italian archaeologists led by Dr. M. A. Fugazzola Delpino (1993). Fugazzola Delpino hypothesized that the seeds had been grown by the inhabitants of a Neolithic farming community on the shores of Lake Bracciano for "food, oil, medicine, and possibly cult use." The last of these uses was predicated on the presence of the poppy seeds in a room that was clearly used for religious purposes (Merlin 2003, 302). Researchers date the seeds to about 5500 BCE.

The next confirmed presence of the poppy plant in antiquity can be traced to the Sumerian civilization, which thrived in the area of the Fertile Crescent between about 4500 and 1900 BCE. The evidence for the cultivation of the plant and harvesting of its seeds dates to a clay tablet containing cuneiform script, sometimes said to be the oldest pharmacopeia in history. This early tablet describes the practice of harvesting the poppy plant early in the morning, presumably to extract opium from its immature seeds. Evidence for the sacramental use of the plant because of its psychoactive powers is also present in the tablet. Part of that evidence is based on the name used by the Sumerians for the poppy plant, *hui gil*, or "plant of joy" (Kritikos and Papadaki 1967; one recent commentator claims to have found actual depictions of the harvesting process in early tablets; see Kanzfeldt 2014).

## Egypt and Crete

Tradition has it that knowledge of the poppy plant and opium was transmitted from the Sumerians to later civilizations, such as the Babylonians (1895–539 BCE) and Assyrians (ca. 2500–609 BCE) but especially to the Egyptians. Opium cultivation and widespread use appear to have become common by the period of the 18th Dynasty (ca. 1550–1350 BCE). Numerous written and pictorial references to the drug are available, such as a necklace made of poppy seeds, a statue of a young boy with ear rings made of poppy seed capsules, a jug that appears to have been used for the preparation of opium solutions, mention of the uses of opium in religious ceremonies (described in *The Book of the Dead*), and a variety of paintings, pictographs, and other artifacts from a number of royal tombs (Merlin 2003). Evidence suggests that opium was used to relieve pain, cure nervous diseases, and put a person to sleep, in addition to its role in religious ceremonies. Most of the opium grown in Egypt at the time was planted in areas around the city of Thebes, a fact that accounts for the name used by Egyptians for the plant, *thebacium* (Rosso 2010).

Not long after the opium plant was first cultivated in Egypt, entrepreneurs began selling and trading the product throughout the eastern Mediterranean. Evidence for this practice, described by one researcher as "the original Medellin cartel, 3,500 years ago," has come from the discovery of many special pots constructed and decorated with poppy themes. The drug trade appears to have been based not primarily for the encouragement of abuse and/or addiction but for the provision of a pain control product, primarily during childbirth and painful diseases (Keyser 2002; for diagrams of the trading pots, see Rosso 2010, 83).

One of the regions to which knowledge of opium may have been carried is the Minoan civilization (ca. 2600–1100 BCE) on the island of Crete. Evidence for this hypothesis comes at least partly from the discovery of a group of five figurines representing Minoan goddesses with their arms uplifted. One of the goddesses wears on her head three moveable objects that appear to be dried pods of the opium plant. The pods have been identified as having coming from the *P. somniferum* plant. In the same room with the statuette is a cylindrical vase with holes in the side that has been associated with the smoking of opium in Minoan and other cultures (Kritikos and Papadaki 1967).

### Greece and Rome

A hint of the transfer of knowledge about opium from Egypt to Greece is found in Homer's *Odyssey*, written in about

720 BCE. In Book 4 of the epic poem, Homer tells of Helen of Troy's putting an opium concoction into the drinks of guests at one of her dinners. She has taken this action because the guests appear to be in a sad mood, and she hopes to lighten their spirits:

> Then Helen, daughter of Zeus, took other counsel. Straightway she cast into the wine of which they were drinking a drug to quiet all pain and strife, and bring forgetfulness of every ill. Whoso should drink this down, when it is mingled in the bowl, would not in the course of that day let a tear fall down over his cheeks, no, not though his mother and father should lie there dead, or though before his face men should slay with the sword his brother or dear son, and his own eyes beheld it. Such cunning drugs had the daughter of Zeus, drugs of healing, which Polydamna, the wife of Thon, had given her, a woman of Egypt. ("Greek Texts and Translations" 2017)

Homer calls the drug used in this incident as *nepenthes*, a substance whose true meaning is not entirely known for sure. The drug, however, is a common part of Greek mythology and probably most commonly associated with opium (Rosso 2010). Some gods and goddesses with whom the poppy or opium are related include

- Hypnos (god of sleep) and Thantos (god of death), twin brothers who are usually represented with a crown of poppies or holding a bouquet of poppies;
- Morpheus (god of dreams), often represented as sleeping on a bed of poppies;
- Demeter (goddess of agriculture), who found peace from her sorrow over losing her daughter Persephone by eating the sap from poppy plants;
- Nyx (goddess of night), mother of Hypnos and Thantos, and the person who delivers opium to her sons.

The use of opium for medical purposes among the ancient Greeks has been the topic of considerable research. It seems clear that the Greeks knew of at least three varieties of poppy plant and discussed them and their medicinal uses in their writings. But it is not always clear when and how they were referring to the medicinal uses of *P. somniferum*. One of the classic studies of the role of opium in ancient Greece mentions a dozen physicians who alluded in some way or another, to some extent or another, to the use of the "poppy" plant in medicine (Kritikos and Papadaki 1967). One name often mentioned in this line of discussion is that of Hippocrates (460–ca. 375 BCE), often called the father of Western medicine. Hippocrates is credited with recommending the use of the opium poppy for a variety of medical uses, such as diseases of women and internal diseases. It is not entirely clear, however, that Hippocrates is actually referring to *P. somniferum*. It is one of Hippocrates's successors, Theophrastus (372–287 BCE), who is often credited with describing the use of *P. somniferum* for a variety of medical purposes (Scarborough 1978).

Possibly the most famous advocate of the poppy plant and opium in the ancient world was the physician Galen (130–210 CE). Galen's influence in the medical world was so strong that it dominated principles and practices in the field for almost 1,500 years. During that time, physicians wishing to treat their patients referred almost without exception to Galen's teachings. In writing about the drug, Galen says that the juice of the poppy, "which physicians are in the habit of calling opium," is "the strongest of the drugs which numb the senses and induce a deadening sleep." He says that it

> resists poison and venomous bites, cures chronic headache, vertigo, deafness, epilepsy, apoplexy, dimness of sight, loss of voice, asthma, coughs of all kinds, spitting of blood, tightness of breath, colic, the lilac poison, jaundice, hardness of the spleen stone, urinary complaints, fever,

dropsies, leprosies, the trouble to which women are subject, melancholy and all pestilences. (Macht 1915, 479)

### The Middle Ages and the Muslim World

Relatively little scholarly research exists on the uses of opium during the Middle Ages. As the period was, in general, something of a desert for learning, this situation is probably not surprising. A reading of the few mentions of opium between 400 and ca. 1600 reveals that opium preparations that would have been familiar to the ancient Greeks and Romans continued to be used throughout the period, primarily for relief from pain (for some brief commentaries on this issue, see Connor 1993; "Opium Poppy: Herb of Heaven or Hell" 1997; and especially Goldberg 2014, Chapter 3, "The Stone of Immortality").

While research and learning gave way to theological musings in most of Europe during the Middle Ages, quite the opposite was true in the Islamic world, where those topics reached the highest point in that culture's history. Much of the learning produced by the ancient Greek and Roman civilizations, though lost to Europe, was preserved and advanced by Muslim scholars. The historical record shows that Muslim scholars, physicians, and pharmacists were well aware of the uses of opium to treat a variety of medical conditions during the whole period between the 9th and 17th centuries. Some examples are the following:

- One Ibn Masawayh (777–857) reported using opium for the treatment of biliary pains, headaches, toothaches, eye aches, and dysentery.
- The physician Ibn Sina (980–1037), whose widespread influence resulted from the publication of his text, *Al-Qanun*, mentioned the use of opium for the treatment of pain and for curing cancers of the eye.
- In his book *Kitab al-Cami al-Müfredat al-Edviye*, the physician and pharmacist Ibn al-Baytar (1197–1248) describes

the use of a pellet of opium "the size of lentil" for the treatment of coughs, headaches, earaches, and gout.

- Turkish surgeon Hugo Von Lucca Borgognoni of Bologne (?–1252) described the use of a sponge soaked in a concoction containing opium to anesthetize a patient for surgery. When placed over the patient's nose, it induced a deep sleep.
- The prominent Ottoman physician Salih bin Nasrallah Ibn Sallum wrote a definitive medical book, *al-Bayan fi al-human* (*Important Measurements of the Human Body*), in which he repeated many of the most common uses of opium for medical treatment, including coughs, pains of various kinds, diarrhea, and headaches (Öncel and Erdemir 2007, 3–5).

Probably the most extensive discussion of opium as a drug in the Muslim world at the time can be found in the writings of the Persian polymath Abu 'Ali al-Husayn ibn Sina, more commonly known by his Westernized name of Avicenna. Avicenna devotes large portions of his medical encyclopedia *al-Qanun fi'l-Tibb* (*Canon of Medicine*) to a discussion of opium. In the book, he refers to the drug as *afion* and recommends its use as an analgesic, hypnotic, and antitussive, and for the treatment of gastrointestinal, cognitive, respiratory, neuromuscular, and sexual dysfunction disorders. He describes a variety of ways in which the drugs can be prepared and used, as a powder, tincture, and smoking material, for example. In the book, he also warns of the dangers of overuse of afion and its possible fatal effects (Heydari, Hashempur, and Zargaran 2013).

### The Far East

The early history of opium in the Far East is less well known than it is for the Middle East and Europe. According to one popular hypothesis, the drug was first introduced to India in about 330 BCE, when Alexander the Great brought opium to that region. There appears to be strong evidence that Alexander regularly used opium to increase his troops' stamina and fighting ability, so that carrying this information to ancient Persia may have been a reasonable consequence of his own practice ("Opium, Morphine, and Heroin" 2011). Other authorities question this history, however, and suggest that Arab traders or other visitors from the Middle East brought knowledge of the drug to parts of India somewhat later. In any case, the use of opium for a variety of medical conditions had become a well-established part of the profession by the early 13th century (Kylebridge 2017; Shahnavaz 2014).

Opium's first appearance in China appears to have occurred during the Tang dynasty (618–907), when the drug was brought to the region by Arab traders following the Silk Road. There appears to be no record of the plant's having been cultivated or used prior to this date. Poppy seeds were apparently exchanged for Chinese goods, and traders demonstrated to their hosts methods for making beverages from the seeds that could be used to cure pain. Shortly thereafter, opium concoctions became a standard part of most Chinese pharmacopeias ("History of Opium, Opium Eating, and Smoking" 1892, 330). (There is virtually no information available on the early introduction of opium to Japan and Korea, except for the brief comment that the drug "was introduced into Japan along with Chinese herbal medicine" at some early date ["Opium in Japan" 2017]. This limitation may be explained by the fact that the borders of both countries were closed to foreign trade until the early 17th century.)

In the history of opium reviewed thus far, the drug was almost always ingested in solid form or in some sort of liquid concoction. The practice of smoking the drug apparently first arose much later, in the early 16th century, when Portuguese sailors started mixing the powdered drug with tobacco. In their travels to India and other parts of the Far East thereafter, they apparently introduced this practice to the region, where it rapidly became a popular method of ingesting the drug (McCoy 1972, Chapter 3). Thereafter, that practice of smoking opium competed with, and eventually became more popular than, the ingestion of opium in a solid or liquid form.

The records of opium use for legal purposes in the years up to the 16th century largely reflect the drug's story told here thus far. It was recognized by physicians and pharmacists as a substance that was effective for a variety of medical conditions, although its misuse was also known to cause severe harmful effects, including, in some cases, death. As long as opium has been used by humans, however, it has also been used for non-medical purposes that produce psychoactive effects that may be recognized by societal norms either as a reasonable social, religious, or ceremonial practice or as a socially inappropriate behavior that requires some form of royal edict, law, or other type of regulation (such as the drug laws that exist in the United States today). Few such formal prohibitions against the use of opium exist in our history of opium thus far, although they do begin to occur in more recent times.

## Laudanum

Probably the most important single event in the history of opium during the late Middle Ages was the invention of laudanum by the Swiss physician Philippus Aureolus Theophrastus Bombastus von Hohenheim, more commonly known as Paracelsus. Laudanum is a tincture (alcoholic solution) of opium along with other ingredients, including powdered gold, crushed pearls, and a variety of other plant and mineral extracts, such as henbane, coral, amber, musk, and bezoar stone. In fact, Paracelsus almost certainly changed his recipe for laudanum on a regular basis, so that no one final list of ingredients is possible (Davenport-Hines 2004, 32). Paracelsus gave the name *laudanum* (from the Latin *laudare*, "to praise") to his product to reflect his belief in its use as a cure for a host of diseases. He is said to have carried a vial of the solution with him at all times and to have used it regularly in his medical practice (Duarte 2005). A further demonstration of his faith in the product was another name he gave to a solid, pill-like form of the product, the stone of immortality (Macht 1915, 478).

The significance of Paracelsus's discovery was a function of his place in medical history. He rejected the basic principles of Galenic medicine that had dominated medical thought for almost 15 centuries and taught instead that metals, minerals, plant materials, and other natural products could and should be used for the treatment of diseases. When he invented, used, and widely recommended his laudanum, his followers also accepted the value of the product in their medical practices and further expanded its use in the field.

Laudanum became the form of opium with which most individuals in Europe became familiar. After Paracelsus, other physicians and pharmacists designed variations of the original formula. The most famous of those variations was a product invented by English physician, Thomas Sydenham, in 1680, a product with a more standardized formula than that of Paracelsus's concoction. Sydenham's laudanum consisted of 1 gram of opium dissolved in 100 milliliters of alcohol. The preparation was made more palatable with the addition of spices such as cinnamon, clover, and saffron. Sydenham's enthusiasm for the product is reflected in what is perhaps his most famous quote on the topic. "Of all the remedies it has pleased almighty God to give man to relieve his suffering," he once wrote, "none is so universal and so efficacious as opium" (Batmanabane 2014, 81).

As with Paracelsus, Sydenham's success in marketing his product was at least partially due to his own reputation in the field of medicine. He was sometimes called the English Hippocrates or the father of English medicine. He described the virtues of his laudanum in his most famous text, *Medical Observations Concerning the History and Cure of Acute Diseases.* (In the book, he also points out the importance of using exactly the right quantity of the drug in order to gain the proper response without harming the patient [Latham 1801]. This reference is a reprint of Sydenham's *Medical Observations*, containing nearly 100 references to laudanum.)

During the 19th century, laudanum became particularly popular among some of the best-known writers and artists of the age. Some used it primarily or at least originally for the treatment of pain or some other condition. But in many cases, an individual used the drug solely for recreational purposes, often claiming that its effect transported a person above and beyond the clutter of everyday life. Among the Victorian personages who used, became addicted to, or even died from the use of laudanum were Elizabeth Barrett Browning, Lord Byron, Wilkie Collins, Samuel Taylor Coleridge, Charles Dickens, Sir Arthur Conan Doyle, George Eliot, Elizabeth Gaskell, John Keats, Edgar Allan Poe, Gabriel Dante Rossetti, and his wife Elizabeth Siddal (who died from an opium overdose), Percy Bysshe Shelley, and Bram Stoker (Diniejko 2002; Milligan 2003, xxxii).

Laudanum was also "the drug of choice" among many ordinary individuals. It was, first of all, easy to obtain. All one had to do was to walk into the nearest pharmacy to purchase a bottle, usually at a very modest price. No prescription or formal monitoring of any kind was necessary. The drug was especially popular among young mothers, as a way of quieting crying babies. Since the tincture also provided users with a "buzz," it also became popular among workers or the unemployed whose life had been made especially difficult by the rise of the Industrial Revolution. For these reasons, laudanum is often called "the aspirin of the nineteenth century" (Diniejko 2002; Hodgson 2008, Chapter 3). In the United States, laudanum was also readily available, often a component of the so-called patent medicines that were so widely popular in the 19th century. (Patent medicines are medicines made under a patent that can be sold "over the counter" [without prescription] [Brecher and the Editors of Consumers Report Magazine 1972; O'Neill 2012].) Laudanum has now been banned in most countries, although it is still available by prescription in the United States, where it is a Schedule II drug ("Controlled Substances" 2017, 8).

## The Opium Wars

Between about 1600 and 1850, perhaps the most interesting story about opium involved its cultivation and trading from countries in Western Europe to the Far East, especially India and China. This story involves a complex relationship among, primarily, England and the Netherlands from Europe and China and India from East Asia. It began as early as the late 16th century when English ships began to buy opium from Indian growers, to be returned to the homeland, where it was used primarily for medicinal purposes. (Many online histories of opium suggest that trading began in 1606, when "ships chartered by Elizabeth I were instructed to purchase the finest Indian opium and transport it back to England." But that would have been impossible, since the queen had died three years earlier, in 1603; see Kienholz 2008.) In any case, the trade situation was complicated by the fact that both the English and the Dutch became intensely engaged in the supervision of the growing of opium in India and its transport back to the home countries and, even more important, to China, with which the English at least had a serious trade deficit. By the end of the 18th century, the English had gained a monopoly on the growing of opium in India and were shipping thousands of cases of opium to China every year. (For a complete discussion of this complex problem, see Derks 2012.)

The center of opium problems that arose during the 19th century, then, was China. While the abuse of opium had occurred in a number of societies before 1800, it had almost never become the subject of formal legislative prohibition. Such was not the case in China. The introduction of smoked opium to the country in the early 18th century had initiated a widespread use of the practice among ordinary citizens. The problem became so serious that one of the first (if not the first) actions ever or anywhere was taken to prohibit the drug's use for any purpose other than medical treatments. In 1729, the emperor Yung-cheng issued an edict prohibiting the use of opium for any purpose except in cases where a license had been issued for medical use (Rhein 1919, 482). Penalties for violation of the edict ranged from 100 strokes of caning with a bamboo stick to death (Booth 1999, 109).

Yung-cheng's edict apparently had little or no effect on China's opium problem. Imports (not mentioned in the edict) continued to flow into the country, and opium smoking continued to be a common practice throughout the nation. By the end of the century, Emperor Kia-king issued the strongest of all imperial edicts to date. That edict prohibited not only the recreational use of opium in the country but also the growing of opium or its importation into the country (Booth 1999, 110). As had been the case with all earlier edicts, Kia-king's decree had no effect on the importation of opium into the country. The volume of the drug delivered to the Chinese port of Canton (the only port through which it was being delivered) rose from 5,000 cases in 1820 to 16,000 cases in 1830 and 20,000 cases in 1838 (Goldfinger 2006).

A crisis occurred in 1838 when a son of the emperor Daoguang died of an opium overdose. Devastated by that event, the emperor appointed a court official, Lin Zexu (also Lin Tsehsu), to bring an end to the importation and use of opium in China once and for all. Lin was successful in the first year of his appointment, arresting more than 1,700 opium users in the country and confiscating 44,000 pounds of the drug. He was less successful, however, in his attempts to bring to an end to the importation of opium by way of British ships arriving at the (previously open) port of Canton. Lin demanded that the British ships at Canton turn over their opium to him. When they refused to do so, he confiscated 21,000 chests of opium, which he ordered destroyed. The British were outraged at this action and called for a fleet of warships to blockade the Chinese coasts. Fighting broke out and continued for a period of nearly three years. Finally, in 1842, the Chinese acceded to British demands in the Treaty of Nanking. In the treaty, China agreed to relax its prohibitions on opium imports, open five ports to trade, and cede Hong Kong to the British (Allingham 2006; Hedman 2012; for a copy of the letter sent by Lin to Queen Victoria about the issue, see "Chinese Cultural Studies: Lin Zixu Lin Tse-Hsu (1839 CE). Letter of Advice to Queen Victoria" n.d.).

That agreement lasted over a decade before hostilities were renewed between China and Great Britain, with France sending forces to support the latter army. The Second Opium War broke out to a considerable extent because of increasing British and French trade efforts around the world, which coincided with civil unrest in China resulting from the Taiping Rebellion of 1850–1864. The British and French forces prevailed in the conflict, which was partly ended in 1858 with the signing of the Treaty of Tientsin (China, Great Britain, and France) and, two years later, with a final agreement, the Convention of Peking (China, Great Britain, France, and Russia). The final treaty essentially opened Chinese ports to the importation of opium, along with ceding additional areas to the three victorious nations (Allingham 2006).

## Morphine and Beyond

Throughout the 19th century, while nations were fighting over the importation, use, and, sometimes, control of opium, other, less well-known (to the general public) developments with regard to the drug were taking place. From a historical standpoint, the most important of these developments was the discovery of morphine by the German chemist Friedrich Wilhelm Adam Sertürner in about 1803. (The exact date of this discovery is a matter of some dispute; see Huxtable and Schwarz 2001.)

### The Discovery and Commercialization of Morphine

In 1800, the science of chemistry was in its very earliest days. Very few scholars even considered the fact that natural products in the world around us, such as opium, might be complex substances consisting of many discrete parts, later to be known as compounds. In fact, the term *compounds* had no precise meaning among early chemists. Sertürner was one of the pioneers in the field of organic chemistry, which includes the study of natural products and their composition. He treated opium powder with some simple chemical actions—dissolving it in hot water and then adding ammonia to the solution. He found that a new substance (compound) precipitated out, a compound to which he gave the name of morphine. He chose the name because of one of the compound's most notable characteristics: the tendency to produce sleepiness in an animal. In Greek mythology, Morpheus was the god of sleep.

Morphine was the first opiate to have been discovered. Historically, the term *opiate* referred to any substance that contained opium or that had chemical or biological effects on a person similar to those produced by opium.

Sertürner announced his discovery to a few of his colleagues, but neither he nor his colleagues bothered to follow up on the compound's properties. When Sertürner decided to do so, he tested the compound on a mouse, three dogs, three young boys, and himself. The mouse and dogs died, and the four humans also became gravely ill. The first symptoms of morphine poisoning, relaxation, and a loss of consciousness, were, however, obvious to Sertürner, leading to the name that he eventually gave the compound. By 1817, Sertürner had isolated and purified morphine and wrote a formal paper on the results of his research, "Ueber eins der Fürchterlichsten Gifte der Pflanzenwelt, als ein Nachtrag zu Seiner Abhandlung über die Mekonsäure und das Morphium; mit Bemerkungen, den Aciden Extractivstoff des Opiums und Seine Verbindungen Betreffend" ("About One of the Most Terrible Poisons of the Plant World, as an Addendum to His Treatise on Meconic Acid and Morphine; with Remarks Concerning the Acid Extract of Opium and Its Compounds"; the original paper is available, in German, at *Annalen der Physik* 1817, 183).

Evidence suggests that Sertürner was still concerned about possible negative effects of morphine in 1817, but he, nonetheless, decided to establish a company to market the drug, Sertürner and Company. He advertised that morphine was an effective analgesic (pain killer) and that it could also be used to treat alcoholism and opium addiction. Sales did not go well for the company, however, at least partly because purity of the drug could not be guaranteed and the process by which it was made was complicated and expensive.

Those problems were solved in 1831 when Scottish chemist William Gregory invented a new method for extracting morphine from opium. The product resulting from his process was called Gregory's salt and was later found to consist of a mixture of morphine chloride and codeine chloride. This was not a problem in terms of its use as an analgesic, but the salt did not solve all the problems associated with the use of morphine in medicine. Two remaining problems were that (1) the drug still had to be administered orally, causing a delay in producing its analgesic effects, and (2) the cost of producing Gregory's salt was no less than the cost of producing laudanum. Therefore, what was the point of using the new process over the well-known process of making laudanum (Doyle 2017)?

One final step in the commercialization of morphine occurred in 1853 with the invention of the hypodermic needle by Scottish physician Alexander Wood. The needle provided a mechanism never before available for injecting a drug directly into a vein, making the drug's access to the body much faster than with oral ingestion. Wood's invention revolutionized not only the use of morphine but also that of many other drugs ("Alexander Wood" 2017; Hamilton and Baskett 2000).

While these improvements in the manufacture and administration of morphine were occurring, the potential value of the drug was not being lost on commercial drug companies. As early as 1827, the Merck pharmaceutical company in Germany (already more than 150 years old) had begun producing morphine, codeine, and cocaine ("Merck & Co., Inc." 2017). Five years later in the United States, the relatively young Zeitler & Rosengarten company began producing opium products also and shortly became the world's largest producer of morphine ("Powers-Weightman-Rosengarten Co." 2007). At about the same time, the first British producers of morphine, MacFarlan Smith, Ltd., began producing morphine for Great Britain (Schaefer 2016, 276–277).

### Heroin: The Wonder Drug

Morphine soon became, quite understandably, a very popular medication. Despite its disastrous side effects (addiction), the drug was used widely by men and women from all aspects of society. The opening lines of the first chapter of the classic study of drugs in America, *Licit and Illicit Drugs*, are, "The United States of America during the nineteenth century could quite properly be described as a 'dope fiend's paradise'" (Brecher and the Editors of Consumer Reports 1972, 3). The authors go on to explain why drugs like morphine and opium were so readily available in the country: (1) they could be obtained directly from a physician, with or without a prescription; (2) they were available at drugstores over the counter, without prescription; (3) grocery and general stores also sold opiate products off their shelves; (4) opiates could be ordered by mail; and (5) opiates were a component of the many thousands of patent medicines readily available to the person on the street (Brecher and the Editors of Consumer Reports 1972, 3).

Hardly any wonder, then, that the nation was experiencing its first "opium epidemic" from about 1850 to the beginning of the 20th century. The evidence seems to suggest that the "epidemic" developed not because so many people wanted to use the drug because of its psychoactive powers but because it solved a wide variety of real medical problems. Cure from disease came first; addiction followed. An 1880 medical textbook, for example, listed 48 diseases and other conditions that could be cured with morphine, including angina pectoris, asthma,

cholera, cardiac diseases, epilepsy, gastric ulcers, malaria, pleu-
ritis, rheumatism, and "vomiting of pregnancy" (Kane 1880,
309–312).

One of the most intriguing points about the "opiate epidemic" was the higher rate of addiction among women than
among men. In the classic study on the history of opiates in
the United States, Terry and Pellens note that the rate of opiate use among women was about three times that among men.
Of course, one factor involved in this number was that many
female prostitutes became addicted to opiates. But, the authors
found, even subtracting that factor, the illicit use of opiates
among women was about twice that of men (Terry and Pellens 1928). The authors and other observers have suggested a
reasonable explanation for these data. One of the most common uses of morphine, they point out, is for the treatment
of "women's disease," which includes normal menstrual-related
conditions, problems of pregnancy, and postpartum issues.
Small wonder that many women turned to opiate nostrums
from release of these normal functions, sometimes leading to
an addiction to the drug (Aldrich n.d.).

Another major factor in the opium epidemic of the late
19th century was the Civil War. In one of the most brutal wars
in modern history, soldiers on both sides of the war suffered
a very large number of injuries that required extreme medical
care, such as the amputation of limbs. Very few effective analgesics were available during this time except for morphine and
laudanum (and opium, when it was available). Consequently,
surgeons commonly injected injured soldiers with morphine,
administered the drug in solid or liquid form, or even had
a man lick the drug of the surgeon's hand, usually the only
analgesic or sedative a person had in preparation for surgery.
And such practices were hardly uncommon. According to one
commonly quoted statistic, a total of 2,245,686 men were
killed by noncombat deaths, compared with 110,070 Union
soldiers who died because of combat (Agnew 2014, 72). The
widespread use of morphine, then, had long-term effects also.

By one estimate, as many as 400,000 veterans returned home, addicted to morphine. What a prescient moment for American wars of the late 20th and early 21st centuries! ("Soldier's Disease" 2011).

### Other Opiates

Morphine was the first psychoactive compound found in opium. Before long, chemists began finding other compounds in opium like morphine, but in smaller quantities. The first such opium derivative, after morphine, was noscapine (called, at the time, narcotine, found by French chemist Jean-François Derosne at about the same time that morphine was first extracted [1803]). Other opium derivatives discovered thereafter were codeine (Pierre Robiquet, 1832), narceine (Pierre-Joseph Pelletier, 1832), thebaine (Pelletier and his factory manager, known today only as Thibouméry, 1835), and papaverine (Georg Merck, 1848) (Robinette 2008, volume II, part 3). Codeine is today said to be the most widely used opiate in the world (Codeine 2017). The other opiate derivatives, however, have largely been replaced by synthetic morphine-like drugs.

The composition of opium differs substantially, depending on the source from which it comes. Generally, morphine makes up about 10–15 percent on an opium sample, followed by lesser amounts of the other opiates. (For the results obtained from one study, see Mohanakrishna Reddy et al. 2003.)

By the end of the 19th century, chemists had a fairly good understanding of opium. That is, they knew what its primary components were, their important physical properties, and their effects on humans and other animals. But understanding the properties of naturally occurring substances, such as opium and its components, is only part of a chemist's job, an activity that is called analytical chemistry. A common second step in chemical research is to make new compounds with chemical structures similar to those of a naturally occurring substance that may have different chemical, physical, and/or biological properties, a process that is called synthetic chemistry or chemical synthesis. Chemists try to make analogs for a couple of reasons: (1) to remove features of the compound that have undesirable effects or (2) to enhance the properties of the compound.

Morphine is a good example of this process. As noted earlier, its discovery brought great satisfaction to physicians who had to deal with pain (and other ailments). It was a highly effective analgesic for use in surgery and a host of other medical procedures. It soon became obvious, however, that individuals could become addicted to the drug relatively easily. The challenge for chemists, then, was to find a compound that was similar to morphine but did not have its addictive properties. The first breakthrough in this search occurred in 1874, when British chemist C. R. Wright (accidentally) synthesized the drug now known as heroin. Wright achieved this result by heating pure morphine with a compound known as acetic anhydride. In that reaction, two acetyl groups from acetic anhydride add to the morphine molecule, making a new compound technically known as diacetylmorphine or "morphine with two acetyl groups." (An acetyl group consists of two carbon atoms, three hydrogen atoms, and one oxygen atom joined to each other.)

Considering its parent compound (morphine), Wright thought that the new compound might be an effective analgesic, like morphine. He tested the drug on dogs and rabbits and observed some troubling responses. It produced, he said, "great prostration, fear, and sleepiness speedily following the administration, the eyes being sensitive, and pupils dilated, considerable salivation being produced in dogs, and slight tendency to vomiting" (Wright 1874). These effects were sufficiently worrisome to convince Wright that he should not proceed with his research on the new compound.

For nearly 25 years, diacetylmorphine was largely ignored by chemists, many of whom felt, as did Wright, that the compound was too dangerous to use as a drug for humans. The drug was rediscovered in about 1897 in the laboratories of the Bayer pharmaceutical company in Elberfeld, Germany. Credit for the discovery goes to German chemist Felix Hoffmann, who was working in the company's research department at the time. Hoffmann was interested especially in the acetylating of compounds, like the work that led to Wright's 1874 discovery. One of Hoffmann's early discoveries was that salicylic acid, obtained from tree bark, could be acetylated to produce an excellent analgesic for mild pain. The chemical name of the product was acetylsalicylate. Bayer began marketing the product in 1900 under the now-more-familiar name of aspirin.

Hoffmann's supervisor at Bayer, Heinrich Dreser, encouraged Hoffmann to study the acetylation of morphine, Wright's experiment about which he may already have known. Hoffmann once again achieved success in his work, this time producing the same diacetylmorphine that Wright had made two decades earlier. (Dreser is sometimes given credit for this discovery, although that is almost certainly not the case; see "Felix Hoffmann" 2015.) Bayer also began marketing this product in 1898 under the name of heroin. That name is said to have come from the drug's ability to make a user "feel like a hero" ("Heroin (n.)" 2017; Rzepa 2015). Heroin is about twice as strong as morphine in terms of pain relief, although its effects last for a shorter time. The specific relative potencies depend on the method of administration, among other factors, with intramuscular injections being more potent than ingestion by mouth ("Two to Three" 2004).

As had been the case with morphine, many medical claims were made for the new drug. Primary among these was its use as a cough medicine, not only for colds and the flu but also for more serious diseases like pneumonia and tuberculosis. While introducing heroin to a medical congress in Germany, Dreser made the claim that heroin was "10 times more effective as a cough medicine than codeine, but had only a tenth of its toxic effects." Other proponents of the new drug even insisted that heroin was an effective treatment for morphine addiction, just as morphine had once been touted as a cure for opium addiction (Askwith 1998). And again, as with morphine, heroin was eventually recommended for a much wider range of medical conditions, including cardiac lesions, cardiac weakness, carcinoma, duodenal ulcer, chronic gastritis, and chronic bronchitis (Einhorn 1899, 168; this reference contains several articles on the medical applications of heroin; images of some of the heroin products available at the time can be viewed at https://www.tumblr.com/search/bayer%20heroin).

## The Criminalization of Opiates

The first decade of the 20th century was a "perfect storm" for the problem of heroin addiction in the United States. First, many reputable physicians and medical groups were recommending the use of heroin for a host of problems. In addition, heroin was easy to obtain in America, both with and without a prescription. Finally, individuals with reasons for wanting to abuse drugs, often to escape the worst aspects of their personal lives, had found that heroin provided that gateway to a "happier" future. Trends in New York City during this period are reflected in the number of admissions to major hospitals. The first person addicted to heroin was admitted for treatment at the city's Bellevue Hospital in 1910. Only five years later, that number had increased to 425 heroin patients. The vast majority of these individuals were, according to one report at the time, "members of gangs who congregate on street corners particularly at night, and make insulting remarks to people who pass" (Scott 1998).

Prior to 1905, the U.S. Congress had passed no laws prohibiting the use of opium or its derivatives. A handful of cities and states had adopted such legislation, but it almost always applied to certain classes of "undesirables," such as Chinese immigrants who brought with them the habit of smoking opium. Probably the first of these laws was the prohibition on the smoking of opium in opium dens, adopted by the city of San Francisco in 1875. All other uses of opium were excluded from the law, and the substance was still widely used by the non-Chinese population for medical and recreational purposes (Gieringer 2005). (Hawaii had passed a similar law in 1856 but had not yet been admitted to the Union as a state [Forbes 1998–2003, 169, #2163].) Other California cities soon followed San Francisco's example, including Oakland, Sacramento, Stockton, and Virginia City. In 1881, the state legislature enacted a similar law applying to all parts of the state (Gieringer 2005).

The first law prohibiting the use of opium in 1905 did not apply to citizens of the United States but to the inhabitants of the Philippine islands. Spain had ceded the Philippines to the United States at the conclusion of the Spanish-American War. Along with the territory, America also inherited a major opium epidemic in the islands (Gieringer 2005). Of far greater importance was a law passed a year later, the U.S. Pure Food and Drug Law 1906 (P.L. 59 384, 34 Stat. 768). The purpose of the law was to prevent "the manufacture, sale, or transportation of adulterated or misbranded or poisonous or deleterious foods, drugs, medicines, and liquors, and for regulating traffic therein" (An Act of June 30, 1906, 1906). Among the reforms included in the law were new restrictions on the labeling of patent medicines, with the aim of letting consumers have a better idea as to the ingredients included in such drugs, along with more rigorous restrictions on the substances that could be used in the manufacture of patent medicines. Passage of the Pure Food and Drug Act took 29 years, the first version of the bill having been introduced in 1879.

Many observers argue that the Pure Food and Drug Act marked "the beginning of the end" of the patent medicine industry. To some extent, this assessment is true. Rates of opiate addiction began to drop after passage of the act. However, a significant problem remained because manufacturers found ways to work around the new regulations. One common solution for manufacturers of patent medicine was to continue including opiates in their products but no longer listing them on labels, thus achieving the letter of the law, if not its intent. (This problem was addressed in later legislative actions; see Baker n.d.; Janssen 1981.) Possibly the most important long-term consequence of adoption of the Pure Food and Drug Act was the creation of the U.S. Food and Drug Administration (FDA), which continues to be today the nation's single most important agency dealing with all aspects of legal and illegal drug use.

Passage of the Pure Food and Drug Act was an indication of the growing concerns in the United States about the harmful effects of opium, morphine, codeine, and other opiates. That concern eventually took on an international flavor as a small group of politicians and religious leaders petitioned President Theodore Roosevelt to call for an international conference about the growing threat of narcotic drugs to the United States and the need for international action to deal with this threat. Because of this concern, Roosevelt called for the creation of an international commission on narcotics trade, to meet in Shanghai from February 5 to 26, 1909. The commission expected originally to deal primarily with the opium trade in China, although discussions very soon evolved to include a much broader canvas, essentially the problems of drug trade throughout the world. In addition, the commission expanded its original charge to include a new non-opioid drug of growing concern, cocaine ("A Century of International Drug Control" 2009; Lowes 1966).

(The strong moral flavor of the U.S. stance against opiates—in contrast to the many possible medical consequences—was reflected in the composition of the U.S. delegation to the Shanghai meeting. It consisted of Charles Henry Brent, Episcopalian bishop in western New York State and the Philippines, and physician Hamilton Wright and pharmacist Henry J. Finger, both of whom had been and continued to be strong advocates in the battle against all types of drug use in the United States, a campaign they conducted for the sake of retaining "ethnic purity" in the nation [see, e.g., Davenport-Hines 2002, Chapter 7; Gieringer 2005].)

In planning for the Shanghai meeting, organizers were careful to point out that the session would not be a formal international conference with the authority to write a binding treaty but an advisory group whose objective it was to learn more about the opium problem and to make recommendations for future actions. The follow-up to the Shanghai meeting, then, was just such a conference, the First International Opium Convention, held at The Hague, the Netherlands, December 1, 1911, to January 23, 1912. On the latter date, attendees adopted a proposed treaty consisting of 6 chapters and 25 articles, dealing not only with opium and morphine, the original drugs of concern, but also with cocaine and heroin, which had received increasing attention during the Shanghai meeting. The conference was hardly an "international" event in the true sense of the word since it was attended by only 13 nations who were most affected by the Chinese opium problem, China itself, France, Germany, Italy, Japan, the Netherlands, Persia, Portugal, Russia, Siam, the United Kingdom, British India, and the United States. The treaty took effect in 1915 when it was ratified by the required five nations, China, Honduras, the Netherlands, Norway, and the United States. It was adopted by most other powers in 1919 when its provisions were incorporated into the Treaty of Versailles, ending World War I ("A Century of International Drug Control" 2009, 50–51; also see Bewley-Taylor 1999).

One of the provisions of the Hague treaty, mentioned in four different articles of the document, was a requirement that signatories to the treaty take such actions as might be necessary to control the manufacture, sale, use, importation, and exportation of opium, morphine, cocaine, and their respective salts ("Suppression of Abuse of Opium and Other Drugs" 1912). In the United States, this provision was met by means of an act of Congress known as the Harrison Narcotic Act of 1914. The act was proposed and adopted not only to meet the requirements of the treaty but also as the first step by the U.S. government to aggressively control the use of opium and opiates in the country.

The act itself seemed somewhat routine, laying out a system for monitoring and controlling the flow of opium products through the U.S. economy. It required anyone who handled opium products in any way—by importing, selling, prescribing, manufacturing, or exporting, for example—to license their business with the federal government and to pay a modest tax for conducting that business. It specifically confirmed the right of physicians to use opiate products in their own practice (King 1953).

Execution of the Harrison Act turned out to be an exercise entirely different from that laid out in the original bill and, perhaps, from the Congress's intention. The U.S. Department of Justice apparently decided to use the provisions of the act to de facto define opium and opiate addiction as a type of criminal behavior rather than a medical problem. It systematically set out to violate the act's stated intent to allow physicians to use opium and opiates to treat addicts therapeutically and to make such behavior criminal equivalent to that of opium patients. In one of the most passionate expressions of this interpretation of post-Harrison history, Rufus King, at the time special counsel to the subcommittee of the U.S. House Committee on the Judiciary to Investigate the Department of Justice and special counsel to the Investigations Subcommittee of the Senate Interstate Commerce Committee, wrote:

> In sum, the Narcotics Division succeeded in creating a very large criminal class for itself to police (i.e., the whole doctor patient addict peddler community), instead of the very small one that Congress had intended (the smuggler and the peddler). Subsequent Division officials have sustained the enforcement oriented propaganda barrage: the addict is a criminal, a criminal type, or laden with criminal tendencies. Addicts can only be dealt with by being

> tracked down and isolated from society in total confine-
> ment; the cure-all is more arrests and stiffer criminal pen-
> alties for all narcotics offenders; and anyone who raises a
> dissenting voice is most likely a bungling "dogooder" or
> one who wants to undermine the foundations of our soci-
> ety. (King 1953, unpaginated text)

This observation is of considerable importance because it clari-
fies the attitude that the U.S. government has, for the most part,
taken about drug abuse, essentially since the adoption of the
Harrison Act in 1914 (see also Brecher and the Editors of Consumer Reports 1972, Chapter 8; Hickman 2007, Chapter 4;
Morgan 1981, Chapters 6 and 7).

The history of federal narcotics legislation in the 20th century, then, is a fascinating chronicle of efforts to reduce or
eliminate the illegal (and sometimes legal) use of opium and
its derivatives by a variety of mechanisms, sometimes just short
of simply declaring the possession and use of those products
as being against the law. Instead, the government usually took
the course of banning the importation or exportation of opium
and its derivatives, the manufacture or transportation of those
products, or their sale or purchase. In addition, federal laws at
first tended to make a distinction between opium and opiates
that were intended for purely recreational purposes—that is,
smoking—in contrast to its medicinal uses (although as the
Harrison experience showed, such distinctions became more
and more murky very early on).

The first federal law formulated on this approach was adopted shortly before the Harrison Act. It was the Smoking
Opium Exclusion of 1909, which was adopted in the spirit of
negotiations occurring simultaneously at the Shanghai opium
meetings. The act explained in the introduction that its purpose was to "prohibit the importation and use of opium for
other than medicinal purposes," a goal it intended to achieve
by banning the importation of any form of opium that could
be used or converted into "smoking opium." At the same time,

all medical uses of opium and opium products were specifically excluded from the act ("Comparison of the Tariffs of 1897 and 1909 in Parallel Columns" 1910).

Throughout the rest of the century, the federal government struggled with a variety of ways for dealing with the nation's "drug problem." That problem gradually evolved over the years to involve a wider range of drugs, such as cocaine, heroin, marijuana, and a host of synthetic drugs, to which the government responded, usually with more severe penalties for trafficking and use and sometimes with more aggressive treatment and prevention programs. Some of the most important laws that were adopted over this period were the following.

*Heroin Act of 1924* banned the manufacture, importation, possession, and use of heroin for any reason whatsoever in the United States, including all medical applications. (Hearings and testimony about the original bill are available at "Prohibiting the Importation of Opium for the Manufacture of Heroin, Hearings before the Committee on Ways and Means of the House of Representatives, on H.R. 7079" 1924.)

*Narcotic Drug Import and Export Act of 1922* extended the existing ban on the import and export of opium products, but added cocaine to the list of prohibited substances. A limited number of exceptions were allowed for legitimate medical use. The act also created the Federal Narcotics Control Board to carry out provisions of this and all previous drug control legislation (Quinn and McLaughlin 1973, 597; for provisions of the law, see "Regulations under the Narcotic Drugs Import and Export Act" 1939, 1064–1084).

*Uniform State Narcotic Act of 1932* was proposed and passed as an effort to bring drug laws in all states into conformity with each other. The law was drafted with the input of a number of medical and pharmaceutical organizations but was largely shaped by the Federal Narcotics Control Board. The act was eventually adopted by all 50 states and has been updated and renewed a number of times since its adoption (Baumohl 2011; "Controlled Substances Act Summary" 2015).

*Boggs Act of 1951* became law on November 2, 1951. It represented a dramatic increase in the severity of penalties for possession and use of and trafficking in narcotic drugs and, for the first time, marijuana. This was occasioned by general concern among legislators and the general public about the increase in illegal drug use after World War II. The act differed from preceding bills in a number of ways, one of which was the lumping of marijuana with opiate drugs for the first time. In addition, the penalties for illegal drug use were increased by about fourfold, with a minimum mandatory sentence of 2 years for simple possession of marijuana, cocaine, or heroin and a maximum sentence of 5 years; a minimum of 5 years and a maximum of 10 years for a second offense; and a minimum of 10 years and a maximum of 15 years for a third offense. The act was also significant in that it provides, for the first time in federal law, mandatory minimum sentencing, removing from judicial discretion the possibility of any less-severe punishments (Erlen and Spillane 2004, 76–92). Another effect of the Boggs Act was the passage by a number of states of similar "mini-Boggs" legislation over succeeding years, many of which imposed even more stringent penalties for drug use (Bonnie and Whitebread 1970, 1074–1076). Finally, the Boggs Act was significant because it specifically recognized the growing threat of drug abuse by young people, a group of drug users who had largely been ignored prior to the time (Bonnie and Whitebread 1970, 1064–1066).

*Narcotic Control Act of 1956* continued the trend of increasing severe penalties for trafficking in and use of illegal drugs. Also introduced by Representative Hale Boggs, the Narcotic Control Act reflected congressional concern that judges were still being too lenient in sentencing drug abusers and eliminated the possibility of suspending sentences or granting parole. One authority in the field of drug history has called the law "the most punitive and repressive anti-narcotics legislation ever adopted by Congress" (McWilliams 1990, 116; also see Cameron and Dillinger 2011; King 1972, Chapter 16).

*Drug Abuse Control Amendment of 1965* was passed primarily in response to concerns about the illicit use of certain types of drugs, such as depressants, stimulants, and hallucinogens that were then legal to use for medical purposes and had not yet been declared illegal for recreational purposes (King 1972, Chapter 26).

## Controlled Substances Act of 1970

The Controlled Substances Act of 1970 is perhaps the most important single piece of drug legislation in the history of the United States. The immediate impetus for the legislation was a ruling by the U.S. Supreme Court that crucial parts of the Marihuana Tax Act of 1937 were unconstitutional. Although the Court's decision did not speak to opium control laws specifically, it did raise questions about the type of drug laws the Congress had been passing over the preceding decades. In commenting on the situation, President Lyndon Johnson remarked in a 1968 speech before Congress that "present Federal laws dealing with these substances are a crazy quilt of inconsistent approaches and widely disparate criminal sanctions" ("59—Special Message to the Congress on Crime and Law Enforcement" 1968).

In response to such concerns, the Congress passed the Comprehensive Drug Abuse Prevention and Control Act of 1970, which President Richard M. Nixon then signed on October 27, 1970. The act had three sections that dealt with rehabilitation programs, control and enforcement, and importation and exportation of drugs. The act was designed to simplify and clarify the morass of drug laws that had been accumulating over the previous six decades. Title II of the act comprises the legislation that is now known simply as the Controlled Substances Act of 1970.

The initial section on rehabilitation programs was especially interesting, since that aspect of drug abuse had received relatively little attention in previous legislation. But the second section turned out to have the most significant impact on federal drug laws to the present day. In that section, five categories ("Schedules") of drugs were created. Each drug was assigned to one of those five categories depending on three criteria: (1) a drug's potential for abuse, (2) its value in accepted medical treatment in the United States, and (3) its safety when used under medical supervision. Thus, substances placed in Schedule I are those that (1) have a high potential for abuse, (2) have no currently accepted use for medical treatments in the United States, and (3) cannot be safely used even under appropriate medical supervision. Drugs traditionally regarded as the most dangerous—cocaine, the opiates, marijuana—are classified under Schedule I of the act. Other examples of Schedule I drugs today are lysergic acid diethylamide, mescaline, peyote, and psilocybin.

In contrast to Schedule I drugs, substances listed in Schedule V (1) have minimal potential for abuse, (2) have accepted medical applications in the United States, and (3) are generally regarded as safe to use under medical supervision (although they may lead to addiction). Examples of Schedule V drugs are certain cough medications that contain small amounts of codeine and products used to treat diarrhea that contain small amounts of opium. In the first announcement of scheduled drugs in the *Federal Register* in 1971, 59 substances were listed in Schedule I, 21 in Schedule II, 22 in Schedule III, 11 in Schedule IV, and 5 in Schedule V (Convention on Psychotropic Substances, 1971, 2015). A complete list of all drugs currently listed under one of the five categories can be found on the Drug Enforcement Administration website, at https://www.deadiversion.usdoj.gov/schedules/orangebook/orangebook.pdf.

The federal government has continued to adopt legislation dealing with all aspects of the drug abuse issue, some fine-tuning penalties for possession, use, and trafficking of illegal drugs, and others relating to the prevention and treatment of drug addiction and with programs of drug education. A useful summary of those laws can be found at "Laws" (2017). Individual states have also passed a very large number of drug laws that supplement federal laws. A good listing of those laws is available at "State Drug Possession Laws" (2017).

## Semisynthetic and Synthetic Opioids

All the opium-related compounds discussed thus far were long called opiates. They could be classified either as natural opiates (substances like opium and codeine that can be extracted from the opium plant) or as semisynthetic opiates (compounds obtained by making changes in a natural opiate, such as morphine and heroin). In the early 20th century, chemists began to make yet another category of opium-like compounds. These substances do not occur in nature, nor are they produced from natural components of opium. They are entirely new, synthetic compounds made from relatively simple compounds. At first, these compounds were called synthetic opiates. Over time, a new terminology has developed. All types of narcotic compounds related in anyway whatsoever to opium are now called opioids. The word is a combination of *opium* and *-oid*, a suffix meaning "similar to."

Of the numerous semisynthetic opioids that have been made, about five stand out in importance: heroin, oxycodone, hydrocodone, hydromorphone (also dihydromorphine), and buprenorphine. The history of heroin has already been discussed. Oxycodone was first synthesized in 1916 by German chemists Martin Freund and Edmund Speyer. As the chemical formulas in Figures 1.1 and 1.2 show, oxycodone's molecular structure is very similar to that of codeine, from which it is derived. Perhaps you can find the difference between the two formulas.

Oxycodone is sold under a number of trade names, including Endodan, OxyContin, Percodan, Percocet, and Roxicet. The compound is about six times as potent as its parent compound, codeine.

Four years later, in 1920, another semisynthetic opioid, hydrocodone, was discovered by German chemists Carl Mannich

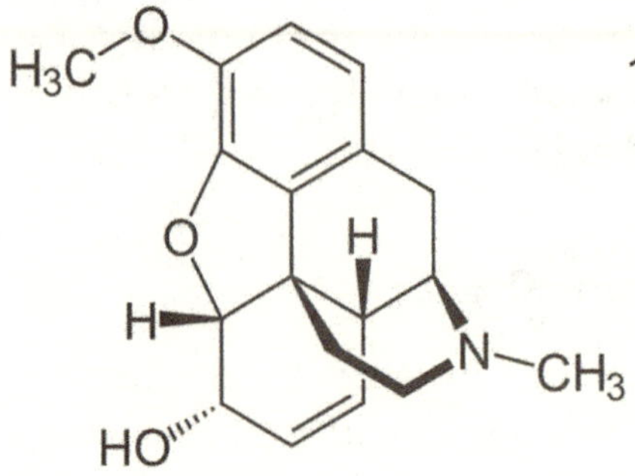

**Figure 1.1  Codeine**
*Source*: NEUROtiker

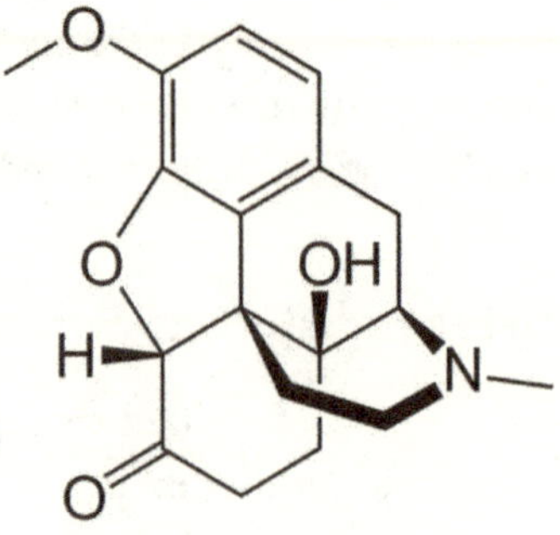

**Figure 1.2  Oxycodone**
*Source*: Fvasconcellos

and Helene Löwenheim. Again, notice the very modest difference between the new product and the codeine from which it was made (Figures 1.3 and 1.4).

Hydrocodone is about six times as potent as its parent, codeine. Probably the most familiar formulation of hydrocodone available on the market today is Vicodin.

Experiments to make semisynthetic analogs of morphine were also conducted. The most important result of those early studies was the synthesis of hydromorphone (also known as dihydromorphone) by researchers at Knoll Pharmaceuticals in 1924. Again, these molecular formulas show how similar these two compounds are to each other (Figures 1.5 and 1.6).

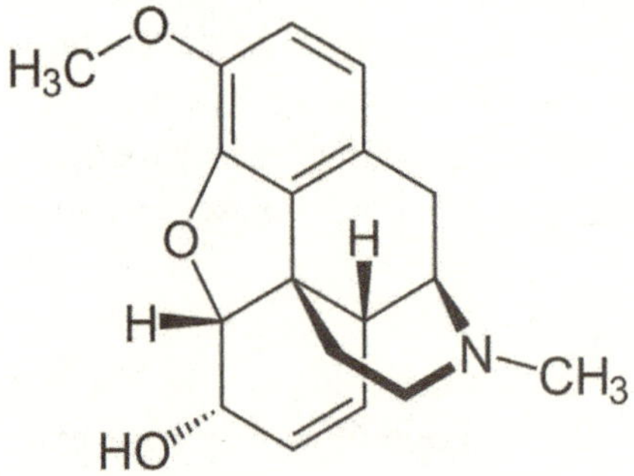

**Figure 1.3  Codeine**
*Source*: NEUROtiker

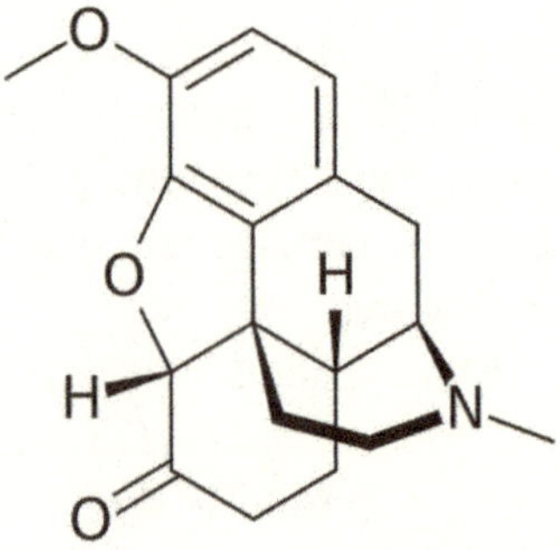

**Figure 1.4  Hydrocodone**
*Source*: Edgar181

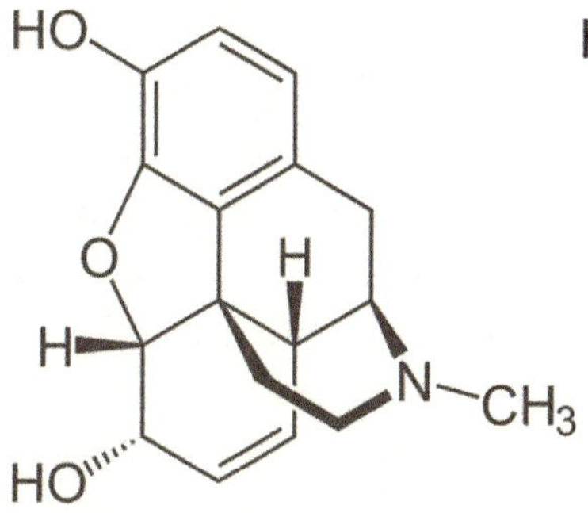

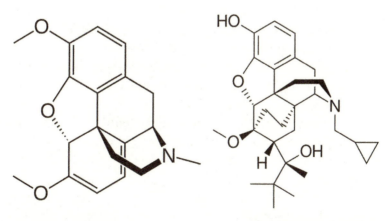

**Figure 1.5   Morphine**
*Source*: NEUROtiker

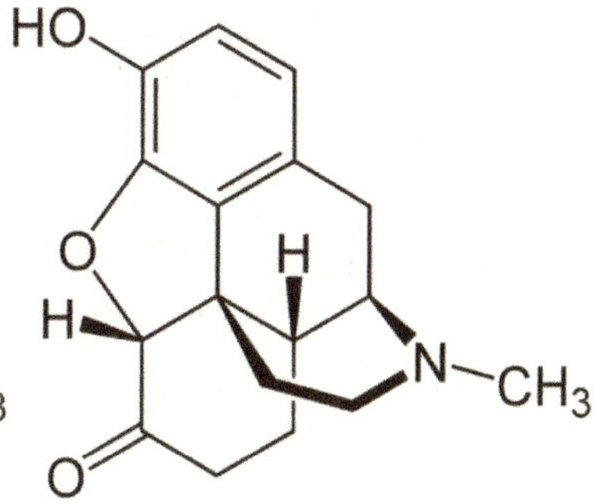

**Figure 1.6   Hydromorphone**
*Source*: Yikrazuul

Probably the best-known form of hydromorphone is sold under the trade name of Dilaudid. It is four to seven times as potent as the parent compound, morphine.

The final compound on this list is buprenorphine, an opioid that developed out of the search for a "safe" compound that would help addicts cut back on and, perhaps, give up their use of more dangerous opioids, such as heroin and oxycodone. It is produced from the parent compound thebaine, and its similarity to that compound can be seen in the following chemical formulas (Figures 1.7 and 1.8).

**Figure 1.7   Thebaine**
*Source*: Fvasconcellos

**Figure 1.8   Buprenorphine**
*Source*: Harbin

The first synthetic opioid to have been discovered was pethidine, also known as meperidine. It was first prepared by German chemist Otto Eisleb in 1932. Eisleb was looking for an anticholinergic/antispasmodic agent (a substance that interrupts nerve action) and did not realize that his new drug might have other applications. The most important of those applications, as an opium-like analgesic agent, was later discovered by German chemist Otto Schaumann in 1939 (Michaelis, Schölkens, and Rudolphi 2007). The drug was given the trade name of Dolantin but has since become better known as Demerol.

Two other synthetic opioids of special importance are methadone and fentanyl. Methadone is one of the many compounds synthesized in the search for a strong analgesic that was not addictive, as was the then most popular product, heroin. A concerted research effort for such a compound was initiated in the 1930s, which resulted in the discovery in 1937 of a compound then called Hoechst 10820 or, more commonly, polamidon. Credit for the first synthesis of the drug goes to German chemists Max Bockmühl and Gustav Ehrhart. When the drug was introduced in the United States after the end of World War II, it was given the name of methadone, by which it is known today. Further research on methadone revealed an unexpected property of the drug: it was effective in aiding individuals abusing or addicted to other opioids. Therefore, a heroin addict who wished to reduce or eliminate his or her use of the drug might be prescribed methadone as a first step in treatment. Although other drugs are now available to assist in addiction treatment for opioids, methadone is still used for such purposes (Defalque and Wright 2007).

The second of these synthetic opioids, fentanyl, is of special interest because of its role in today's opioid epidemic. Its history begins in the Belgian town of Beerse, where a local researcher by the name of Paul Janssen had decided to create a new company, to be called Janssen Pharmaceutica. The main interest of the company was to find new, more potent, and faster-acting analgesics. Janssen decided that a part of the heroin and meperidine molecules, called the piperidine ring, was the key to his search. He tested dozens and dozens of compounds made from a piperidine ring to which various changes had been made. In 1957, he made a major breakthrough when he discovered a compound that he called phenopiperidine that was 25 times more potent than morphine and 50 times more potent than the parent compound, meperidine. As impressive as this result was, Janssen continued to look for even more powerful and faster-acting analgesics. In 1960, he found such a compound, fentanyl. Fentanyl was found to be more than 10 times as potent as phenopiperidine and 100–200 times as potent as morphine. The drug was finally approved for use in the United States by the FDA in 1968. In today's world, it is one of the most problematic compounds in the nation's opioid epidemic (Stanley 2014).

A second opioid of importance synthesized by the Janssen lab in 1974 is carfentanil or carfentanyl, marketed under the trade name Wildnil. The drug was intended for use as an anesthetic for the treatment of large animals, such as horses and elephants. It is reputed to be 10,000 times as potent as morphine and 100 times as potent as fentanyl. The intake of as little as 2 milligrams is lethal to the average human ("Carfentanil: A Dangerous New Factor in the Opioid Crisis" 2016). Carfentanil has come to public attention only within the past few years. It has hit a handful of communities and states more severely than others. For example, the drug apparently first reached the streets of Akron, Ohio, on July 5, 2016. On that date, the city's police department reported 17 cases of carfentanil overdose and 1 death within a nine-hour period. During the next six months, 140 deaths from the drug were reported in the county (Katz 2017; for a graphic that illustrates the relative strengths of major opioids, see Keating and Granados 2017).

## The Brain Chemistry of Opioids

When a person takes a drug, a complex series of chemical reactions occur in the brain that result in the signs and symptoms associated with drug dependence, addiction, withdrawal, tolerance, and death by overdose. A brief overview of those changes follows here.

A major component of these changes is a group of compounds known as *endogenous opioids*. The endogenous opioids consist of three chemical families, known as the endorphins, enkephalins, and dynorphins. These compounds produce a variety of effects on the brain, including relief from pain, a reduction in the rate of respiration, and a general sense of calmness. Some experts believe that endogenous opioids may be responsible for an even wider array of effects that result in positive emotions not only about oneself but also toward other people. These views were put forward, for example, by one of the discoverers of endogenous opioids, Candace Pert, in a series of books that included *Molecules of Emotion, Why You Feel the Way You Feel*, and *Everything You Need to Know to Feel G(o)od* (Freedman 2007).

Endogenous opioids exert their influence on the brain by transmitting electrical impulses from one neuron (nerve cell) to an adjacent neuron. They are released from the end (axon) of one neuron, pass through the space between the two neurons (the synaptic gap), and attach to the head (dendrite) of the second neuron. Because of the way in which they act, endogenous opioids belong to a class of compounds known as *neurotransmitters* ("carriers of a nerve message"). Attachment occurs at specialized parts of the receiving neuron known as *receptor sites*. A receptor site is a portion of the neuron that has a very distinctive three-dimensional shape that matches the shape of an opioid molecule. The most common analogy used for the process is a lock-and-key model, in which a key (the opioid molecule) fits very tightly into the lock (the receptor site). (For a video of this process, see Kuhar 2017.)

*Exogenous opioids* are substances that do not occur naturally in the brain but act in the same way as do endogenous opioids. That is, once introduced into the brain, they attach to receptor sites on neurons in the same manner as do endogenous opioids. One important difference is that they tend to bind more tightly to a receptor site than do their natural cousins, thus reducing the efficacy of the system by which endogenous opioids normally operate. Among the exogenous opioids familiar to readers of this book are buprenorphine, codeine, heroin, hydrocodone, hydromorphone, methadone, morphine, oxycodone, and oxymorphone.

In a person who uses opioid drugs on a regular basis, for either legal or illegal purposes, the brain eventually becomes *tolerant* to the drug. That is, physical changes in the nervous system become adjusted to the presence of an exogenous opioid and, in the process, begin to require ever-increasing levels of the drug. Thus, a person who may originally use a single dose per day of an opioid drug will eventually need two doses a day, or three or four.

In other words, the brain slowly becomes *physically dependent* on the drug. That is, exogenous opioids have come to take the place of endogenous opioids, which no longer function normally in the brain. The condition of physical dependence is diagnosed by certain *withdrawal symptoms*. When the brain no longer receives the exogenous opioid to which it has become accustomed—or to the level of opioid needed—the nervous system begins to "fall apart," unable to carry out the normal functions on which the body depends. Typical withdrawal signs and symptoms are a sense of unease, irritability, sweating, nausea, runny nose, tremor, vomiting, muscle pain, and craving for another opiate dose. Left untreated, additional symptoms that may develop include abdominal cramping, diarrhea, dilation of the pupils, and "goose bumps." These symptoms are unpleasant, but they are not generally life threatening, and they can be treated rather easily by drugs and maintenance programs ("Withdrawing from Opiates and Opioids" 2017).

Opioid *addiction* was once considered to be a moral or psychological issue. Individuals often argued that persons could quit drug use if they simply tried hard enough or if they had the best-available counseling or pharmaceutical services. That viewpoint is now largely obsolete. The present view about opioid addiction is that it is a symptom of brain disease. The continuing use of exogenous opioids leads to a wide variety of structural changes in the human brain, some of which may not be reversible without profound medical treatment of some kind. Research now provides clear evidence that ongoing opioid drug use can result in changes in the homeostasis (maintenance of balanced functions) and allostasis (ability to adjust to changes) of the brain, as well as alterations in the mechanisms by which neuronal messages are transmitted in the brain and structural changes in the brain itself. (For an excellent visual presentation of this topic, see "Understanding Addiction Reward and Pleasure in the Brain" 2017.)

As this discussion illustrates, the terms *dependence* and *addiction* are not synonymous: They refer to two different conditions present in the brain after the use of opioids ("Physical Dependence and Addiction" 2016). Yet another term that is sometimes used to describe abnormal brain functions because of opioid use is *opioid use disorder* (OUD). *OUD* is a psychiatric term used to describe a condition that meets at least two of about a dozen different signs and symptoms within a 12-month period. Among those signs and symptoms are a persistent desire or unsuccessful efforts to cut down or control opioid use, a craving or strong desire to use opioids, recurrent opioid use in situations that are physically hazardous, and symptoms of tolerance and/or withdrawal ("DSM 5 Opioid Use Disorder Checklist" 2017).

## Conclusion

Opioids have been an integral part of human society since the beginning of recorded time. They have been used primarily for two purposes: for the cure of medical conditions, primarily the relief of pain, and for recreational purposes. Opioids have had a mixed success as a medicine. They have, in fact, turned out to be among the most powerful and effective of all analgesics for a variety of purposes. But they have never lived up to the more extravagant claims for their curative powers. Today, they continue to hold a place of priority in the arsenal of drugs used by physicians and surgeons for treating severe and/or chronic pain. Overall, therapeutic uses of opioids have occupied a place of respect in human civilization.

The value of opioids for recreational uses is more problematic. There is no question that various cultures have regarded opioids as anything from a relatively harmless form of relaxation or even a tool to creative thought. Overall, however, the physical and mental harm caused by this group of drugs has either prevented societal approval of such applications or prompted the passage of severe laws against their production, distribution, and use.

The United States in the early 21st century is experiencing what is probably the most widespread and serious set of problems created by the abuse of and addiction to opioids. Chapter 2 explores how the opium epidemic came about, the problems it poses for society, and methods that have been and are being developed to treat and prevent the misuse of opioids.

### References

"Abuse of Prescription (Rx) Drugs Affects Young Adults Most." 2016. National Institute on Drug Abuse. https://www.drugabuse.gov/related-topics/trends-statistics/infographics/abuse-prescription-rx-drugs-affects-young-adults-most. Accessed on November 28, 2017.

"An Act of June 30, 1906, Public Law 59-384, 34 STAT 768, for Preventing the Manufacture, Sale, or Transportation of Adulterated or Misbranded or Poisonous or Deleterious Foods, Drugs, Medicines, and Liquors, and for Regulating Traffic Therein, and for Other Purposes." 1906. National Archives. http://research.archives.gov/description/5716297. Accessed on December 6, 2017.

Agnew, Jeremy. 2014. *Alcohol and Opium in the Old West: Use, Abuse, and Influence.* Jefferson, NC: McFarland & Company, Inc.

Aldrich, Michael R. n.d. "Historical Notes on Women Addicts" (CNS Productions). https://www.cnsproductions .com/pdf/Aldrich.pdf. Accessed on December 4, 2017.

"Alexander Wood." 2017. Royal College of Physicians of Edinburgh. https://www.rcpe.ac.uk/heritage/college-history/alexander-wood. Accessed on December 4, 2017.

Allingham, Philip V. 2006. "The Opium Trade, Seventh through Nineteenth Centuries." The Victorian Web. http://www.victorianweb.org/history/empire/opiumwars/ opiumwars1.html. Accessed on December 3, 2017.

Annalen der Physik. 1817. Google Books. https://books .google.com/books?id=EF9ZAAAAcAAJ&pg=PP13&lpg=P P13&dq#v=onepage&q&f=false. Accessed on December 3, 2017.

Askwith, Richard. 1998. "How Aspirin Turned Hero." *Sunday Times.* https://www.opioids.com/heroin/heroinhistory .html. Accessed on December 5, 2017.

Baker, Peggy M. n.d. "Patent Medicines: Cures and Quacks." Pilgrim Hall Museum. http://www.pilgrimhallmuseum .org/pdf/Patent_Medicine.pdf. Accessed on December 6, 2017.

Batmanabane, Gitanjali. 2014. "Why Patients in Pain Cannot Get 'God's Own Medicine'?" *Journal of Pharmacology and Pharmacotherapeutics.* 5(2): 81–82.

Baumohl, Jim. 2011. "Uniform State Narcotics Act." In Mark A. R. Kleiman and James E. Hawdon, eds. *Encyclopedia of Drug Policy.* Thousand Oaks, CA: Sage Publications, 795–797.

Bewley-Taylor, David R. 1999. *The United States and International Drug Control, 1909–1997.* New York: Pinter.

Blau, Max. 2017. "Stat Forecast: Opioids Could Kill Nearly 500,000 Americans in the Next Decade." STAT@JPM. https://www.statnews.com/2017/06/27/opioid-deaths-forecast/. Accessed on November 28, 2017.

Bonnie, Richard J., and Charles H. Whitebread. 1970. "The Forbidden Fruit and the Tree of Knowledge: An Inquiry into the Legal History of American Marijuana Prohibition." *Virginia Law Review*. 56(6): 971–1203. http://www.votehemp.com/PDF/The_Forbidden_Fruit_and_The_Tree_of_Knowledge.pdf. Accessed on December 6, 2017.

Booth, Martin. 1999. *Opium: A History*. New York: St. Martin's Griffin.

Brecher, Edward M., and the Editors of Consumer Reports. 1972. *Licit and Illicit Drugs*. Boston; Toronto: Little, Brown. http://www.druglibrary.org/schaffer/library/studies/cu/cumenu.htm. Accessed on December 2, 2017.

Bushak, Lecia. 2016. "Civilization's Painkiller: A Brief History of Opioids." *Newsweek*. http://www.newsweek.com/civilization-painkiller-brief-history-opioid-486164. Accessed on November 29, 2017.

Cameron, Jennifer M., and Ronna J. Dillinger. 2011. "Narcotic Control Act." In Mark A. R. Kleiman and James E. Hawdon, eds. *Encyclopedia of Drug Policy*. Thousand Oaks, CA: Sage Publications.

"Carfentanil: A Dangerous New Factor in the Opioid Crisis." 2016. Officer Safety Alert. Drug Enforcement Agency. https://www.dea.gov/divisions/hq/2016/hq092216_attach.pdf. Accessed on December 10, 2017.

"A Century of International Drug Control." 2009. United Nations Office on Drugs and Crime. http://www.unodc.org/documents/data-and-analysis/Studies/100_Years_of_Drug_Control.pdf. Accessed on December 6, 2017.

"Chinese Cultural Studies: Lin Zixu Lin Tse-Hsu (1839 CE). Letter of Advice to Queen Victoria." n.d. https://www

.coursehero.com/file/27214024/Chinese-Cultural-Studies-Lin-Tse-Hsu-1785-1850-Letter-to-Queen-Victoria-1839pdf/ Accessed on March 19, 2018.

"Codeine." 2017. Global Information Network about Drugs. http://www.ginad.org/en/drugs/drugs/237/codeine. Accessed on December 5, 2017.

"Comparison of the Tariffs of 1897 and 1909 in Parallel Columns." 1910. Washington, DC: Government Printing Office. https://archive.org/details/cu31924018727697. Accessed on December 6, 2017.

Connor, Steve. 1993. "Science/A Day in the Life of a Medieval Hospital: On a Windswept Hill in Scotland, Archaeologists Are Excavating the Site of an Infirmary Run by Monks. Their Finds Shed New Light on Medical Practice in the Middle Ages, Says Steve Connor." *Independent*. http://www.independent.co.uk/arts-entertainment/science-a-day-in-the-life-of-a-medieval-hospital-on-a-windswept-hill-in-scotland-archaeologists-are-1484182.html. Accessed on November 29, 2017.

"Controlled Substances." 2017. Drug Enforcement Administration. https://www.deadiversion.usdoj.gov/schedules/orangebook/e_cs_sched.pdf. Accessed on December 2, 2017.

"Controlled Substances Act Summary." 2015. Uniform Law Commission. http://www.uniformlaws.org/ActSummary.aspx?title=Controlled%20Substances%20Act. Accessed on December 6, 2017.

Convention on Psychotropic Substances, 1972. United Nations. 2015. https://www.unodc.org/pdf/convention_1971_en.pdf. Accessed on March 19, 2018.

"Data Brief 166: Drug-Poisoning Deaths Involving Opioid Analgesics: United States, 1999–2011." 2016. https://www.cdc.gov/nchs/data/databriefs/db166_table.pdf#1.

https://www.cdc.gov/nchs/data/databriefs/db273_table.pdf. Accessed on November 9, 2017.

Davenport-Hines, Richard Peter Treadwell. 2002. *The Pursuit of Oblivion: A Global History of Narcotics*. New York: Norton.

Davenport-Hines, Richard Peter Treadwell. 2004. *The Pursuit of Oblivion: A Global History of Narcotics*. New York: Norton.

Defalque, Ray J., and Amos J. Wright. 2007. "The Early History of Methadone. Myths and Facts." *Bulletin of Anesthesia History.* 25(3): 13–16.

De Quincey, Thomas. 1821. "Confessions of an Opium Eater." Project Gutenberg. https://www.gutenberg.org/files/2040/2040-h/2040-h.htm. Accessed on November 25, 2017. This essay originally appeared in *London Magazine* on September and October 1821 and was revised and republished again in book form in 1822 and, in revised form, 1856.

Derks, Hans. 2012. *History of the Opium Problem: The Assault on the East, ca. 1600–1950*. Boston: Leiden.

Diniejko, Andrzej. 2002. "Victorian Drug Use." The Victorian Web. http://www.victorianweb.org/victorian/science/addiction/addiction2.html. Accessed on December 1, 2017.

Doyle, W. P. 2017. "William Gregory (1803–1858)." The University of Edinburgh. School of Chemistry. http://www.chem.ed.ac.uk/about-us/history/professors/william-gregory. Accessed on December 4, 2017.

"DSM 5 Opioid Use Disorder Checklist." 2017. Buppractice. https://www.buppractice.com/node/19556. Accessed on January 9, 2018.

Duarte, Danilo Freire. 2005. "Una Historia Breve Del Opio Y De Los Opioides; Opium and Opioids: A Brief History." *Revista Brasileira De Anestesiologia.* 55(1):

135–146. http://www.scielo.br/scielo.php?pid=S0034-70942005000100015&script=sci_arttext&tlng=en.

Einhorn, Max. 1899. "Heroin and Heroin Hydrochlor." *Clinical Excerpts.* 5(10): 168–169. https://books.google.com/books?id=kcxXAAAAMAAJ&printsec=frontcover&source=gbs_ge_summary_r&cad=0#v=onepage&q&f=false. Accessed on December 5, 2017.

Erlen, Jonathon, and Joseph F. Spillane. 2004. *Federal Drug Control: The Evolution of Policy and Practice.* New York: Pharmaceutical Products Press.

"Felix Hoffmann." 2015. Chemical Heritage Foundation. https://www.chemheritage.org/historical-profile/felix-hoffmann. Accessed on December 5, 2017.

"59—Special Message to the Congress on Crime and Law Enforcement: 'To Insure the Public Safety.'" 1968. American Presidency Project. http://www.presidency.ucsb.edu/ws/?pid=29237#axzz1k1QdB1Wg. Accessed on December 6, 2017.

Forbes, David W., ed. 1998–2003. *Hawaiian National Bibliography, 1780–1900.* Honolulu: University of Hawaii Press.

Freedman, Joshua. 2007. "The Physics of Emotion: Candace Pert on Feeling Go(o)d." sixseconds. http://www.6seconds.org/2007/01/26/the-physics-of-emotion-candace-pert-on-feeling-good/. Accessed on December 30, 2017.

Fugazzola Delpino, M. A., et al. 1993. "La Marmotta (Anguillara Sabazia, RM). Scavi 1989: Un Abitato Perilacustre De Età Neolitica." *Archeozoologia della Grotta dell'Uzzo.* Sicilia, S: 181–304.

Gieringer, Dale. 2005. "125th Anniversary of the First U.S. Anti-Drug Law: San Francisco's Opium Den Ordinance (Nov. 15, 1875)." http://www.drugsense.org/dpfca/opiumlaw.html. Accessed on December 6, 2017.

Goldberg, Jeff. 2014. *Flowers in the Blood: The Story of Opium.* New York: Skyhorse Publishing.

Goldfinger, Shandra. 2006. "Opium Trade in China." https://www.mtholyoke.edu/~goldf20s/politics116/trade.html. Accessed on December 2, 2017.

"Greek Texts and Translations." 2017. http://perseus.uchicago.edu/perseus-cgi/citequery3.pl?dbname=GreekFeb2011&query=Hom.%20Od.%204.220&getid=2. Accessed on November 28, 2017.

Hamilton, Gillian R., and Thomas F. Baskett. 2000. "History of Anesthesia—In the Arms of Morpheus: The Development of Morphine for Postoperative Pain Relief." *Canadian Journal of Anaesthesia.* 47(4): 367–374. https://link.springer.com/content/pdf/10.1007/BF03020955.pdf. Accessed on December 4, 2017.

Hedman, Jason. 2012. "Commissioner Lin Zexu and the Opium War." Jasonhedman. https://jasonhedman.wordpress.com/2012/11/28/commissioner-lin-zexu-and-the-opium-war/. Accessed on December 3, 2017.

"Heroin (n.)." 2017. *Online Etymology Dictionary.* https://www.etymonline.com/word/heroin. Accessed on December 3, 2017.

Heydari, M., M. H. Hashempur, and A. Zargaran. 2013. "Medicinal Aspects of Opium as Described in Avicenna's Canon of Medicine." *Acta Medico-historica Adriatica.* 11(1): 101–112.

Hickman, Timothy Alton. 2007. *The Secret Leprosy of Modern Days: Narcotic Addiction and Cultural Crisis in the United States, 1870–1920.* Amherst: University of Massachusetts Press.

"History of Opium, Opium Eating, and Smoking." 1892. *The Journal of the Anthropological Institute of Great Britain and Ireland.* 21: 329–331.

Hodgson, Barbara. 2008. *In the Arms of Morpheus: The Tragic History of Laudanum, Morphine and Patent Medicines*. New York: Greystone Books.

Huxtable, Ryan J., and Stephan K. W. Schwarz. 2001. "The Isolation of Morphine—First Principles in Science and Ethics." *Molecular Interventions*. 1(4): 189–191. https://www.researchgate.net/publication/5419568_The_Isolation_of_Morphine-First_Principles_in_Science_and_Ethics. Accessed on December 3, 2017.

Janssen, Wallace F. 1981. "The Story of the Laws behind the Labels." U.S. Food and Drug Administration. https://www.fda.gov/AboutFDA/WhatWeDo/History/Overviews/ucm056044.htm. Accessed on December 6, 2017.

Kane, H. H. 1880. "The Hypodermic Injection of Morphine." New York: Chas. L. Bermingham & Co. https://ia800203.us.archive.org/25/items/hypodermicinject00kaneuoft/hypodermicinject00kaneuoft.pdf. Accessed on December 4, 2017.

Kantzveldt. 2014. "Annunaki and the Cultivation of Opium." abovetopsecret. http://www.abovetopsecret.com/forum/thread1043294/pg1. Accessed on November 28, 2017.

Katz, Josh. 2017. "Drug Deaths in America Are Rising Faster Than Ever." *New York Times*. https://www.nytimes.com/interactive/2017/06/05/upshot/opioid-epidemic-drug-overdose-deaths-are-rising-faster-than-ever.html. Accessed on December 10, 2017.

Keating, Dan, and Samuel Granados. 2017. "See How Deadly Street Opioids Like 'Elephant Tranquilizer' Have Become." *Washington Post*. https://www.washingtonpost.com/graphics/2017/health/opioids-scale/?utm_term=.54ec367f21c2. Accessed on December 26, 2017.

Keyser, Jason. 2002. "Vessels Offer Windows into Ancient Use of Drugs." *Los Angeles Times*. http://articles.latimes

.com/2002/aug/11/news/adfg-narcs11. Accessed on
November 28, 2017.

Kienholz, Mary. 2008. *Opium Traders and Their Worlds*.
Vol. 1. New York: iUniverse.

King, Rufus. 1953. "The Narcotics Bureau and the Harrison
Act: Jailing the Healers and the Sick." *The Yale Law Journal*.
62(5): 784–787. http://druglibrary.org/special/king/king1
.htm. Accessed on December 6, 2017.

King, Rufus. 1972. *The Drug Hang-Up: America's Fifty Year
Folly*. New York: Norton. http://druglibrary.org/special/
king/dhu/dhumenu.htm. Accessed on December 6, 2017.

Kritikos, P. G., and S. P. Papadaki. 1967. "The History
of the Poppy and of Opium and Their Expansion in
Antiquity in the Eastern Mediterranean Area." https://
www.unodc.org/unodc/en/data-and-analysis/bulletin/
bulletin_1967-01-01_3_page004.html. Accessed on
November 28, 2017.

Kuhar, Michael. 2017. "The Addicted Brain." Emory
University. https://www.coursera.org/learn/addiction-and-
the-brain/lecture/RMkZR/cocaine-nicotine. Accessed on
December 30, 2017.

Kylebridge. 2017. "Opium, Empire, and India (Part I)."
Points: The Blog of the Alcohols & Drugs History Society.
https://pointsadhsblog.wordpress.com/2017/04/04/opium-
empire-and-india-part-i/. Accessed on November 30, 2017.

Latham, R. G. 1801. *The Works of Thomas Sydenham, M. D.*
London: The Sydenham Society. https://ia902604.us
.archive.org/11/items/worksofthomassyd02sydeuoft/
worksofthomassyd02sydeuoft.pdf. Accessed on December 1,
2017.

"Laws." 2017. The National Alliance of Advocates for
Buprenorphine Treatment. https://www.naabt.org/laws
.cfm. Accessed on December 6, 2017.

Lowes, Peter D. 1966. *The Genesis of International Narcotics Control*. Geneva: Librairie Droz.

Macht, David I. 1915. "The History of Opium and Some of Its Preparations and Alkaloids." *The Journal of the American Medical Association*. 64(6): 477–481. https://books.google .com/books?id=0ZJMAQAAMAAJ&pg=PA477&lpg=PA4 77&dq#v=onepage&q&f=false. Accessed on November 29, 2017.

Martin, Steven. 2012. *Opium Fiend: A 21st Century Slave to a 19th Century Addiction*. New York: Villard Books.

McCoy, Alfred W. 1972. *The Politics of Heroin in Southeast Asia*. New York: Harper & Row. http://renincorp.org/ bookshelf/politics-of-heroin-in-south.pdf. Accessed on March 19, 2018.

McWilliams, John C. 1990. *The Protectors: Harry J. Anslinger and the Federal Bureau of Narcotics, 1930–1962*. Newark: University of Delaware Press.

"Merck & Co., Inc." 2017. Lehman Brothers Collection. Harvard Business School. https://www.library.hbs.edu/hc/ lehman/company.html?company=merck_co_inc. Accessed on December 4, 2017.

Merlin, M. D. 2003. "Archaeological Evidence for the Tradition of Psychoactive Plant Use in the Old World." *Economic Botany*. 57(3): 295–323. https://ia601605.us.archive.org/ 23/items/Merlin2003AncientPsychoactivePlantUse/Merlin_ 2003_Ancient_Psychoactive_Plant_Use.pdf. Accessed on November 28, 2017.

Michaelis, Martin, Bernward Schölkens, and Karl Rudolphi. 2007. "An Anthology from Naunyn-Schmiedeberg's Archives of Pharmacology: O. Schaumann (1940) Über eine Neue Klasse von Verbindungen mit Spasmolytischer und Zentral Analgetischer Wirkung unter Besonderer Berücksichtigung des 1 methyl 4 phenyl piperidin 4 carbonsäure äthylesters (Dolantin). Archiv f. Experiment.

Path. u. Pharmakol. 196: 109–36." *Naunyn-Schmiedeberg's Archives of Pharmacology*. 375(2): 81–84.

Milligan, Barry. 2003. "Introduction." *Confessions of an Opium Eater. Thomas De Quincey*. London: Penguin Books.

Mohanakrishna Reddy, Mudiam, et al. 2003. "Application of Capillary Zone Electrophoresis in the Separation and Determination of the Principal Gum Opium Alkaloids." *Electrophoresis*. 24(9): 1437–1441.

Morgan, H. Wayne. 1981. *Drugs in America: A Social History, 1800–1980*. Syracuse, NY: Syracuse University Press.

Öncel, Öztan, and Demirhan Erdemir. 2007. "A View of the Development of Some Anaesthesic and Anaelgesic Drugs in the Western World and in Turkey and Some Original Documents." 38th International Conference for the History of Pharmacy. https://idus.us.es/xmlui/bitstream/handle/11441/39548/101.pdf?sequence=1. Accessed on November 29, 2017.

O'Neill, Tony. 2012. "10 Old-Timey Medicines That Got People High." *Alternet*. https://www.alternet.org/drugs/10-old-timey-medicines-got-people-high. Accessed on December 2, 2017.

"The Opening to China Part II: The Second Opium War, the United States, and the Treaty of Tianjin, 1857–1859." 2017. Office of the Historian. https://history.state.gov/milestones/1830-1860/china-2. Accessed on December 3, 2017.

"Opium, Morphine, and Heroin." 2011. Hooked: Illegal Drugs, episode 2. https://www.youtube.com/watch?v=mT8fiAn74t0. Accessed on November 30, 2017.

"The Opium Alkaloids." 1953. United Nations Office on Drugs and Crime. https://www.unodc.org/unodc/en/data-and-analysis/bulletin/bulletin_1953-01-01_3_page005.html. Accessed on December 3, 2017.

"Opium in Japan." 2017. Cannabis in Japan. http://www
.japanhemp.org/en/opium.htm. Accessed on December 1,
2017.

"Opium Poppy: Herb of Heaven or Hell." 1997. Sacred
Earth. http://www.sacredearth.com/ethnobotany/
plantprofiles/poppy.php. Accessed on November 29, 2017.

"Origins and History of Opium." 1994. The Herb Museum.
http://www.herbmuseum.ca/content/origins-and-history-
opium. Accessed on November 26, 2017.

"Physical Dependence and Addiction." 2016. NAAB. http://
www.naabt.org/addiction_physical-dependence.cfm.
Accessed on December 15, 2017.

"Powers-Weightman-Rosengarten Co." 2007. Bottlebooks
.com. http://www.bottlebooks.com/wholesale%20
druggists/powers-weightman-rosengarten.html. Accessed
on December 4, 2017.

"Prohibiting the Importation of Opium for the Manufacture
of Heroin, Hearings before the Committee on Ways
and Means of the House of Representatives, on H.R.
7079." 1924. Hathi Trust. https://catalog.hathitrust.org/
Record/100668043. Accessed on December 6, 2017.

Quinn, Thomas M., and Gerald T. McLaughlin. 1973. "The
Evolution of Federal Drug Control Legislation." *Catholic
University Law Review*. 22(3): 586–627. http://scholarship
.law.edu/cgi/viewcontent.cgi?article=2622&context=lawrev
iew. Accessed on December 6, 2017.

"Regulations under the Narcotic Drugs Import and Export
Act." 1939. In The Code of Federal Regulations of the
United States of America. Vol. 5. https://books.google
.com/books?id=beuyAAAAIAAJ&pg=PA1065&lpg=PA10
65&dq=%2242+stat.+596%22+heroin&source=bl&ots=p
2Boe4f72s&sig=8cLwlV5zo3T0XOZkN8bEj65yFqc&hl=
en&sa=X&ei=dyk0VaD8KMzUoATDvIDwBg&ved=0C

DQQ6AEwBQ#v=snippet&q=%22narcotic%20drug%20 import%22&f=false. Accessed on December 6, 2017.

"Remarks by President Trump on Combatting [*sic*] Drug Demand and the Opioid Crisis." 2017. https://www .whitehouse.gov/the-press-office/2017/10/26/remarks-president-trump-combatting-drug-demand-and-opioid-crisis. Accessed on November 13, 2017.

Rhein, John H. W. 1919. "Federal and State Laws in Relation to the Drug Habit." *Archives of Neurology and Psychiatry.* 2(4): 482–483. https://books.google.com/ books?id=1ZNGAAAAYAAJ. Accessed on December 2, 2017.

Robinette, Glenn W. 2008. *Did Lin Zexu Make Morphine?* Valparaiso, Chile: Graffiti Militante Press. https:// archive.org/stream/bub_gb_QReYAQos2goC/bub_gb_ QReYAQos2goC_djvu.txt. Accessed on December 5, 2017.

Rosso, Ana Maria. 2010. "Poppy and Opium in Ancient Times: Remedy or Narcotic?" *Biomedicine International.* 1: 81–87.

Rudd, Rose A., et al. 2016. "Increases in Drug and Opioid Overdose Deaths—United States, 2000–2015." *Morbidity and Mortality Weekly.* 65(50–51): 1445–1452. https:// www.cdc.gov/mmwr/volumes/65/wr/mm655051e1.htm. Accessed on November 9, 2017.

Rzepa, Henry S. 2015. "Opium, Morphine and Heroin." http://www.ch.ic.ac.uk/rzepa/mim/drugs/html/morphine_ text.htm. Accessed on December 3, 2017.

Scarborough, John. 1978. "Theophrastus on Herbals and Herbal Remedies." *Journal of the History of Biology.* 11(2): 353–385.

Schaefer, Bernd. 2016. *Natural Products in the Chemical Industry.* Berlin: Springer-Verlag.

Scott, Ian. 1998. "Heroin: A Hundred Year Habit." *History Today*. 48(6). http://cbm.msoe.edu/markMyweb/ ddtyResources/documents/opioidReceptorHeroin.pdf. Accessed on December 5, 2017.

Shahnavaz, S. 2014. "Afyun." *Encyclopædia Iranica*. I(6): 594–598. http://www.iranicaonline.org/articles/afyun-opium. Accessed on November 30, 2017.

"Soldier's Disease." 2011. Civil War Rx. http://civilwarrx .blogspot.com/2016/06/soldiers-disease.html. Accessed on December 4, 2017.

Stanley, Theodore H. 2014. "The Fentanyl Story." *The Journal of Pain*. 15(12): 1215–1226.

"State Drug Possession Laws." 2017. FindLaw. http:// statelaws.findlaw.com/criminal-laws/drug-possession.html. Accessed on December 6, 2017.

"Supply of Opiate Raw Materials and Demand for Opiates for Medical and Scientific Purposes." 2015. International Narcotics Control Board. https://www.incb.org/ documents/Narcotic-Drugs/Technical-Publications/2015/ part_3_SandD_E.pdf. Accessed on November 26, 3017.

"Suppression of Abuse of Opium and Other Drugs." 1912. United States Treaties. Library of Congress. http://www.loc .gov/law/help/us-treaties/bevans/m-ust000001-0855.pdf. Accessed on December 6, 2017.

Terry, Charles E., and Mildred Pellens. 1928. *The Opium Problem*. Camden, NJ: The Haddon Craftsmen. https:// babel.hathitrust.org/cgi/pt?id=mdp.39015006502523;view =1up;seq=8. Accessed on December 4, 2017.

"Two to Three." 2004. Heroin Helper. https://www.hero inhelper.com/curious/chemistry/2to3.shtml. Accessed on December 3, 2017.

"Understanding Addiction Reward and Pleasure in the Brain." 2017. InspireMalibu. https://www.inspiremalibu.com/blog/ alcohol-addiction/understanding-addiction-reward-and-pleasure-in-the-brain/. Accessed on December 30, 2017.

"Withdrawing from Opiates and Opioids." 2017. Healthline. https://www.healthline.com/health/opiate-withdrawal. Accessed on December 30, 2017.

"World Drug Report 2016." 2016. Vienna: United Nations Office on Drugs and Crime. https://www.unodc.org/doc/wdr2016/WORLD_DRUG_REPORT_2016_web.pdf. Accessed on December 1, 2017.

Wright, C. R. A. 1874. "On the Action of Organic Acids and Their Anhydrides on the Natural Alkaloids." *Journal of the Chemical Society*. 27: 1031–1043. https://web.archive.org/web/20040606103721/http://adhpage.dilaudid.net/heroin.html. Accessed on December 5, 2017.

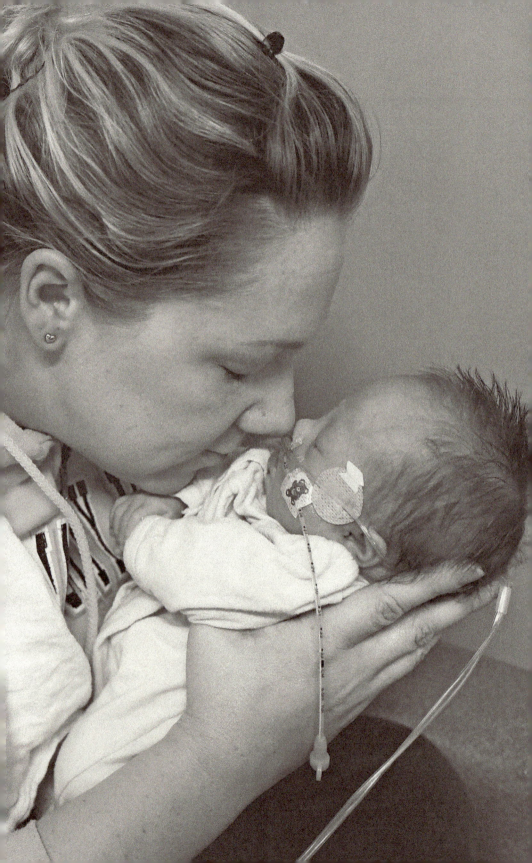

# 2  Problems, Controversies, and Solutions

In June 2017, the national publication STAT announced the results of a study about the future of the opioid epidemic. The study involved interviews with individuals who specialize in epidemiology, clinical medicine, health economics, and pharmaceutical use, as well as politicians, patient advocates, providers, health care payers, doctors, and drug makers. Based on these interviews, STAT developed a set of 10 forecasts for possible future trends in the opioid epidemic. The most optimistic of those forecasts predicted that the number of deaths from opioid overdoses would peak in about 2020 and then drop off to a total, in 2027, of about 21,300 deaths annually from opioid abuse. That result would represent a decrease of 36 percent over totals for 2015. The median forecasts of trends (forecasts #4 and #5) predict death rates of 45,000 and 46,740 for 2027, representing increases of 36 percent and 41 percent over 2015 rates. The most pessimistic forecast suggests a death rate in 2027 of 93,613, an increase of 183 percent of 2015 numbers. That number of deaths translates into an average of about 250 opioid deaths per day, two and a half times of today's rate (Blau 2017).

---

Rachel, 30, holds her newborn baby Isabella and lovingly rubs noses together. Isabella was born with a mild case of neonatal abstinence syndrome because of her mother's recovery from an opioid addiction. Rachel was taking a synthetic opioid prescription during her pregnancy as she recovered from an addiction to heroin. (Andy Cross/The Denver Post via Getty Images)

## Numbers Tell the Story

### Mortality and Morbidity

There are many ways in which one can tell the story of the opioid epidemic. For example, the very personal stories of men and women who have been opioid abusers at some time in their lives, or who have lost a loved one or close friend, can "put a face" on the epidemic. Some of the essays in Chapter 3 of this book attempt to do that. Perhaps the most common method of defining "the opioid epidemic" is in terms of numbers, the number of deaths, emergency department admissions, or clinical referrals, or the financial cost to individuals, businesses, and the government. These data are less personal than are individuals' stories. But they do provide an overview of the extent to which the abuse of opioids has become an "epidemic." For example, the total number of opioid deaths in the United States in 2015 was 33,091. That number has been increasing steadily since 1999, when the total number of opioid overdose deaths was 8,048. Those numbers represent an increase of 311 percent during that period of time. The rate of opioid deaths has also been increasing more rapidly over the past five years. Between 2014 and 2015, for example, the death rate increased by 15.5 percent ("Overdose Death Rates" 2017; see Excel spreadsheet at the end of article for details).

Among all opioids, two drugs, in particular, have contributed to this rapid increase in death rates: heroin and fentanyl. The number of deaths from heroin overdose in 1999 was 1,960. By 2015, it had risen to 12,989, an increase of 562 percent. In just the five-year period from 2010 to 2015, that death rate increased by 119 percent. Deaths from fentanyl in the early 2000s were so low that national agencies collected only a limited amount of data. In 2001, the number of deaths attributed to fentanyl poisoning was 66. That number hovered around 300–400 from then through 2006 and then between 500 and 1,000 from 2007 through 2013. The number of deaths then began to increase rapidly, to 4,697 in 2014, 14,440 in 2015, and 20,100 in 2016 (Jones et al. 2015; Rudd et al. 2016; also see Table 2.1).

Table 2.1    Trends in Fentanyl Overdose Death Numbers, 2001–2016

| Year | Number of Deaths |
|------|------------------|
| 2001 | 66 |
| 2002 | 262 |
| 2003 | 334 |
| 2004 | 395 |
| 2005 | 404 |
| 2006 | 3,317 |
| 2007 | 966 |
| 2008 | 543 |
| 2009 | 652 |
| 2010 | 678 |
| 2011 | 648 |
| 2012 | 677 |
| 2013 | 979 |
| 2014 | 4,697 |
| 2015 | 14,440 |
| 2016 | 34,204 |

Source: "NFLIS Brief: Fentanyl, 2001–2015." National Forensic Laboratory Information System. https://www.deadiversion.usdoj.gov/nflis/2017fentanyl.pdf. "NFLIS Brief: Fentanyl and Fentanyl-Related Substances Reported in NFLIS, 2015–2016." National Forensic Laboratory Information System. https://www.nflis .deadiversion.usdoj.gov/DesktopModules/ReportDownloads/Reports/11350_ R1_NFLIS_Research_Brief_Fentanyl.pdf. Accessed on December 10, 2017.

Another measure of the opioid epidemic is the number of individuals who experience an opioid overdose but do not die from that overdose. Those individuals may take one of two actions because of the overdose: be admitted to a hospital for inpatient care or visit an emergency department for immediate care. Significant upward trends in both measures have occurred over the past decade. The rate of inpatient cases has increased between 2005 and 2014 from 136.8 cases per 100,000 to 224.6 cases per 100,000. That change amounts to a 64.1 percent increase over that period and an average increase of 5.7 percent

**Table 2.2  Rate of Inpatient Stays (IS) and Emergency Department (ED) Visits for Opioid Overdose, 2005–2014 (cases per 100,000)**

| Year | Rate | |
|------|------|------|
|      | IS   | ED   |
| 2005 | 136.8 | 89.1 |
| 2006 | 164.2 | 91.8 |
| 2007 | 159.0 | 82.6 |
| 2008 | 165.7 | 94.1 |
| 2009 | 181.4 | 107.4 |
| 2010 | 197.1 | 117.5 |
| 2011 | 207.8 | 131.2 |
| 2012 | 210.4 | 146.8 |
| 2013 | 213.7 | 166.2 |
| 2014 | 224.6 | 177.7 |

*Source*: Weiss et al. (2017).

average annual growth rate. The rate of increase in emergency department visits has experienced a similar increase, from 89.1 cases per 100,000 in 2005 to 177.7 cases per 100,000 in 2014. Those numbers reflect an almost doubling (99.4 percent) in cases between 2005 and 2014 or an annual average increase of 8.0 percent (Weiss et al. 2017; also see Table 2.2).

## Who Uses Opioids?

While the opioid epidemic the United States is currently experiencing is clearly a national problem, it does not affect all citizens in the same way. Ongoing demographic studies have shown that the epidemic has affected individuals differently based on sex, age, race, and geographic location. As Table 2.3 shows, men are more likely than women to use opioids illegally, those from 18 to 34 years of age are more likely to do so, and Hispanics are more likely than whites or blacks. There appear to be similarities depending on the region of the country in which one lives and

Table 2.3   Death Rates from Opioid Overdose Persons 12+ Years Old for 2015 (Rate per 100,000)

| Characteristic | Rate |
|---|---|
| All | 3.9 |
| Sex | |
| Male | 4.4 |
| Female | 3.4 |
| Age (years) | |
| 0–14 | 0.1 |
| 15–24 | 1.6 |
| 25–34 | 5.3 |
| 35–44 | 6.9 |
| 45–54 | 8.1 |
| 55–64 | 6.4 |
| ≥65 | 1.5 |
| Race | |
| White, non-Hispanic | 5.3 |
| Black, non-Hispanic | 2.1 |
| Hispanic | 1.8 |
| Region | |
| Northeast | 3.6 |
| Midwest | 3.4 |
| South | 4.4 |
| West | 3.8 |
| County type* | |
| Large metropolitan | 1.3 |
| Small metropolitan | 1.3 |
| Nonmetropolitan | 1.5 |

*"Annual Surveillance Report of Drug-Related Risks and Outcomes." 2017. CDC National Center for Injury Prevention and Control, Table 2B, pages 45–46. https://www.cdc.gov/drugoverdose/pdf/pubs/2017-cdc-drug-surveillance-report.pdf. Accessed on December 22, 2017.

Source: Rudd et al. (2016). Table 1. Accessed on December 22, 2017.

the effect of population size on opioid use. But these numbers are deceiving. Researchers have long known that the opioid crisis affects specific counties, widespread throughout the country, in very different ways. For example, the death rate from opioid overdose in 2016 in Siskiyou County, California, was three times that in neighboring Klamath County, Oregon, with 37 deaths per 100,000 in the former and 12 deaths per 100,000 in the latter. Other counties with high death rates were Clark County, Ohio (59 deaths per 100,000), Wyoming County, West Virginia (69 deaths per 100,000), and Rio Arriba County, New Mexico (77 deaths per 100,000). (For complete U.S. data on opioid deaths by country, see Katz and Goodnough 2017.)

Some of the most recent data on demographic trends for opioid deaths (December 2017) provide insights not previously available on trends among specialized populations. Perhaps most significant was the increase in opioid-related deaths from 2015 to 2016 among African Americans, an increase of 41 percent in a single year. By contrast, the increase in death rate among whites was 19 percent. Some observers have suggested that this change has largely been due to the increase in availability of fentanyl in metropolitan areas. The same report also highlighted the difference by which the epidemic affects various parts of the nation. The death rate in West Virginia, the state hit most severely by the epidemic, increased from 42 per 100,000 in 2015 to 52 per 100,000. Other high-death-rate states were Ohio (39 per 100,000), New Hampshire (39 per 100,000), and Pennsylvania (38 per 100,000). By contrast, opioid death rates were much lower in Midwest states, such as Nebraska (7 per 100,000), South Dakota (8 per 100,000), and North Dakota (11 per 100,000) (Katz and Goodnough 2017).

### Economic Costs

As disturbing as the cost in deaths and illness from opioid overdoses may be, the epidemic has other types of costs—such as economic costs——to individuals and the general public. The costs arise from a number of sources, such as

- direct health care costs, the cost of treating an individual with an opioid-related medical condition;
- substance abuse treatment, the cost of helping individuals to recover from a substance abuse problem;
- criminal justice costs, which may include the cost of law enforcement agencies in responding to overdoses and other opioid-related problems; legal costs in processing a drug-related case; costs for the operation of correctional facilities; and property losses because of opioid abuse–related crimes;
- loss in productivity, because of a person's death, incarceration, or treatment for opioid abuse (Florence et al. 2016).

Placing a dollar value on the total economic costs of opioid abuse because of these factors can be difficult, and various economists have come up with different numbers. Among the most recent and probably most valuable are the estimates from the President's Council of Economic Advisors, issued in November 2017. Recognizing the challenges in producing a specific dollar value on the economic costs of opioid abuse, the council provided a range of numbers, depending on the method by which data were analyzed. The report estimated that the cost of opioid-related deaths alone ranged from $221.6 billion to $549.8 billion annually. For nonfatal events, the council provided a single "best estimate" of $72.3 billion for the year 2015 ("The Underestimated Cost of the Opioid Epidemic" 2017).

**The Innocent Bystanders**

The worst aspects of the current opioid epidemic extend far beyond those who fall into dependence and/or addiction and who may die from the problem; their parents, sons and daughters, siblings, friends, and other loved ones; the general population whose economic interests may be influenced by the crisis;

the public health system that becomes overly burdened by the epidemic; and other individuals and organizations that have been affected by the crisis. One group that is sometimes forgotten in this assessment of the problem is the children born to women who have become dependent on or addicted to opioids. Those children may be born with a condition known as neonatal abstinence syndrome (NAS). The condition develops when a child in the womb is exposed to opioids (or other drugs) that the mother is taking. When the baby is born, it no longer has access to those drugs and experiences the symptoms of drug withdrawal. Those signs and symptoms include the following:

- Tremors
- Irritability
- Excessive crying, often high pitched
- Sleep problems
- Tight muscle tone
- Hyperactive reflexes
- Seizures
- Yawning
- Stuffy nose and sneezing
- Inability or unwillingness to suck
- Vomiting
- Diarrhea
- Dehydration
- Sweating
- Fever or unstable temperature
- Slow weight gain
- Blotchy skin

These signs and symptoms may vary from case to case depending on a number of factors, such as the type of drug used by the mother, the length of time she has been using, and the birth time of the baby (normal or premature) ("Neonatal Abstinence Syndrome" 2017).

The incidence of NAS has increased dramatically over the past decade. One of the most comprehensive measures of this increase followed the number of NAS cases in 28 states between 1999 and 2013. (Not all states collect data on the incidence of NAS; 2013 is the latest year for which data were available.) Researchers found that the rate of NAS in the 28 states increased fourfold between 1999 and 2013, from 1.5 cases per 1,000 hospital births in the former year to 6.0 cases per 1,000 hospital births in the latter year. As is often the case with opioid statistics, data differed substantially among states. The rate of NAS cases in Hawaii in 2013, for example, was 0.7 cases per 1,000 hospital births. By contrast, the rate for West Virginia in 2013 was 33.4 cases per 1,000 hospital births (Ko et al. 2016). One explanation for these trends was the significant greater use of opioids among women in rural areas compared to urban areas. A recent study on this phenomenon found that rates of births complicated by opioid use increased from 1.3 per 1,000 hospital births in 2004 to 8.1 per 1,000 hospital births in 2013 in rural areas. Comparable figures for urban hospitals were 1.6 and 4.8 per 1,000 births, respectively. Authors of the study concluded that "the incidence of NAS and maternal opioid use in the United States increased disproportionately in rural counties from 2004 to 2013 relative to urban counties" (Villapiano et al. 2017).

Studies on the long-term effects of NAS are somewhat sparse, at least partly, because the condition has been recognized so recently. Those studies that have been complete suggest that a baby who has NAS may experience both physical and mental effects later in life. These effects may include the following:

- Vision problems
- Motor development problems
- Behavioral problems

- Cognitive problems
- Risk for future substance abuse
- Chronic stress
- Mistrust of health care systems
- Otitis media (inflammation of the middle ear)
- Increased risk for environmental problems ("Long-Term Out-comes of Infants with Neonatal Abstinence Syndrome" 2017)

Another aspect of the NAS issue involves fostering and adoption. Many parents of NAS babies are themselves addicted and, therefore, not able to take care or interested in taking care of their new child. A basic question that arises in such instances is whether the NAS baby should remain with his or her biological parents or some other option be considered. The most common options are placing the baby with another family member, such as grandparents or siblings, transferring the child to foster care, or making the baby available for adoption. Such decisions are, of course, likely to be emotional wrenching, as well as a major concern for public health agencies. In one recent study, for example, researchers found that workers at the Massachusetts Department of Children and Families in 2016 were devoting about 10,000 hours on this one problem alone (França, Mustafa, and McManus 2016, 80).

Some experts argue that leaving an NAS baby with its biological parents (or, at least, the biological mother) is the best choice in most such cases. They recognize that risks are involved in such a decision, such as behavioral and emotional problems, aggression, attention deficit, and attention deficit hyperactivity disorder. (For a review of these outcomes, see Nygaard et al. 2016.) But they contend that such risks are less important than the benefits that accrue to both mother and child by maintaining the close biological bond that exists between the two (Beal, Bauer, and Diedrick 2014).

The fact remains, however, that significant numbers of NAS babies do not remain with their biological mothers but, instead, are assigned to a foster home. Recent data confirm this trend in several states and nationwide. A 2017 report from the Child Welfare League of America to the President's Commission on Combating Drug Addiction and the Opioid Crisis noted that the number of children assigned to foster care in recent years because of NAS births increased nationwide by 8 percent between 2012 and 2015. Those numbers differed significantly, however, from state to state. In Montana, for example, the number of children in foster care in 2015 was equal to the total in care in 2009 and 2010 combined, and the number in foster care in Georgia increased by 44 percent between 2013 and 2015, from 7,607 to 10,935 ("To: President's Commission on Combating Drug Addiction and the Opioid Crisis 2017"; also see Lachman 2017).

### An Underlying Theme

Laudanum, morphine, heroin, noscapine, codeine, oxycodone, hydromorphone, buprenorphine—the long story of opioid drug discovery has a familiar ring to it. In every case, the drug discovery has been motivated by the search for a "better" analgesic. By *better*, we mean a strong (or stronger) analgesic that can be used with no or very low likelihood of its use being followed by addiction. Each chemist or pharmaceutical company that posted a breakthrough in this line of research was confident that progress had been made toward that goal. And each chemist or pharmaceutical company was eventually disappointed.

And, in every case, another step occurred. The new drug always found (often a great deal of) legitimate medical use. But the drug has always found its way into a country's black market, available for sale to and abuse by individuals who eventually became dependent on or addicted to the drug. The pathway from discovery to use occurred along both routes: through legitimate medical use by individuals who later became addicted to the drug's use and through the black market to individuals who may already have developed a substance abuse problem of another. As an example, some people who begin abusing opioids may already have been abusing or become addicted to alcohol, marijuana, cocaine, or amphetamines. Such multifactorial conditions are known as comorbidities.

The challenge for legislators, law enforcement officers, drug treatment centers, and other individuals and organizations trying to reduce illicit drug use is trying to catch up with, or at least stay current with, new drug options that continue to arise in society. The discussion of opioid laws in Chapter 1, for example, illustrates that pattern. A company begins to manufacture a potentially useful new analgesic drug. Individuals then begin to abuse the drug through legitimate medical procedures or in the search for a new recreational drug. Government officials attempt to reduce this trend by adopting new laws and regulations to control the illicit drug use. A new drug appears on the market, and the process repeats. The Controlled Substances Act (CSA) of 1970 was the nation's most ambitious effort to interrupt this recurring chain of events. And it didn't work. The review of opioid laws in Chapter 1 also illustrates how legislators and administrators have continually amended the CSA and adopted new laws to achieve this objective, so far without success.

This process of discovery, release, and abuse did not end with the drugs listed at the end of Chapter 1. Indeed, it continues today, constituting an element of today's opioid epidemic. Two recent additions to the list of troubling opioids are carfentanil (described in Chapter 1) and U-47700. U-47700 was originally developed by chemists at Upjohn pharmaceutical company and patented by American chemist Jacob Szmuszkovicz in 1976. Once again, the discovery arose out of the hopes of a pharmaceutical company—Upjohn—to develop a more powerful analgesic for moderate to severe pain but without the risk of addiction. The drug was tested on laboratory animals but never on humans. The animal evidence, however, confirmed the drug's analgesic potential, and laboratories outside the United States began producing the substance for human use.

It was found to be about eight times as potent as equal amounts of morphine. By 2016, individuals interested in the sale and/ or use of morphine-like drugs were making U-47700 available to substance abusers. (By that time, the compound was often being called Pink, Pinky, or U4 [Anderson 2016].)

Very shortly after the drug became available, reports of poisoning cases and deaths from use of U-47700 began to arrive. In most cases, the drug was used in combination with fentanyl and often sold to users as "pure fentanyl." Perhaps the most famous case of Pink poisoning was the death of pop star Prince in April 2016, a case in which the performer is thought to have ingested a mixture of Pink and fentanyl. By October of that year, more than 80 deaths from the use of Pink had been reported, and the U.S. Drug Enforcement Agency had announced its intent to list the drug as a Schedule I substance. (At the time, the drug was still legal in all but a handful of states [O'Hara 2016; "Rules—2016" 2016].) Of course, Pink is not the end of the cat-and-mouse game over illicit drugs. In 2017, yet another new product became available for drug abusers and addicts, a drug called Gray Death (Anderson 2017). Nor is Gray Death likely to be the last chapter in this story.

## The History of OxyContin

If there is a face to the present opioid epidemic in the United States, it is probably the drug called OxyContin. OxyContin is the trade name for a formulation of the opioid oxycodone first marketed by Purdue Pharma pharmaceutical company in 1996. The history of the drug's role in the development of today's opioid crisis has been told and argued in several books and articles. Among the most complete of these descriptions and discussions are Eban (2011), Gunderman (2016), Jayawan and Balkrishnan (2005), Keefe (2017), Meier (2003), Quinones (2015), and Van Zee (2009).

The beginnings of this story can be traced to 1921 and the creation of the Committee on Drug Addiction, created by the

Bureau of Social Hygiene in New York City. The committee's goal was to find ways of encouraging researchers to find a drug with analgesic effects at least as good as those of the existing opioids but without the risk of addiction to users. The committee continues to function in 2018, having gone through several name changes, culminating in today's title of College on Problems of Drug Dependence ("About CPDD" 2017; May and Jacobson 1989). The college has expanded its mission to include a more general line of research on brain chemistry and the way it is affected by drugs. Obviously, relatively little progress has been made toward the organization's original objective.

One family that has long been inspired by the college's aims, as well as the general problem of pain relief among humans, has been the Sackler family, consisting of brothers Arthur (1913–1987), Mortimer (1916–2010), and Raymond (1920–2017), all physicians, and their families. The Sacklers' contribution to the drug industry was their emphasis on solid business practices, rather than simply sound chemical and pharmaceutical issues in the marketing of their drugs. The eldest brother, Arthur, got his start in this field early, working as an ad copy writer for the advertising firm Williams Douglas MacAdams while he was still in medical school. (He later became president and chief executive officer of the company.)

For a period, Sackler focused on medical research, working as a psychiatrist at the Creedmoor State Hospital in New York State where, in 1949, he founded the Creedmoor Institute of Psychobiological Studies. At the same time, he was pursuing his interests in the advertising of medical products, eventually founding an industry newsletter, *Medical Tribune*, in 1960. His first great success in the commercialization of the drug industry came while he was at Williams Douglas MacAdams. He convinced the pharmaceutical firm Charles Pfizer and Company to take a new approach to the marketing of its new antibiotic, Terramycin. He recommended that the company provide a very large advertising budget to send information directly to individual doctors. This was a revolutionary approach in an industry that traditionally provided only a limited amount of low-key advertising about a product. Sackler's proposal was adopted by Pfizer, however, and the drug became a huge commercial success, with sales of $45 million in just one year, 1952 (Castagnoli 1999, 17–18; Podolsky 2014, Chapter 1; Quinones 2015, 29).

Sackler and his brothers first became involved in the opioid side of the pharmaceutical market in 1952 when they purchased a small, little-known drug company called Purdue Frederick, a name they later changed to Purdue Pharma. One of the products developed in the company's research laboratories was a drug that they called MS Contin.

MS Contin was Purdue's first venture into the analgesic drug market. It was a formulation of morphine using a patented slow-release system developed by the British firm Napp Pharmaceuticals. An important advantage of MS Contin was that, with this formulation, a person had to take only one pill a day, with the active ingredient being released continuously ("Contin") throughout the day. MS Contin was approved for use as a treatment from pain due to cancer in 1984 and made an estimated $475 million for the company over the next decade (Eban 2011; "Joint Meeting of the Anesthetic and Life Support Drugs Advisory Committee and Drug Safety & Risk Management Advisory Committee. Table of Contents" 2008, 8).

One challenge with which Purdue soon had to deal, however, was that its patent for MS Contin, as with all drugs, was good for only 20 years. At the end of that time, the company would need to have another proprietary drug with which to replace MS Contin. That drug turned out to be OxyContin, approved by the FDA (U.S. Food and Drug Administration) for treatment of chronic pain in 1996. (The FDA medical review of the drug found that it was no more effective than conventional oxycodone formulations but had reduced risk of addiction because of its time-release formula [Van Zee 2009].) As with MS Contin, Purdue marketed the new drug aggressively. The company reportedly held many meetings at which more than 5,000 physicians, pharmacists, and nurses were in attendance, touting the new "gold standard" for analgesics, OxyContin. Again, it made its pitch directly to individual physicians, the majority of whom were not pain specialists, through a network of sales representatives who made more than $40 million in sales incentive bonuses in 2001 (Van Zee 2009).

A problem arose in 2000, when reports began to arise about some deleterious side effects of OxyContin use. These side effects included respiratory depression, nausea, sedation, constipation, euphoria or dysphoria, inconsistent improvement in functioning and quality of life, opioid-induced hyperalgesia, hormonal deficiency, diminished immune function, and an increased risk of opioid addiction (Ballantyne 2006). Quite understandably, Purdue initiated a substantial campaign to dispute or discredit these reports (Van Zee 2009, footnotes 43–49). One of the articles frequently cited by the company was a letter to the *New England Journal of Medicine* published in 1980 by Jane Porter and Hershel Jick, from the Boston University Medical Center (Porter and Jick 1980). The five-sentence letter concluded with the authors' observation that "despite widespread use of narcotic drugs in hospitals, the development of addiction is rare in medical patients with no history of addiction." In fact, they claimed to have found "only four cases of reasonably well documented addiction in [11,882] patients who had a history of addiction" (Porter and Jick 1980). The company also referred to another early study that found no cases of addiction among more than 10,000 patients who had been treated for severe burns in the United States (Perry and Heidrich 1982). With this evidence in hand, Purdue recommended to its sales representatives that the risk of addiction arising out of the use of narcotics such as OxyContin was "less than one percent" (Meier 2003, 67, 173).

As reports of addiction resulting from the use of OxyContin continued to appear, Purdue came across another argument to refute the drug's role in those adverse events. It turned to an article written in 1989 by David E. Weissman and J. David Haddox at the Medical College of Wisconsin. Reporting on a single case of a young man whose behavior mimicked the behavior of drug addiction, Weissman and Haddox said that this change in behavior was a result of *inadequate* treatment with narcotics. They called the condition *pseudoaddiction* and suggested that the appropriate treatment was a higher dose of narcotics such as OxyContin (Greene and Chambers 2015). This suggestion provided Purdue with an additional argument for an even extended use of OxyContin in cases of pain that went beyond the drug's original use for chronic pain.

A portent of Purdue's future problems appeared in a 2005 article in the *American Journal of Industrial Medicine* by researchers at the University of Washington. The article begins by noting that a number of states had loosened their regulations on the use of opioids for a variety of purposes in the late 1990s. That change appeared to have caused a somewhat dramatic increase in the use of such opioids, at least in the state of Washington. The number of prescriptions for drugs like OxyContin for employees of the Washington State workers' compensation system increased about two and a half times, from 23,000 annually in 1996 to 57,000 annually in 2002 (Franklin et al. 2005). During the same time, according to the researchers, the average dose of opioids prescribed for patients increased by 50 percent, and the number of deaths attributable, or probably attributable, to opioid overdose was 32 (Franklin et al. 2005, 247). The researchers concluded that "it is possible that tolerance or opioid-induced abnormal pain sensitivity may be occurring in some workers who use opioids for chronic pain. Opioid-related deaths in this population may be preventable through use of prudent guidelines regarding opioid use for chronic pain" (Franklin et al. 2005, 247).

Over the years, Purdue has attempted to make changes in its formulation methods, labeling, and advertising to reduce the risk of overdose by users of OxyContin. (For a complete history of these efforts, see "Timeline of Selected FDA Activities and Significant Events Addressing Opioid Misuse and Abuse" 2017.) Statistics provided earlier in this book suggest that those efforts have been less than successful, and some critics have questioned the sincerity of Purdue's concerns about the opioid epidemic.

Purdue is by no means the only corporation about which questions have been raised regarding the opioid crisis. In December 2017, an investigative team from *The Washington Post* and the CBS news program *60 Minutes* reported on the activities of McKesson Corporation, the largest distributor of drugs in the United States. The team found that McKesson apparently filled very large opioid orders for several pharmacies across the United States without reporting such irregular activity to the DEA (Drug Enforcement Administration), as required by law. One example the team cited involved the Platte Valley Pharmacy in Brighton, Colorado, a town of 38,000 inhabitants. DEA found that pharmacist Jeffrey Clawson at the store was selling as many as 2,000 pain pills per day. The overriding issue for DEA investigators was that the agency's attorneys decided not to pursue a case against McKesson and settled with the company for a fine of $150 million. (The DEA investigators had suggested a fine of $1 billion [Bernstein and Higham 2017]; also see Whitaker 2017 for the *60 Minutes* segment; for McKesson's response to the story, see Hammergren 2017.)

Legal actions against opioid manufacturers and distributors increased significantly in 2017. By the end of that year, more than 100 cities, counties, and states had filed suit against companies such as Allergan, AmerisourceBergen, Cardinal Health, Endo, the Janssen unit of Johnson & Johnson, McKesson, Purdue Pharma, and Teva Pharmaceutical. (For a list and interactive map of these governmental units, see Quinn 2017, at http://www.governing.com/gov-data/health/states-city-gov ernments-opioids-lawsuits-map.html.) In many cases, states and localities are simply requesting further information, such as access to a company's e-mails, about their opioid activities.

In other cases, they are actually suing one or more companies in district or federal court to obtain the information they want or to pursue legal action on the matter. In one case, an Indian tribe, the Cherokee Nation, is even bringing suit in tribal court against entities such as AmerisourceBergen, Cardinal Health, CVS Health, McKesson, Walgreen's, and Walmart for ignoring federal regulations on the monitoring of opioid prescription sales to members of its tribe (Hofmann 2017; also see Smith and Davey 2017).

## A Flood of Opioids

However one feels about the business practices of some pharmaceutical companies, the fact remains that the prescribing and sales of opioid drugs continued to mushroom after the early 1990s. According to one study, the number of prescriptions for opioids increased from 107.26 million in 1992 to 172.46 million in 2000 to 225.27 million in 2005 to 273.29 million in 2010 and to 277.29 in 2012. After that date, it began to drop off to an estimated 238.98 in 2016 (Pezalla et al. 2017, Table S1). Despite efforts to promote the prescribing of extended-release formulations, the more traditional immediate-release products outsold the new type of drug by about nine to one (Pezalla et al. 2017, Table S1).

Other changes in prescribing patterns changed considerably over the last decade of this period. Although the rate of opioid prescriptions dropped by about 0.8 percent, the rate of high-dose opioids dropped by eight times that amount, 6.6 percent. The number of 30-day prescriptions written also dropped by about 3.2 percent, although the number of prescriptions for more than 30 days increased by 4.3 percent ("Annual Surveillance Report of Drug-Related Risks and Outcomes" 2017, Table 1D, page 43). These data suggest that physicians continued to rely over this period on opioid analgesics for the treatment of all kinds of pain, not just cancer and chronic pain, for which they were originally designed.

One of the most basic questions asked by experts interested in the current opioid epidemic is how these legal prescriptions translate into instances of abuse, addiction, and death. That is, how does a person get access to the opioid pills that might eventually lead to his or her addiction and/or death? One answer to that question is that some individuals who are prescribed opioid drugs for medical conditions (such as postsurgical pain) continue to use those drugs even after they no longer need them for that pain. That is, they have become dependent on or addicted to the drugs. It follows then that physicians need to be more conservative about their prescribing of opioids even for legitimate medical purposes.

But, according to some observers, this scenario contains two serious flaws. In the first place, data do not support the contention that most individuals who become dependent on or addicted to opioids get them for legitimate medical reasons. As an example, some 277.29 million prescriptions for opioids were written in 2012. But the Centers for Disease Control and Prevention (CDC) estimated that only about 2.1 million individuals were dependent on or addicted to those drugs in that year (Pezalla et al. 2017, Table S1; "Results from the 2012 National Survey on Drug Use and Health: Summary of National Findings" 2013, 6; for a more detailed discussion of this issue, see Sullum 2016).

Government studies have also found that the major reason that people give for abusing an opioid is to deal with ongoing pain. By contrast, only a fraction of those interviewed said that their own dependence or addiction was the reason for their misuse ("Key Substance Use and Mental Health Indicators in the United States: Results from the 2016 National Survey on Drug Use and Health" 2017, Table A13.B, page A-11; also see Table 2.4).

Another reason to question this explanation is that, when one asks people who are dependent on or addicted to an opioid the source from which they got their drugs, they most commonly cite sources other than their own medical prescriptions. In the

Table 2.4   Main Reasons for Pain Reliever Misuse for the Last Episode of Misuse among Individuals Aged 12 or Older Who Misused Pain Relievers in the Past Year

| Main Reason for Misuse | Percentage of Misusers |
| --- | --- |
| Relieves physical pain | 62.3 |
| Feels good or gets high | 12.9 |
| Relieves tension | 10.8 |
| Helps with emotions | 3.9 |
| Helps with sleep | 3.3 |
| To experiment with opioids | 3.0 |
| Because of an addiction | 2.1 |
| Increases or decreases effect of another drug | 0.9 |
| Some other reason | 0.9 |

Source: "Key Substance Use and Mental Health Indicators in the United States: Results from the 2016 National Survey on Drug Use and Health" (2017), Table A13.B.

2016 survey cited earlier, for example, more than half of those surveyed said that they got their drugs from a friend or relative ("Key Substance Use and Mental Health Indicators in the United States: Results from the 2016 National Survey on Drug Use and Health" 2017, Table A14.B, page A-11; also see Table 2.5).

The question as to how people who are dependent or addicted get their opioids has some very practical and important implications. As the misuse of opioids and other prescription drugs has mushroomed over the past two decades, states and the federal government have adopted legislation and regulations that make opioids more difficult to get, even for those who need the drugs for pain. A review of this legislation can be found on pages 244–273. In any case, the concern of physicians, other health care workers, and patients is that people who are really in need of pain medications such as opioids may find it more and more difficult to get those drugs for legitimate purposes.

Some individuals have medical conditions that result in their facing a lifetime of constant pain, a pain that can be treated only with the most powerful analgesics, such as opioid drugs. Such conditions include slipped or bulging discs, spinal stenosis, compression fractures, scoliosis, migraine, cluster headaches, osteoarthritis, sciatica, and various types of neuropathies. In a 2012 study, researchers found that about 25.3 million Americans (11.2 percent of the population) have chronic pain ("NIH Analysis Shows Americans Are in Pain" 2015).

For many of these people, opioids provide some measure of relief from their inescapable pain. But news about today's opioid epidemic has made this practice more problematic for many pain sufferers. For one thing, they may be exposed by ridicule and stigma from family and friends because they are thought of as "addicts." Such individuals may or may not be dependent on opioids, but they are very seldom addicted to the drugs. Some opioid users may also develop their own concerns about becoming addicted to opioids.

This problem has been made even more challenging as a result of new laws, regulations, and guidelines from governmental and professional associations. The statements are usually designed to reduce the number of opioid prescriptions and, then presumably but perhaps inaccurately, reduce the number of deaths from opioids. But these efforts have sometimes had the harmful effects of withholding opioids from patients who quite legitimately need them for relief from pain. The media is filled today with statements such as "I think [the CDC guidelines, discussed below] go much too far and a) will leave many in pain and b) will drive some seeking pain relief into the illicit market with all its hazards" (Professor Jerrold Winter, professor of pharmacology and toxicology at the University at Buffalo, as quoted in Smith 2016).

New laws and recommendations have seemingly influenced the nature of the opium epidemic in ways unanticipated by their authors. Many experts have been pleased to note that death rates from most opioids appear to have begun leveling off.

At the same time, however, death rates from the use of heroin and fentanyl have begun to skyrocket. One possible explanation for these trends, according to some experts, is that, as legal opioids become more difficult to get from legal sources, individuals in pain may switch to illegal options, such as heroin and fentanyl and its derivatives. To the extent that this is true, patients who need and take opioids for legitimate medical reasons are perhaps being "sacrificed" to shortsighted new regulations (Katz 2017; "Overdose Death Rates" 2017).

## Regulating the Use of Opioids

### Guidelines

For almost two decades, interested professional and governmental groups have been considering ways of reducing the nation's illicit use of opioids. These groups have devised position statements, guidelines, and other policy statements suggesting ways of monitoring legal and illegal opioid use. Some of these statements are now quite old and, at least to some extent, out of date and, therefore, of limited usefulness. For example, the U.S. DEA released its Proposed Model Guidelines for the Use of Controlled Substances in Pain Management in 1998, before many of the most recent opioid issues appeared (Good 1998; for an extended, but not complete, list of such statements, see "Database of Statutes, Regulations, & Other Policies for Pain Management" n.d.).

Perhaps the most widely mentioned and most recent of pain and opioid guidelines was a document issued in March 2016 by the CDC (Dowell, Haegerich, and Chou 2016). This 50-page document with 223 references goes into considerable detail in suggesting policies and practices for dealing with prescribing opioids for pain. Some of the major features of the report are as follows:

- Clinicians should consider possible risks and benefits in prescribing opioids for pain and proceed based on the relative importance of each. They should also include other forms of therapy in case one chooses to write a prescription for an opioid (also, sections in this list come from Dowell, Haegerich, and Chou 2016, Box 1, page 16).

- In concert with patients, clinicians should set realistic goals for the treatment program and reconsider that program if the risk–benefit ratio changes along the way.

- Before starting treatment, clinicians should discuss with patients possible risks involved in the use of opioid for the treatment of pain.

- Clinicians should prescribe immediate release (IR) rather than extended release (ER) for patients.

- Clinicians should prescribe only the lowest effective dosage of opioids for a patient. If increases are necessary, to levels as high as ≥50 MME (milligram morphine equivalents), the risk–benefit ratio should be reconsidered. Dosages of ≥90 MME should not be prescribed.

- For cases of acute pain, duration of a prescription should generally be no less than three and no more than seven days.

- Risks and benefits of opioid use should be reevaluated within one to four weeks of the original prescription and at least every three months thereafter.

- Clinicians should evaluate possible risks of opioid use for any specific patient both before prescribing and during the period of treatment. If indications of addiction appear, the patient should be offered treatment with naloxone. (This treatment is discussed later.)

- Prescribers should review a patient's previous drug use record, using the prescription drug monitoring program, which will be discussed later in this chapter), before beginning treatment.

- When considering prescribing opioids for chronic pain, a clinician should first conduct a urine test for other drugs the patient may have been taking. Urine tests may also be indicated during the treatment period.

- Clinicians should avoid prescribing opioid pain medication and benzodiazepines concurrently whenever possible.
- Patients who show symptoms of opioid overdose use should be offered medication-assisted treatment with buprenorphine and/or methadone, along with behavioral therapy.

**Reactions to the Guidelines**

Publication of the CDC guidelines elicited a substantial number of responses, many unfavorable to the recommendations they contain. Perhaps the most fundamental of all complaints was that the CDC authors had ignored or misrepresented scientific information about opioids and their effects on patients. One writer said that the CDC authors *deliberately distorted the evidence they gathered* (emphasis in original, Lawhern 2017). The title of one paper illustrates the authors' views on the issue, "Neat, Plausible, and Generally Wrong: A Response to the CDC Recommendations for Chronic Opioid Use" (Martin, Potee, and Lazris 2016).

One problem with the guidelines that has been mentioned often is the one discussed earlier, namely that sufficient evidence now exists to indicate that prescription opioids are not a major cause of the opioid epidemic and that people who use opioids for chronic pain or other legitimate medical problems are not very likely to become addicts. For example, authors of one article concluded that

> the CDC frames the recommendations as being for primary care clinicians and their individual patients. Yet the threat of addiction largely comes from diverted prescription opioids, not from long-term use with a skilled prescriber in a longitudinal clinical relationship. By not acknowledging the role of diversion—and instead focusing on individuals who report functional and pain benefit for their severe chronic pain—the CDC misses the target. (Martin, Potee, and Lazris 2016)

In other cases, experts objected to more technical points in the CDC report. For example, one research team focused on the report's concern that evidence about opioid abuse for chronic pain was inadequate to make informed recommendations because existing studies had not continued over a long-enough period. Researchers followed up on this point by examining the duration of other trials that have been conducted on the treatment of chronic pain. They concluded that "no common nonopioid treatment for chronic pain has been studied in aggregate over longer intervals of active treatment than opioids. . . . Considering only duration of active treatment in efficacy or effectiveness trials, published evidence is no stronger for any major drug category or behavioral therapy than for opioids" (Tayeb et al. 2016).

A recurrent theme in criticisms of the CDC guidelines is that they will almost certainly make it more difficult for individuals with chronic pain and other medical conditions to obtain the medications they need—opioids—to deal with their problem. A substantial number of clinicians are now concerned that the simple act of prescribing opioids carries with it some measure of criminal prosecution for malpractice. The basis of that fear is in the nature of the guidelines themselves. Originally published as "suggestions" for the prescribing of opioids, the guidelines soon gained stronger force. Almost immediately, the DEA began to increase monitoring of clinicians' prescription behaviors for opioids and instituting cases against those who were thought to be "overprescribing." Even before the guidelines were published, the DEA had quadrupled the number of cases brought against physicians in the period from 2011 to 2014, from 88 to 371 cases. The guidelines appear to some, then, to have legitimized the DEA's de facto, if not de jure prescribing practice as the basis for criminal proceedings (Yang, Larochelle, and Haffajee 2017).

The "voluntary" nature of the CDC guidelines soon became eroded in other ways. In fact, before those guidelines were ever formally published in the Federal Register, the U.S. Congress had adopted legislation requiring those recommendations to be enforced in the U.S. Department of Veterans Affairs. The 2016 omnibus spending bill passes in December required the Department of Veterans Affairs to "adopt the opioid prescribing guidelines developed by the Centers of Disease Control; to develop IT systems to track and monitor opioid prescriptions; to ensure all VA medical facilities are equipped with opioid receptor antagonists to treat drug overdoses; and to provide additional training to medical personnel who prescribe controlled substances" (Boyle 2016). In early 2017, the Centers for Medicare and Medicaid Services announced that it would also make the guidelines for compensation of medical services involving the use of opioids (Anson 2017).

## Legislation

### Federal

The federal government began to deal with opioid issues in the 114th Congress (2014), when the U.S. Congress passed two laws, the Comprehensive Addiction and Recovery Act (CARA, P.L. 114–198) and the 21st Century Cures Act (Cures Act; P.L. 114–255). CARA consisted of four sections ("Titles") dealing with the following aspects of the opioid crisis:

- Title I (section 107): Reauthorization NASPER, the National All Schedules Prescription Electronic Reporting. This section is not specific to opioids but applies to all types of description drugs ($10 million per year for five years).
- Title I (section 109): Opioid Overdose Reversal Medication Access. This allocation is for training of first-responders in the use of drugs used for opioid overdoses ($5 million for the period FY 2017–FY 2019).
- Title II: First Responder Training for Emergency Treatment of Known or Suspected Opioid Overdose ($12 million per year for five years).

- Title III (section 301): Evidence-Based Prescription Opioid and Heroin Treatment and Interventions Demonstration ($25 million per year for FY 2017–FY 2021 [$125 million for the entire period]).
- Title III (section 302): Building Communities of Recovery. Not specific to opioids ($1 million per year for five years).
- Title V: Reauthorization of Residential Treatment Program for Pregnant and Postpartum Women. Not specific to opioids ($17 million per year for five years).
- Title VI: State Demonstration Grants for Comprehensive Opioid Abuse Response ($5 million per year for five years) (Sacco and Bagalman 2017, 20–21).

Provisions regarding the opioid crisis in the Cures Act are to be found in Title I, Section 1003, of the act. That section creates an account in the U.S. Treasury called the Account for the State Response to the Opioid Abuse Crisis. Funds in this account are to be used for state demonstration programs for dealing with the opioid crisis, such as prevention programs; training for health care practitioners with regard to best practices for prescribing opioids, pain management, recognizing potential cases of drug abuse, referral of patients to treatment programs, and overdose prevention; supporting access to health care services; and other public health-related activities, as a state determines appropriate, related to addressing the opioid abuse crisis within the state (Public Law 114–255. 114th Congress 2017). (The federal government spends money through other agencies for opioid programs beyond these specific laws; see Sacco and Bagalman 2017, 22.)

*State*

Individual states and multistate groups have been more aggressive about passing laws to control the opioid epidemic. One of the most popular approaches to the prevention of opioid

Table 2.5   Source Where Pain Relievers Were Obtained for Most Recent Misuse among Individuals Aged 12 or Older Who Misused Pain Relievers in the Past Year

| | |
|---|---|
| By prescription or stolen from a health care provider | 37.5 |
| Prescription from one doctor | 35.4 |
| Prescription from more than one doctor | 1.4 |
| Stolen from doctor's office, hospital, clinic, etc. | 0.7 |
| From friend or relative | 53.0 |
| From friend or relative for free | 40.4 |
| Bought from friend or relative | 8.9 |
| Stole from friend or relative | 3.7 |
| Bought from drug dealer or other strangers | 6.0 |
| Some other way | 3.4 |

Source: "Key Substance Use and Mental Health Indicators in the United States: Results from the 2016 National Survey on Drug Use and Health" (2017), Table A14.B.

abuse has been tracking and monitoring of prescription drug sales. This approach has a high chance of success because many people who obtain opioids illegally do so by stealing a physician's prescription pad; stealing opioids from a physician's office, hospital, or pharmacy; or stealing a family member or friend's prescription (see Table 2.5).

The principle behind this approach to opioid abuse prevention had its origin in the creation of the California Triplicate Prescription Program (TPP) in 1939. In that program, every prescription for Schedule II drugs had to be written in triplicate, one copy of which went to a central state recording office (the office of the state attorney general), a second copy remained with the prescriber, and a third copy stayed with the dispensing pharmacy. Over time, the California TPP developed more efficient methods of carrying out this program, changing from written prescriptions to electronic transmissions. Also, additional states adopted programs like the California TPP, all with a similar philosophy and similar goals but with a variety of details as to how they operate. Today, such programs are called PDMPs. They exist in all 50 states and the District of Columbia ("Prescription Drug Monitoring Programs" 2017).

PDMPs have several benefits. Most important, they allow governmental agencies ranging from public health offices to law enforcement agencies to keep track of prescriptions that are being written for opioids and other drugs that have the potential for nonmedical use. They alert these agencies to the possibility that specific prescribers, dispensers, and/or users may be involved in the nonmedical use of these drugs. PDMPs also make possible a variety of educational programs for prospective abusers of prescription drugs as well as for the general public. They also provide the data and statistics on which such educational programs can be based ("CURES/PDMP" n.d.).

Although the federal government has no part in the administration, operation, or other activity of state PDMPs, it does provide financial assistance to states for the development and enhancement of those programs. The primary source of funding for this activity is the Harold Rogers Prescription Drug Monitoring Grant Funding Program, named for Representative Harold Rogers (R-KY). Rogers introduced the legislation in 2001 to the U.S. Congress that was eventually adopted the following year, creating the program that now carries his name. States that receive grants from the program are free to use them for any one of a variety of purposes, such as collecting and using data to determine drug abuse trends in a state, developing and carrying out the evaluation of existing drug prevention programs, contributing to the development of prescription drug abuse prevention programs, and enabling Native American communities to create and operate prescription drug abuse prevention programs and coordinating their efforts with those of the state in which they are located ("Harold Rogers Prescription Drug Monitoring Program (CFDA #16.754)" 2016).

As concerns over the opioid epidemic have increased in the past few years, many states have responded with more aggressive legislation that attempts to control the flow of opioids in the state. Some examples from 2017 are the following (citations refer to relevant state law):

- Alaska: Seven-day limit on all opioid prescriptions; training in pain managements and opioid prescribing for all candidates for medical, dental, and pharmaceutical licenses (http://www.legis.state.ak.us/basis/get_fulltext.asp?session= 30&bill=HB159).
- Colorado: Seven-day limit, with approval from state Department of Health Care Policy and Financing for more than three prescriptions. New rules apply to the state's Health First Program (https://www.colorado.gov/pacific/hcpf/news/ colorado-medicaid-tighten-opioid-usage-policy).
- Delaware: A very extensive and detailed program for preventing opioid abuse that includes a seven-day limit for all first prescriptions and a physical examination and other procedures for additional prescription; close monitoring of the PDMP for possible previous use of opioids by the patient (https://news.delaware.gov/2017/02/01/new-protections-for-safe-prescribing-of-opiates/).
- Illinois: In a first-in-the-nation pilot program, prescribed medications for some drugs will be delivered in containers that can be locked and opened with a special code, preventing the drugs from getting into the hands of individuals for whom the drugs were not intended (http://www.ilga.gov/ legislation/publicacts/fulltext.asp?Name=099-0473).
- New Hampshire: For a state with one of the largest opioid problems in the nation, a new report in 2016 on a host of policies and practices designed to reduce the epidemic. Included are sections on emergency and prescribing rules, naloxone distribution, "Good Samaritan" policies for anyone assisting

a person in an opioid crisis, a statewide addiction crisis line, a New Hampshire alcohol and drug treatment locator system, and a system of regional access point systems (https://gal lery.mailchimp.com/5b9be11abdba5b61e47d79a2f/files/Opiate_gov_Response_8_23_16.pdf).

- Oregon: A new set of guidelines that includes ways of determining when to initiate or continue use of opioids for chronic pain; methods of opioid selection, dosage, duration, follow-up, and discontinuation; assessment of risks and addressing potential harms of opioid use; and additional issues, such as possible comorbidities with marijuana and storage and disposal of opioids (http://www.oregon.gov/obnm/rules/opioidprescribingguidelines.pdf).

- Pennsylvania: The Department of Drug and Alcohol Programs and Department of Health issues detailed guidelines for use of opioids by dentists (http://www.health.pa.gov/my%20health/diseases%20and%20conditions/m-p/opi oids/pages/prescribing-guidelines.aspx#.WrAe6OjwY2w).

*Multistate*

On some occasions, states have concluded that regional efforts to fight the opioid epidemic can be more effective than, or contribute to, the work of individual states. In 2016, four states—Delaware, Minnesota, New Mexico, and Rhode Island—signed a compact to share information about the opioid epidemic in their states. Each state would make available to other states in the group data on trends in incidence and information about programs of prevention and treatment that are under investigation ("States Stem Opioid Overdose through Information Sharing" 2016). Other state associations are even more ambitious, apparently filling the gap by the federal government's efforts thus far to deal with the opioid epidemic. Also in 2016, 46 governors signed the Compact to Fight Opioid Addiction, agreeing to redouble their efforts to fight the opioid epidemic with new steps to reduce inappropriate prescribing, change the nation's understanding of opioids and addiction, and ensure a pathway to recovery for individuals suffering from addiction ("A Compact to Fight Opioid Addiction" 2016).

## Prevention

The fundamental goal of programs for dealing with opioid dependence and addiction is, of course, prevention. If methods are available for preventing individuals from using opioids for nonmedical purposes in the first place, the risk of addiction and its consequences (such as death) can be avoided. Therefore, it is small wonder that very substantial efforts have been expended in trying to find ways of preventing people from misusing opioids to begin with.

Recommendations for controlling the nonmedical use of opioids have come from a wide variety of sources, including governmental agencies at the federal, state, and local levels; many professional organizations; nongovernmental associations; academic organizations and institutions; and concerned professionals and laypersons from every part of society. Some common themes appear in these recommendations, themes that are reflected, for example, in a report issued by the Substance Abuse and Mental Health Services Administration's Center for the Application of Prevention Technologies in 2016. That report lists four areas in which prevention programs can be developed: education, tracking and monitoring, proper medication disposal, and enforcement, as well as some combination of these approaches ("Preventing Prescription Drug Abuse" 2016).

## Education

### Health Care Workers

Perhaps the group that can benefit most from education about opioid issues is health care workers: physicians, dentists, pharmacists, nurses, physician assistants, and other individuals who write or fill prescriptions for opioids and/or who deal with patients who may be at risk for misuse, abuse, or addiction. One of the basic problems with education at this level is that the topic of drug abuse, in general, and opioid abuse, in particular, is seldom discussed adequately in a professional's training experience. Many health care workers report having had only a few hours or, in some cases, no instruction at all on the topic of drug abuse in their medical, dental, nursing, public health, or other training programs. In a 2011 White House report on the opioid epidemic, researchers noted that

> prescribers and dispensers, including physicians, physician assistants, nurse practitioners, pharmacists, nurses, prescribing psychologists, and dentists, all have a role to play in reducing opioid misuse and abuse. Most receive little training on the importance of appropriate prescribing and dispensing of opioids to prevent adverse effects, diversion, and addiction. Outside of specialty addiction treatment programs, most healthcare providers have received minimal training in how to recognize substance abuse in their patients. Most medical, dental, pharmacy, and other health professional schools do not provide in depth training on substance abuse; often, substance abuse education is limited to classroom or clinical electives. Moreover, students in these schools may only receive limited training on treating pain. ("Epidemic: Responding to America's Prescription Drug Abuse Crisis" 2011, 2–3)

A number of states and professional associations have studied this problem and devised recommendations for ways of dealing with the inadequate level of education about opioids and other drugs. As of early 2018, only one state—Massachusetts—has translated these recommendations into a specific program for including a study of the opioid crisis in the regular medical, dental, nursing, pharmaceutical, and other health care educational programs. In 2016, a committee consisted of representatives

from the Baker–Polito administration (governor and lieutenant governor of the state) and the Massachusetts Medical
Society, and the deans of the Commonwealth's four medical
schools—Boston University School of Medicine, Harvard
Medical School, Tufts School of Medicine, and the University
of Massachusetts Medical School. The committee's report laid
out a series of competencies that they felt every graduate from
these four institutions should have. Those competencies were
to be achieved through whatever curricular devices the schools
considered appropriate, spread out over a student's four years
of medical training.

The competencies were categorized into three general categories: primary, secondary, and tertiary prevention domains.
Elements of the first category involved attention to screening,
evaluation, and prevention. An example of the specific competency expected in this domain was the ability to determine
the appropriate approach for treating a person's substance abuse
problem, on the basis of his or her physical condition and
medical history. The goal of the second domain was to "engage
patients in safe, informed, and patient-centered treatment planning." One approach to this objective would be to better inform
patients about the nature of their problem and methods for
dealing with the problem. The third domain is entitled "Managing Substance Use Disorders as a Chronic Disease." The goal
of this domain is to help eliminate the stigma associated with
drug abuse and better understand how social factors contribute
to attitudes about the condition (Governor's Medical Education Working Group on Prescription Drug Misuse 2016).

Until medical, dental, and other health care training schools
adopt clearly stated objectives and programs like those adopted in Massachusetts, most individuals in the field will need
to take responsibility for their own training in the treatment
of opioid abuse. Among the recommendations regarding this
issue made by various boards, committees, review groups, and
other organizations is one offered by the Center for Lawful Access and Abuse Deterrence in its National Prescription Drug

Abuse Prevention Strategy position paper, published in 2010. That paper recommended continuing education for prescribers to maintain and increase competency over time. In order to promote best practices in pain management, providers must continually learn new information and stay abreast of emerging policies and standards of care. Events and training sessions on the management of pain, safe prescribing, and abuse prevention are necessary to ensure and enhance quality across the spectrum of care ("National Prescription Drug Abuse Prevention Strategy" 2010, 32).

Some examples of the courses that have been designed by various organizations to meet this recommendation include the following:

- "Clinical Challenges in Opioid Prescribing: Balancing Safety and Efficacy." Substance Abuse and Mental Health Services Administration. https://www.samhsa.gov/medica tion-assisted-treatment/training-resources/opioid-courses/ clinical-challenges-opioid-prescribing.
- "Protecting Your Practice and Patients from Prescription Drug Abuse." PharmCon. https://www.freece.com/freece/CE Catalog_Details.aspx?ID=d13bc174-55a8-48bd-be5f-9549c 971d551.
- "Prescriber's Summit on Prescription Drug Abuse/Misuse." Ohio Pharmacists Association. http://www.ohiopharmacists .org/aws/OPA/pt/sd/calendar/38758/_PARENT/layout_ interior_details/true.
- "Performance in Practice" (two courses). American Academy of Addiction Psychiatry. https://www.aaap.org/education-training/cme-opportunities/.
- "Drug Diversion Training and Best Practice Prescribing." Wild Iris Medical Education, Inc. http://www.nursingceu .com/courses/486/index_nceu.html.
- "Safe and Competent Opioid Prescribing: Optimizing Office Systems" and "Making Sense of Massachusetts Opioid

Prescribing Laws and State and National Guidelines." OpioidPrescribing.org. https://www.opioidprescribing.com/overview.

- Multiple courses: American Society of Pain Management Nursing. https://www.pathlms.com/aspmn/courses.
- Various topics: PCSS-O Training. http://pcss-o.org/modules.

Another aspect of education for physicians, nurses, dentists, and other prescribers of medication is the Risk Evaluation and Mitigation Strategy (REMS) program administered by the FDA. This program was authorized by the Food and Drug Administration Amendments Act of 2007. The law allows the FDA to require that drug manufacturers institute programs (REMSs) for drug prescribers about new or existing products. These programs must consist of some type of educational plan by which the relative risks and benefits of a drug are explained to drug prescribers. These programs go beyond the normal statements provided by manufacturers with regard to a drug's safety and possible risks. An acceptable (to the FDA) REMS must include one or more "elements to assure safe use" (ETASU) that provide information above and beyond that which is normally provided by a manufacturer to a prescriber. Some ETASUs that are recommended include specialized training materials for the drug, specific procedures for the drug's use, patient/physician agreements or statements of informed consent, safety protocols for the drug's use, and required laboratory testing (Merenda 2011; a detailed description of the type of REMS procedure that might be used for long-acting and extended-release opioid products can be found at "Extended Release (ER) and Long Acting (LA) Opioid Analgesics Risk Evaluation and Mitigation Strategy (REMS)" 2014).

### Schools and Colleges

Many experts in the field of opioid abuse prevention stress that educational programs for boys and girls and young men and women should be available at every level, from prekindergarten to college. Programs to meet these expectations are available from commercial publishers, professional organizations, governmental agencies, state departments of education, and individual school districts and schools. One of the best such approaches to a comprehensive prevention curriculum is the one developed by the state of Ohio Department of Education. The program provides requirements, recommendations, and resources for opioid education from kindergarten through 12th grade ("Opioid Abuse Prevention" 2017). The department's website provides a summary of learning goals and links to useful resources for grades K-3, 4–5, 6–8, and 9–12. The learning objectives for the lowest grades, for example, call for "'differences among foods, poisons, medicines and drugs; personal responsibility for ones [as in the original] actions'; and rules regarding who provides, distributes, accesses and monitors medication in the home and community" ("Opioid Abuse Prevention" 2017). The website then provides links to specific curriculum developed by the FDA, CDC, and Kids' Health web pages that contain specific lesson plans for programs that meet these objectives. The Kids' Health curriculum for this age group, for example, includes lessons on "Trusted Adults" and "What Should You Do?" ("K to Grade 2 • Health Problems Series. Drugs" 2016). The FDA lesson is extensive (46 pages), dealing with all aspects of the topic "Medicines in My Home" ("Medicines in My Home" 2017). Similar resources are available from nonprofit organizations for other precollege-grade levels. See, for example, "An Educational Program Designed to Prevent First Use and Save Lives" (2017) and "Opioid Education Resources" (2017).

Colleges and universities across the nation have devised a variety of approaches for dealing with the opioid crisis. One such approach is the creation of substance-free dormitories, housing facilities in which students may live where the use of any illegal substance is prohibited. Rutgers University, for example, has created Recovery House, a facility where students at risk for drug and/or alcohol abuse may live with reduced opportunities to be exposed to illegal substances ("Recovery Housing" 2017). Other institutions offer one-time lectures or presentations explaining the nature of the opioid epidemic and ways of dealing with the crisis. In November 2017, for example, D'Youville College in Buffalo, New York, offered a presentation, "Opioid Crisis in WNY Part I: Community Intervention and Narcan Training," conducted by experts in the field, followed by training in the use of Narcan for opioid overdoses ("D'Youville Assists in Quest to Treat Opioid Epidemic" 2017).

One of the most creative approaches to opioid abuse prevention at the college level can be found at Harford Community College, in Bel Air, Maryland. Its approach to meeting state requirements for opioid educational programs was to adopt a new college policy requiring all incoming full-time students "to participate in and in-person or electronic heroin and opioid addiction and awareness training" ("Approved Minutes. Harford Community College" 2017).

Perhaps the most common approach to training in opioid abuse at the college level is use of free online courses on the topic provided by a variety of organizations and institutions. The Harvard University Online Learning website, for example, offers a course called "The Opioid Crisis in America" as part of its Global Health and Medicine series. The course consists of seven lessons and can be accessed free of charge ("The Opioid Crisis in America" 2017). A for-profit company based in Washington, D.C., EverFi, may be the largest single provider of online courses on opioid abuse prevention. In November 2017, the company announced the launch of a new addition to its large selection of online prevention courses, "Prescription Drug Abuse Prevention." The company reported that more than 30,000 students had already enrolled for the course by the end of November 2017 ("Prescription Drug Safety Network" 2017).

**Proper Medication Disposal**

By far, the most common source of illegal prescription pain-killers is a close friend or relative. In a 2017 study, researchers reported that 65.2 percent of all individuals over the age of 12 who abused opioids obtained them for free, by paying for them, or by stealing from a friend or relative. For teenagers between the ages of 12 and 17, that number was 61.5 percent (Lipari and Hughes 2017, Figure 3). The inference from these data is that many individuals who had received those drugs legitimately for medical purposes then failed to take them all and stored them in a medicine cabinet or some other location in their homes from which they made their way to an unauthorized user. The solution to such a pattern, many experts say, is to develop and put into use simple, accessible systems through which a person can dispose of unwanted or unneeded medications.

Prior to 2014, the only legal methods for disposing of unused or unwanted prescription drugs was to flush them down the toilet, dispose of them in the trash, surrender them to law enforcement agencies, or seek some other method of disposal from the DEA. Many people decided, by intent or not, simply to store these drugs in their homes, often in locations that were readily available to other family members and friends. In September 2014, under authority of the 2010 Secure and Responsible Drug Disposal Act, the DEA announced a new rule concerning the secure disposal of prescription drugs. The rule established a variety of disposal techniques for such drugs, ranging from mail-back programs (in which drugs could be sent back at no cost to manufacturers) to take-back events (community-based occasions at which individuals could turn in unused drugs) to specially designed and situated disposal centers (where drugs could be dropped off). The new rule provided detailed instructions for the development and implementation of these systems of drug disposal ("Disposal Act: General Public Fact Sheet" 2014).

Since the DEA action, a number of governmental bodies, nonprofit organizations, drug suppliers, and other groups have developed guidelines, recommendations, formal programs, or other ways to reduce the availability of opioids among the public. For example, Partnership for Drug-Free Kids has developed an online publication for general use on the topic, "Safe Drug Disposal: A Guide for Communities Seeking Solutions." The brochure includes sections on "Why Does Safe Drug Disposal Matter?" "What Is a Safe Drug Disposal Program?" "Who Is Involved in Safe Drug-Disposal Programs?" "How Can Community Officials and Organizers Build Support for Safe Drug-Disposal Programs?" and "Promoting Safe Drug-Disposal Programs" ("Safe Drug Disposal: A Guide for Communities Seeking Solutions" 2015).

In late 2017, CVS, a pharmaceutical company, announced that it was partnering with Partnership for Drug-Free Kids to initiate, in February 2018, a variety of programs to reduce illegal access to opioids. The program involves an increased limitation on the availability of opioid drugs, an expanded drug disposal system, and funding for drug abuse programs and support services (Maynard 2017). As of early 2018, several options are now available for the safe disposal of illegal opioids and other prescription drugs ("Disposal of Unused Medicines: What You Should Know" 2017; this site not only contains good information on drug disposal but also provides links to other websites with more detailed information).

### Enforcement

One aspect of the nation's opioid-control efforts involves more aggressive implementation of existing state and federal laws that may apply to the crisis. The range of laws that may be invoked in this effort is large. In a 2015 enforcement action across the states of Arkansas, Alabama, Louisiana, and Mississippi, for example, investigations and arrests involved agents from the U.S. Drug Enforcement; the Federal Bureau of Investigation;

the Department of Homeland Security; the Bureau of Alcohol, Tobacco, Firearms, and Explosives; FDA; U.S. Marshals Service; and the Internal Revenue Service, along with the U.S. Attorneys offices in the four states, and law enforcement officers at the state and local levels ("DEA Announces Largest-Ever Prescription Drug Operation" 2015).

*Pill Mill Laws*

Many of these operations are aimed at two types of pill-distribution activities, pill mills and doctor-shopping practices. According to one definition, a pill mill is "a doctor's office, clinic, or health care facility that routinely conspires in the prescribing and dispensing of controlled substances outside the scope of the prevailing standards of medical practice in the community or violates the laws of [a state] regarding the prescribing or dispensing of controlled prescription drugs" ("Pill Mill Initiative" 2011). The term *doctor shopping* refers to the practice of a person's "obtaining controlled substances from multiple healthcare practitioners without the prescribers' knowledge of the other prescriptions" ("Doctor Shopping Laws" 2012). The practice allows a person to obtain large quantities of a prescription drug for which he or she has no medical use.

One of the first states to adopt a pill mill law was Florida. In 2010, the state had the nation's highest rate of diversion of opioids for illegal use. One consequence of that dubious record is that an estimated seven Floridians were dying every day in the state because of this problem ("Pill Mill Initiative" 2011). In 2011, the state legislature adopted a so-called anti-pill mill bill whose provisions included increasing administrative and criminal penalties for doctors and clinics convicted of prescription drug trafficking, establishing new standards for doctors who prescribe narcotic drugs, adding requirements for the registration of such drugs, banning doctors from prescribing certain drugs especially likely to be used for non-medical purposes, increasing the monitoring of pharmacies and companies that dispense prescription drugs, and improving the system for monitoring prescription drug dispensing ("Florida's Prescription Drug Diversion and Abuse Roadmap 2012–2015" 2012; a copy of the bill is available at http://www.flsenate.gov/Session/Bill/2011/7095/BillText/er/PDF, accessed on December 26, 2017).

As of early 2018, 11 states had adopted some form of legislation designed to identify, monitor, and (usually) close pill mills: Alabama, Florida, Georgia, Indiana, Kentucky, Louisiana, Mississippi, Ohio, Tennessee, Texas, and West Virginia ("Menu of Pain Management Clinic Regulation" n.d., 1). Other states continue to consider similar types of pill mill legislation.

Several studies have attempted to determine whether pill mill laws are effective in reducing opioid overdose deaths and, if so, by how much. One of the most recent of those studies compared the number of expected deaths in the state of Florida, based on trends in a nearby state (North Carolina). Researchers found that the laws saved 1,029 deaths in the 34 months following the law's adoption, in comparison to the number that would have been expected based on North Carolina numbers. Those data improved over time, with the rate of deaths falling by 0.6 per 100,000 in the first year following the law's adoption, by 1.8 per 100.000 in the next year, and by 3.0 per 100,000 in the third year (Kennedy-Hendricks 2016; also see Johnson et al. 2014; Rutkow et al. 2015; Surrett et al. 2014).

Some observers have pointed out that, despite their apparent success, anti-pill mill bills are not without their undesirable and sometimes unexpected consequences. On the one hand, as discussed earlier, some patients who have legitimate needs for certain opioids or other prescription drugs, usually for the control of pain, are unable to get their prescriptions filled. On the other hand, pharmacists may feel so pressured by the pill mill laws that they refuse to fill such prescriptions for fear of running afoul of the law (Ault 2017).

Another unintended consequence of pill mill and similar prescription drug laws is that people who have become dependent on or addicted to prescription drugs may switch to other drugs, at least as dangerous as the prescription drugs to which they no longer have access. In many cases, the drug of choice is an old, familiar, and illegal substance: heroin. Several studies have now shown that pill mill laws may produce decreases—often rapid and large—in the number of facilities where prescription drugs may be illegally obtained but that such successes are countered by comparable rapid and large increases in the use of illegal drugs such as heroin (Blackwell 2013; Huecker and Shoff 2014).

Perhaps the most dramatic illustration of this possibility is the rise in overdoses from the use of fentanyl. The number of deaths from overdoses, admissions to emergency departments, and positive blood tests for fentanyl among arrestees has skyrocketed in the past few years. At least three factors contribute to this trend. First, the cost of synthetic drugs like fentanyl and carfentanil is substantially less than it is for more traditional opioids, such as oxycodone and hydromorphone. Second, new laws and more aggressive enforcement have often made it more difficult for users to obtain legal medical opioids. Third, drug manufacturers have begun to add fentanyl to less-harmful traditional drugs and marketed them to users as Percocet or Oxy-Contin. All of these factors have made fentanyl and its analogs more popular and more widely used in the past few years than in all of U.S. history (McGreal 2016; also see "NFLIS Brief: Fentanyl, 2001–2015" 2017, Figure 1).

*Doctor Shopping Laws*

All 50 states and the District of Columbia also have some type of legislation dealing with doctor shopping. Those laws differ from state to state and can be classified as "general" doctor shopping laws or "specific" doctor shopping laws. General doctor shopping laws tend to adopt language from the federal Uniform Controlled Substances Act ("Uniform Controlled Substances Act (1994)" 1994) or the much older Uniform

Narcotic Drug Act (which it supplanted) that restricts the sale and purchase of all and any kinds of drugs. The relevant Delaware law, for example, is based on the former statute and the California law on the latter statute. Other states, such as Rhode Island, have two general doctor shopping laws, one based on each of the two federal statutes ("Doctor Shopping Laws" 2012). General doctor shopping laws tend to use phrases such as "it is unlawful for any person knowingly or intentionally . . . [t]o acquire or obtain or attempt to acquire or obtain, possession of a controlled substance or prescription drug by misrepresentation, fraud, forgery, deception or subterfuge" (Title 16. Health and Safety. Food and Drugs. Chapter 47, 2017).

Other states have more specific and more rigorous laws that make it clear that they refer specifically to the practice of doctor shopping. These laws generally describe and prohibit the practices used by individuals in doctor shopping, as in the Montana law that makes it illegal for a person to

> knowingly or purposefully failing to disclose to a practitioner, . . . that the person has received the same or a similar dangerous drug or prescription for a dangerous drug from another source within the prior 30 days; or . . . knowingly or purposefully communicating false or incomplete information to a practitioner with the intent to procure the administration of or a prescription for a dangerous drug. ("45-9-104. Fraudulently Obtaining Dangerous Drugs" 2014)

While many public health and law enforcement agencies are generally enthusiastic about the potential for doctor shopping laws as a way of reducing the illegal use of prescription drugs, some legal and civil rights specialists have expressed concerns about the possible intrusion of such laws on an individual privacy. They argue that a person's medical records should be sacrosanct, and developing databases that can be shared among doctors, pharmacists, law enforcement officers, and others is a substantial threat to anyone's privacy ("ACLU Asks Court to Protect Confidentiality of Rush Limbaugh's Medical Records" 2004; Schwartzapfel 2017; for a very interesting exchange among individuals involved in doctor shopping, also see "I've Been Caught Doctor Shopping . . . What Next?" 2017).

## Treatment

Opioid addiction was first recognized as a serious national problem in the early 20th century. At first, the problem was regarded as a moral issue, like burglary or perjury, and not a situation with which the medical profession should become involved. Indeed, physicians who attempted to treat addicts could be (and were) arrested and convicted (Nevius 2016).

That view slowly began to change, and by about 1920, the problem had become serious enough that federal, state, and local entities were beginning to establish facilities at which opioid dependence and addiction could be treated. Health care workers usually tried one (and sometimes both) of two therapies for the treatment of dependence and addiction: detoxification and abstinence or maintenance. The two approaches sprang from two different views about the nature of opioid dependence and addiction. On the one hand, some experts believed that addiction was an incurable problem, and the best one could hope for was to help an addict to function as best as possible on as low a dose of medication as possible (maintenance). The medication typically used in this form of therapy was methadone. The second approach assumed that addicts could be cured, and the best way to do that was to wean them off their problematic drug (detoxification) and then train them to get on with their lives by remaining completely drug free (abstinence). The drugs most commonly used for the detoxification stage were heroin and cocaine, given in decreasing concentrations over time. Training in abstinence has most often involved a patient's introduction and commitment to the 12-step program developed by Alcoholics Anonymous for abstinence from that substance ("Medication-Assisted Treatment for Opioid Addiction in Opioid Treatment Programs" 2005).

(An even more effective agonist than methadone is levacetylmethadol [also known as levomethadyl acetate, LAAM, or its trade name ORLAAM]. It acts on the same general principle of methadone but is even more effective. Compared to methadone, which a patient normally takes once a day, LAAM needs to be taken only about every three days. The commercial form of the drug, ORLAAM, was discontinued in 2003 because of life-threatening side effects. LAAM treatment is still available under very carefully controlled conditions to individuals for whom methadone treatment is unsuccessful ["Orlaam" 2017].)

Unfortunately, studies have shown that the detoxification/abstinence approach to treatment tends not to be very successful. The author of one recent review of efficacy studies concluded that detoxification followed by abstinence "carries the risk of a very high relapse rate and treatment failure." He noted that about two-thirds of opioid-dependent patients relapse unless they then have maintenance therapy (Yan 2010). Nonetheless, at least some form of detoxification/abstinence programs remain popular methods of opioid addiction treatment in the United States today (see, e.g., "Top 3 Goals of Drug Detox" 2017; for a detailed discussion of this issue, see Mehendalen et al. 2016).

The treatment of choice in many instances today is based on the agonist/antagonist theory of the way opioids work in the brain. (For a good overview and discussion of this theory, see Stotts, Dodrill, and Kosten 2009.) As noted in Chapter 1, neurons in the brain contain certain receptor sites whose physical shape closely matches those of specific endogenous opioids. When an endogenous opioid is released into the brain, it searches out and attaches to a complementary receptor site. When the connection between opioid and receptor site is made, the receptor site is stimulated to initiate other changes in the brain that are responsible for the clinical symptoms of opioid function, such as pleasure or emotion. (For a simplified explanation of this process, see "Full Opioid Agonists and Opioid Antagonists" 2017.)

According to current theory, a person feels pain when, usually, a compound known as substance P is released from one neuron, travels to a second neuron, and binds to a receptor site on that neuron. That action initiates a sensation that we call "pain" (see Ontiveros 2012, slide 17). Agonists and antagonists inhibit that process by preventing substance P (and other pain-causing substances) from completing that pathway. Three types of agonists and antagonists are involved in this process: agonists, partial agonists, and antagonists. An agonist (or full agonist) is a substance that binds to a receptor site and prevents any other substance (such as an opioid) from binding to the same site. Some examples of agonists are morphine, heroin, oxycodone, hydromorphone, and fentanyl. When one of these substances reaches the brain, it travels to pain receptor sites, attaches to them, and prevents the transmission of substance P. This is the mechanism by which exogenous opioids control pain. The opioid–receptor bond, at the same time, initiates other sensations through the second neuron, such as euphoria and relaxation, the feelings one has when taking opioids into the body for reasons other than pain. This description explains why early methods for treating opioid addiction with other opioids are not successful. Suppose a person is addicted to morphine. Substituting heroin for morphine as a treatment method is not going to work because both substances work in the same way on brain cells.

The opioid agonist probably most commonly used for treatment of addiction is methadone. When a person ingests methadone, it goes to the brain and binds to opioid receptors in the same way as do heroin and other opioids. The difference between methadone and other opioids, however, is that its stimulating effects are more moderate than are those of heroin and other opioids. Receptors to which methadone is attached release dopamine, as they do with heroin. But the "high" produced is less intense and smoother than that from heroin. A person on methadone therapy needs to take a methadone dose only once a day, during which time he or she no longer feels the intense desire for heroin or other opioids. Methadone therapy has been in use for nearly half a century and generally works very well with most patients, provided it is accompanied by regular supportive counseling and therapy sessions (Payte, Smith, and Woods 2001).

A partial agonist works in essentially the same way as a full agonist, except that it does not completely deactivate the receptor site. As its name suggests, it reduces the activity of that site but does not interrupt it completely. (For a detailed explanation of this process, see "Mechanism of Action of a Partial Opioid Agonist" 2017.) The most commonly used partial agonist today is buprenorphine. Other members of the family include nalmefene, norclozapine, buspirone, and aripiprazole. Partial agonists not only produce a decreased effect on the brain but also prevent full agonists, such as heroin and oxycodone, from attaching to receptor cells and producing their own effect.

From a therapeutic perspective, the most important of the partial agonists currently known is buprenorphine. When buprenorphine reaches the brain, it attaches to receptor cells in a less-than-complete (partial) fashion. Its first effect is to prevent other agonists, such as heroin or oxycodone, from attaching to those same receptors. That is, it "protects" the brain from developing an addiction to those agonists. At the same time, it produces an effect on the brain that is similar to, but less pronounced than, that caused by full agonists. As a treatment modality, then, a program of controlled buprenorphine administration provides a patient with some of the same effects as full agonists but in a less-intense form that is less likely to lead to addiction. (For an illustrated explanation of the process by which buprenorphine works in the brain, see "Buprenorphine. A Treatment for Opioid Addiction in the Privacy of a Doctor's Office" 2015.)

Buprenorphine treatment typically lasts anywhere from six months to a year, although it can take longer than that for a person to recover from one's addiction. The drug was first approved for therapeutic use in October 2002 under the brand names Suboxone® and Subutex®. Those two formulations were later discontinued and replaced by a new form of the drug, Suboxone Film®. The FDA has also approved some generic forms of the drug ("Buprenorphine. A Treatment for Opioid Addiction in the Privacy of a Doctor's Office" 2015).

An antagonist operates on a different principle. An antagonist attaches to a receptor site without producing any effect on the neuron to which it is attached; that is, it does not produce any of the sensations normally associated with agonist use. Providing an antagonist to a person, then, essentially prevents the presence of any agonist from affecting brain function. Furthermore, the antagonist binds more strongly to the receptor site than does an agonist. Thus, it not only prevents an agonist from binding to the receptor site but actually replaces any agonists already present at that site (see "Full Opioid Agonists and Opioid Antagonists" 2017 for an illustration of the process).

The two most common antagonists used today for the treatment of opioid addiction are naloxone and naltrexone. These drugs are available in two formulations, injectable and inhalant. They tend to be used most commonly with patients who have overdosed on an opioid. Their effect is generally quite remarkable; in many instances, a person who has turned blue and stopped breathing may experience an almost complete recovery in a matter of minutes ("Administer Naloxone" 2017). The two drugs are available under a variety of trade names, such as Evzio®, Nalone®, Narcan®, Narcanti®, Narcon® (injectable or spray naloxone), and Vivitrol (extended-release injectable naltrexone) ("Opioid Antagonists" 2017).

Treatment of infants for NAS often makes use of the same pharmacological options as those used by adults who are dependent on or addicted to opioids. Those options most commonly involve the use of methadone or buprenorphine, with adjustments in procedure appropriate to the special needs of very young children (Kocherlakota 2014, Table 4, page e555). Other drugs have been tried but with less satisfactory outcomes.

In fact, studies have now shown that nonpharmacological procedures are more effective than pharmacological approaches. These procedures include gentle and frequent handling of children, feeding on demand, as much physical contact with mother as possible, avoiding wakening a sleeping baby, swaddling of the child, a frequent high-nutritional feeding schedule, music and massage therapy, pacifiers and kangaroo-style carrying, low-level stimulation with dim light and low levels of noise, and water beds (Kocherlakota 2014, page e553).

Although a nonpharmacological approach for NAS infants is obviously preferable for treatment of their condition, anywhere from 27 to 91 percent of those with the condition do not adequately respond to this approach, and pharmacological tools are needed. Although clinical evidence is still incomplete, studies suggest that methadone, buprenorphine, morphine, clonidine, and phenobarbital may all be useful, depending on individual circumstances of an infant's case (Hamdan 2017).

The discussion of opioid addiction treatments presented here may have given the impression that many aspects of such programs, or at least the available options, are generally agreed upon. Of course, some providers prefer one approach and others a different approach. Yet it is possible that the topic of treatment is considerably more complex and unsettled than it may appear. In its issue of December 28, 2017, *The New York Times* included a complete section dedicated to opioid treatment issues. Authors of the article concluded that "there is great debate about which treatment approaches work best, and even how to measure their efficacy." They went on to quote the director of business development at the widely respected Hazelden Betty Ford Foundation on the subject. "A lot of organizations," he said, "say they have the cure, but they have no incentive to try to prove it through the data" (Corkery and Silver-Greenberg 2017, F6).

The primary theme of *The New York Times* article, however, went beyond that assessment of current treatment strategies. Instead, it was the commercialization of treatment programs that has taken place in the United States over the past two decades. Most of the reporting in the article pointed to the fact that a number of business entrepreneurs had taken advantage of the opioid crisis to create businesses that have prospered—in some cases quite dramatically—from the need for addiction and dependence treatment. The authors again concluded from their research that new insurance laws dealing with payment for opioid treatment programs in 2008 and 2010 had "transformed what had largely been a government-funded and charitable-minded field into an enticing for-profit business" that now operated "a $35 billion industry of inpatient programs" (Corkery and Silver-Greenberg 2017, F6).

Another fundamental concern about the use of medications to treat opioid dependence and addiction is that the approach is not widely used in the United States. According to the most recent data available, less than half of all privately funded treatments for opioid dependence and/or addiction offer medication-assisted treatment (MAT), and only a third of the patients enrolled in these programs receive some type of MAT. Furthermore, as the number of those needing opioid treatment increases, the number in such programs is decreasing, falling from 35 percent in 2002 to 28 percent in 2012 (the latest date for which data are available) ("Effective Treatments for Opioid Addiction" 2016).

A number of factors have been suggested for this set of circumstances. First, there is the (erroneous) belief that the use of methadone or buprenorphine may lead to new forms of opioid addiction. Second, many people who could benefit from MAT do not have the insurance coverage needed to pay for such treatments. Third, there are not a sufficient number of physicians trained in the use of MAT compared to the number of patients who could benefit from the treatment. Fourth, there are also too few facilities licensed to offer MAT treatments for opioid abusers.

## Alternative Forms of Treatment

Beyond research efforts to improve the efficacy and safety of existing medications available for the treatment of opioid dependence and addiction, some workers are looking at entirely new approaches for dealing with the problem. One suggestion has been that it may be possible to synthesize a vaccine that could prevent an opioid from having its deleterious effects on the brain. Some early research has produced promising results. The approach used is to find a substance that, when added to the body, interacts and inactivates opioid molecules, preventing them from reaching the brain. In an experiment reported in December 2017, for example, researchers at the U.S. Military HIV Research Program found that an experimental heroin vaccine induced antibodies that prevented the drug from crossing the blood-brain barrier in mice and rats, thus preventing it from acting on the nervous system in the brain ("New Vaccine Technology Shows Promise as a Tool to Combat the Opioid Crisis" 2017).

The goal of another line of research is to find ways of reducing postoperative and other types of pain, thus avoiding the use of opioids entirely for pain control. One such method is called transcranial direct current stimulation. The procedure involves the application of very small electric current to the brain. The effect of such a treatment is to induce the release of endogenous opioids that alter the pain process in the brain in much the same way as that achieved by exogenous opioids, such as heroin and oxycodone (Knotkova et al. 2017). A similar procedure, transcranial magnetic stimulation, uses a magnetic field instead of an electrical field to induce such changes in the brain ("Transcranial Magnetic Stimulation" 2018). Yet a third procedure is called deep brain stimulation. It also involves the application of an electrical current to the brain, with somewhat different parameters than those used for transcranial direct current stimulation (Wichmann and DeLong 2006; for a similar procedure, see Usichenko et al. 2006; for yet another and perhaps unexpected alternative treatment method, see the essay by Anjali Sarkar in Chapter 3).

## Conclusion

Trends in the nation's current opioid epidemic have not been encouraging. As of early 2018, the number of opioid-related deaths has continued to rise. Researchers have learned a great deal about the ways in which opioid dependence and addiction develop and have suggested a variety of methods by which these conditions can be prevented or ameliorated. But the evidence for success of these procedures in the everyday world is mixed. Research continues on ways in which prevention and treatment approaches can be made more effective and more available to a larger group of men and women and boys and girls at risk for this terrible disease.

## References

"About CPDD." 2017. The College on Problems of Drug Dependence. http://cpdd.org/about-us/. Accessed on December 12, 2017.

"ACLU Asks Court to Protect Confidentiality of Rush Limbaugh's Medical Records." 2004. American Civil Liberties Union. https://www.aclu.org/news/aclu-asks-court-protect-confidentiality-rush-limbaughs-medical-records. Accessed on December 27, 2017.

"Administer Naloxone." 2017. Harm Reduction Coalition. http://harmreduction.org/issues/overdose-prevention/overview/overdose-basics/responding-to-opioid-overdose/administer-naloxone/. Accessed on December 29, 2017.

Anderson, L. 2016. "U-47700 (Pink)." Drugs.com. https://www.drugs.com/illicit/u-47700.html. Accessed on December 11, 2017.

Anderson, L. 2017. "Gray Death." Drugs.com. https://www .drugs.com/illicit/graydeath.html. Accessed on December 11, 2017.

"Annual Surveillance Report of Drug-Related Risks and Outcomes." 2017. Centers for Disease Control and Prevention. https://www.cdc.gov/drugoverdose/pdf/pubs/ 2017-cdc-drug-surveillance-report.pdf. Accessed on December 14, 2017.

Anson, Pat. 2017. "Medicare Planning to Adopt CDC Opioid Guidelines." Pain News Network. https://www.painnews network.org/stories/2017/2/3/medicare-planning-to- adopt-cdc-opioid-guidelines. Accessed on December 16, 2017.

"Approved Minutes. Harford Community College." 2017. https://www.harford.edu/~/media/PDF/President/ BoardOfTrustees/Minutes/2017/Minutes2017_06_13 .ashx. Accessed on December 23, 2017.

Ault, Alicia. 2017. "Pharmacists May Be Legally Liable for Opioid Overdoses." Medscape. https://www.medscape .com/viewarticle/882358#vp_1. Accessed on December 26, 2017.

Ballantyne, Jane C. 2006. "Opioids for Chronic Nonterminal Pain." *Southern Medical Journal.* 99(11): 1245–1255. http://www.thblack.com/links/RSD/SouthMedJ2006_99_ 1245_opioidsInNonterminalPain-12p.pdf. Accessed on December 13, 2017.

Beal, Judy, Jill A. Bauer, and Lee A. Diedrick. 2014. "Should Infants with Neonatal Abstinence Syndrome Be Discharged with Their Mothers Rather Than Placed in a Foster-Care Environment?" *MCN, The American Journal of Maternal/ Child Nursing.* 39(4): 218–219.

Bernstein, Lenny, and Scott Higham. 2017. "'We Feel Like Our System Was Hijacked': DEA Agents Say a Huge Opioid Case Ended in a Whimper." *Washington Post.*

https://www.washingtonpost.com/investigations/mckesson-dea-opioids-fine/2017/12/14/ab50ad0e-db5b-11e7-b1a8-62589434a581_story.html?utm_term=.d50f9641fe69. Accessed on December 20, 2017.

Blackwell, Brandon. 2013. "The Heroin Epidemic: Death Toll from Drug Continues to Soar in Cuyahoga County." Cleveland.com. http://www.cleveland.com/metro/index.ssf/2013/09/heroin_epidemic_cuyahoga_count.html. Accessed on December 26, 2017.

Blau, Max. 2017. "STAT Forecast: Opioids Could Kill Nearly 500,000 Americans in the Next Decade." https://www.statnews.com/2017/06/27/opioid-deaths-forecast/. Accessed on December 11, 2017.

Boyle, Annette M. 2016. "CDC Opioid Guidelines Could Cause Problems for VA Patients, Clinicians." U.S. Medicine. http://www.usmedicine.com/clinical-topics/addiction/cdc-guidelines-could-cause-problems-for-va-patients-clinicians/. Accessed on December 16, 2017.

"Buprenorphine. A Treatment for Opioid Addiction in the Privacy of a Doctor's Office." 2015. The National Alliance of Advocates for Buprenorphine. https://www.naabt.org/documents/naabt_brochure%20Version%202.pdf. Accessed on December 29, 2017.

Castagnoli, William G. 1999. *Medicine Ave.: The Story of Medical Advertising in America*: Huntington, NY: Medical Advertising Hall of Fame.

"A Compact to Fight Opioid Addiction." 2016. National Governors Association. https://www.nga.org/cms/news/2016/opioid-compact. Accessed on December 20, 2017.

Corkery, Michael, and Jessica Silver-Greenberg. 2017. "Addiction, Inc." *New York Times*. December 28, 2017, F1–F16.

"CURES/PDMP." n.d. Office of the Attorney General. California Department of Justice. http://oag.ca.gov/sites/

all/files/agweb/pdfs/pdmp/brochure.pdf. Accessed on December 19, 2017.

"Database of Statutes, Regulations, & Other Policies for Pain Management." n.d. Pain & Policies Study Group. http://www.painpolicy.wisc.edu/database-statutes-regulations-other-policies-pain-management. Accessed on December 15, 2017.

"DEA Announces Largest-Ever Prescription Drug Operation." 2015. Drug Enforcement Administration. https://www.dea.gov/divisions/no/2015/no052015.shtml. Accessed on December 24, 2017.

"Disposal Act: General Public Fact Sheet." 2014. Drug Enforcement Administration. https://www.deadiversion.usdoj.gov/drug_disposal/fact_sheets/disposal_public.pdf. Accessed on December 23, 2017.

"Disposal of Unused Medicines: What You Should Know." 2017. U.S. Food and Drug Administration. https://www.fda.gov/Drugs/ResourcesForYou/Consumers/Buying UsingMedicineSafely/EnsuringSafeUseofMedicine/Safe DisposalofMedicines/ucm186187.htm. Accessed on December 23, 2017.

"Doctor Shopping Laws." 2012. Centers for Disease Control and Prevention. http://www.cdc.gov/phlp/docs/menu-shoppinglaws.pdf. Accessed on December 19, 2017.

Dowell, Deborah, Tamara M. Haegerich, and Roger Chou. 2016. "CDC Guideline for Prescribing Opioids for Chronic Pain—United States, 2016." *Morbidity and Mortality Weekly Report.* 65(1): 1–49. https://www.cdc.gov/mmwr/volumes/65/rr/pdfs/rr6501e1.pdf. Accessed on December 15, 2017.

"D'Youville Assists in Quest to Treat Opioid Epidemic." 2017. D'Youville College. http://www.dyc.edu/news/2017/1127-dyouville-assists-in-opiod-training.aspx. Accessed on December 23, 2017.

Eban, Katherine. 2011. "OxyContin: Purdue Pharma's Painful Medicine." *Fortune*. http://fortune.com/2011/11/09/oxycontin-purdue-pharmas-painful-medicine/. Accessed on December 12, 2017.

"An Educational Program Designed to Prevent First Use and Save Lives." 2017. Overdose Lifeline, Inc. https://www.overdose-lifeline.org/opioid-heroin-prevention-education-program.html. Accessed on December 23, 2017.

"Effective Treatments for Opioid Addiction." 2016. National Institute on Drug Abuse. https://d14rmgtrwzf5a.cloudfront.net/sites/default/files/opioidaddictiontreatment.pdf. Accessed on January 3, 2018.

"Epidemic: Responding to America's Prescription Drug Abuse Crisis." 2011. Washington, DC: The White House. http://publications.iowa.gov/12965/1/NationalRxAbusePlan2011.pdf. Accessed on December 21, 2017.

"Extended Release (ER) and Long Acting (LA) Opioid Analgesics Risk Evaluation and Mitigation Strategy (REMS)." 2014. U.S. Food and Drug Administration. https://www.fda.gov/downloads/Drugs/DrugSafety/PostmarketDrugSafetyInformationforPatientsandProviders/UCM311290.pdf. Accessed on December 22, 2017.

Florence, Curtis S., et al. 2016. "The Economic Burden of Prescription Opioid Overdose, Abuse, and Dependence in the United States, 2013." *Medical Care*. 54(10): 901–906.

"Florida's Prescription Drug Diversion and Abuse Roadmap 2012–2015." 2012. Florida Office of the Attorney General. http://myfloridalegal.com/webfiles.nsf/wf/kgrg-8t8l5k/$file/prescriptiondrugdiversionandabuseroadmap.pdf. Accessed on December 26, 2017.

"45-9-104. Fraudulently Obtaining Dangerous Drugs." 2017. Montana Code Annotated 2017. http://leg.mt.gov/bills/mca/title_0450/chapter_0090/part_0010/section_0040/0450-0090-0010-0040.html. Accessed on December 19, 2017.

França, Urbano L., Shaheer Mustafa, and Michael L. McManus. 2016. "The Growing Burden of Neonatal Opiate Exposure on Children and Family Services in Massachusetts." *Child Maltreatment*. 21(1): 80–84. http://journals.sagepub.com/doi/pdf/10.1177/1077559515615437. Accessed on December 31, 2017.

Franklin, Gary M., et al. 2005. "Opioid Dosing Trends and Mortality in Washington State Workers' Compensation, 1996–2002." *American Journal of Industrial Medicine*. 48(2): 91–99.

"Full Opioid Agonists and Opioid Antagonists." 2017. UBC CPD. https://www.youtube.com/watch?v=W2kL0nPPbII. Accessed on December 29, 2017.

Good, Patricia M. 1998. "The Drug Enforcement Administration and Proposed Model Guidelines for the Use of Controlled Substances in Pain Management." http://www.painpolicy.wisc.edu/sites/www.painpolicy.wisc.edu/files/dea98.pdf. Accessed on December 15, 2017.

Governor's Medical Education Working Group on Prescription Drug Misuse. 2016. "Medical Education Core Competencies for the Prevention and Management of Prescription Drug Misuse." http://www.mass.gov/eohhs/docs/dph/stop-addiction/governors-medical-education-working-group-core-competencies.pdf. Accessed on December 21, 2017.

Greene, Marion S., and R. Andrew Chambers. 2015. "Pseudoaddiction: Fact or Fiction? An Investigation of the Medical Literature." *Current Addiction Reports*. 2(4): 310–317.

Gunderman, Richard. 2016. "Oxycontin: How Purdue Pharma Helped Spark the Opioid Epidemic." The Conversation. http://theconversation.com/oxycontin-how-purdue-pharma-helped-spark-the-opioid-epidemic-57331. Accessed on December 12, 2017.

Hamdan, Ashraf H. 2017. "Neonatal Abstinence Syndrome Treatment & Management." Medscape. https://emedicine

.medscape.com/article/978763-treatment#d6. Accessed on December 29, 2017.

Hammergren, John. 2017. "Setting the Record Straight: McKesson's Efforts to Help Address the Opioid Crisis." LinkedIn. https://www.linkedin.com/pulse/setting-record-straight-john-hammergren/. Accessed on December 20, 2017.

"Harold Rogers Prescription Drug Monitoring Program (CFDA #16.754)." 2016. Bureau of Justice Assistance. U.S. Department of Justice. https://www.bja.gov/funding/PDMP16.pdf. Accessed on December 19, 2017.

Hofmann, Jan. 2017. "In Opioid Battle, Cherokee Want Their Day in Tribal Court." *New York Times*. https://www.nytimes.com/2017/12/17/health/cherokee-opioid-addiction-pharmacies.html?mtrref=www.google.com. Accessed on December 21, 2017.

Huecker, Martin R., and Hugh W. Shoff. 2014. "The Law of Unintended Consequences: Illicit for Licit Narcotic Substitution." *Western Journal of Emergency Medicine*. 15(4): 561–563. https://www.ncbi.nlm.nih.gov/pmc/articles/PMC4100869/#b11-wjem-15-561. Accessed on December 26, 2017.

"I've Been Caught Doctor Shopping . . . What Next?" 2017. Drugs.com. https://www.drugs.com/forum/featured-conditions/ive-been-caught-doctor-shopping-what-next-34036.html. Accessed on December 27, 2017.

Jayawan, Sujata S., and Rajesh Balkrishnan. 2005. "The Controversy Surrounding OxyContin Abuse: Issues and Solutions." *Therapeutics and Clinical Risk Management*. 1(2): 77–82. https://www.ncbi.nlm.nih.gov/pmc/articles/PMC1661612/. Accessed on December 12, 2017.

Johnson, Hal, et al. 2014. "Decline in Drug Overdose Deaths after State Policy Changes—Florida, 2010–2012." *Morbidity and Mortality Weekly Report*. 63(26): 569–574.

https://www.cdc.gov/mmwr/preview/mmwrhtml/
mm6326a3.htm. Accessed on December 26, 2017.

"Joint Meeting of the Anesthetic and Life Support Drugs
Advisory Committee and Drug Safety & Risk Management
Advisory Committee. Table of Contents." 2008. Food and
Drug Administration. https://www.fda.gov/ohrms/dockets/
ac/08/briefing/2008-4395b1-01-FDA.pdf. Accessed on
December 12, 2017.

Jones, Christopher M., et al. 2015. "Vital Signs: Demographic
and Substance Use Trends among Heroin Users—United
States, 2002–2013." *Morbidity and Mortality Weekly Report.*
64(26): 719–725. https://www.cdc.gov/mmwr/preview/
mmwrhtml/mm6426a3.htm?s_cid=mm6426a3_w.
Accessed on December 11, 2017.

"K to Grade 2 • Health Problems Series. Drugs." 2016. Kids'
Health in the Classroom. http://kidshealth.org/classroom/
prekto2/problems/drugs/drugs.pdf. Accessed on December 23,
2017.

Katz, Josh. 2017. "The First Count of Fentanyl Deaths in
2016: Up 540% in Three Years." *New York Times.* https://
www.nytimes.com/interactive/2017/09/02/upshot/fentanyl-
drug-overdose-deaths.html. Accessed on December 15,
2017.

Katz, Josh, and Abby Goodnough. 2017. "The Opioid Crisis
Is Getting Worse, Particularly for Black Americans." *New
York Times.* https://www.nytimes.com/interactive/2017/
12/22/upshot/opioid-deaths-are-spreading-rapidly-into-
black-america.html?_r=0. Accessed on December 22,
2017.

Keefe, Patrick Radden. 2017. "The Family That Built an
Empire of Pain." *New Yorker.* October 30, 2017, 34–49.
https://www.newyorker.com/magazine/2017/10/30/the-
family-that-built-an-empire-of-pain. Accessed on March 19,
2018.

Kennedy-Hendricks, Alene. 2016. "Opioid Overdose Deaths and Florida's Crackdown on Pill Mills." *American Journal of Public Health*. 106(2): 291–297.

"Key Substance Use and Mental Health Indicators in the United States: Results from the 2016 National Survey on Drug Use and Health." 2017. Substance Abuse and Mental Health Services Administration. https://www.samhsa.gov/ data/sites/default/files/NSDUH-FFR1-2016/NSDUH-FFR1-2016.pdf. Accessed on December 15, 2017.

Knotkova, Helena, et al. 2017. "Transcranial Direct Current Stimulation (tDCS): What Pain Practitioners Need to Know." Practical Pain Management. https://www.practical painmanagement.com/treatments/interventional/stimulators/ transcranial-direct-current-stimulation-tdcs-what-pain. Accessed on January 3, 2018.

Ko, Jean Y., et al. 2016. "Incidence of Neonatal Abstinence Syndrome—28 States, 1999–2013." *Morbidity and Mortality Weekly*. 65(31): 799–802. https://www.cdc.gov/ mmwr/volumes/65/wr/mm6531a2.htm. Accessed on December 27, 2017.

Kocherlakota, Prabhakar. 2014. "Neonatal Abstinence Syndrome." *Pediatrics*. 134(2): e547–e561. http://pediatrics .aappublications.org/content/pediatrics/134/2/e547.full .pdf. Accessed on December 29, 2017.

Lachman, Sherry. 2017. "The Opioid Plague's Youngest Victims." *New York Times*. https://www.nytimes.com/ 2017/12/28/opinion/opioid-crisis-children-foster-care .html?_r=0. Accessed on December 31, 2017.

Lawhern, Richard "Red." 2017. "The CDC Opioid Guidelines Violate Standards of Science Research." American Council on Science and Health. https://www.acsh.org/news/2017/ 03/25/cdc-opioid-guidelines-violate-standards-science-research-11050. Accessed on December 16, 2017.

Lipari, Rachel N., and Arthur Hughes. 2017. "How People Obtain the Prescription Pain Relievers They Misuse."

The CBHSQ Report. https://www.samhsa.gov/data/
sites/default/files/report_2686/ShortReport-2686.html.
Accessed on December 23, 2017.

"Long-Term Outcomes of Infants with Neonatal Abstinence
Syndrome." 2017. Seattle Children's. http://www.seattle
childrens.org/healthcare-professionals/education/continuing-
medical-nursing-education/neonatal-nursing-education-
briefs/long-term-outcomes-of-infants-with-nas/. Accessed
on December 27, 2017.

Martin, Stephen A., Ruth A. Potee, and Andrew Lazris.
2016. "Neat, Plausible, and Generally Wrong: A Response
to the CDC Recommendations for Chronic Opioid
Use." Medium. https://medium.com/@stmartin/neat-
plausible-and-generally-wrong-a-response-to-the-cdc-
recommendations-for-chronic-opioid-use-5c9d9d319f71.
Accessed on December 16, 2017.

May, Everette L., and Arthur E. Jacobson. 1989. "The
Committee on Problems of Drug Dependence: A Legacy
of the National Academy of Sciences. A Historical Account."
*Drug and Alcohol Dependence*. 23(3): 183–218. http://
cpdd.org/wp-content/uploads/2016/02/mayarticle.pdf.
Accessed on December 12, 2017.

Maynard, Christopher. 2017. "CVS Announces Initiatives
to Curb Opioid Abuse." *Consumer Affairs*. https://www
.consumeraffairs.com/news/cvs-announces-initiatives-to-
curb-opioid-abuse-092517.html. Accessed on December 23,
2017.

McGreal, Chris. 2016. "How Cracking Down on America's
Painkiller Capital Led to a Heroin Crisis." *Guardian*.
https://www.theguardian.com/science/2016/may/25/
opioid-epidemic-prescription-painkillers-heroin-addiction.
Accessed on December 26, 2017.

"Mechanism of Action of a Partial Opioid Agonist." 2017.
UBC CPD. https://www.youtube.com/watch?v=qeVNcNf8
orE. Accessed on December 28, 2017.

"Medication-Assisted Treatment for Opioid Addiction in Opioid Treatment Programs." 2005. Treatment Improvement Protocol (TIP) Series, No. 43. Center for Substance Abuse Treatment. https://www.ncbi.nlm.nih .gov/books/NBK64157/. Accessed on December 28, 2017.

"Medicines in My Home." 2017. Food and Drug Administration. https://www.fda.gov/downloads/Drugs/ ResourcesForYou/Consumers/BuyingUsingMedicineSafely/ UnderstandingOver-the-CounterMedicines/UCM094874 .pdf. Accessed on December 23, 2017.

Mehendalen, Anand W., et al. 2016. "The Problem of Outcomes in Addiction Treatments, the Inconvenient Truths." *Journal of Addiction and Preventive Medicine*. http://www.elynsgroup.com/journal/article/the-problem- of-outcomes-in-addiction-treatments-the-inconvenient- truths. Accessed on March 19, 2018.

Meier, Barry. 2003. *Pain Killer: A "Wonder" Drug's Trail of Addiction and Death*. Emmaus, PA: Rodale.

"Menu of Pain Management Clinic Regulation." n.d. Public Health Laws. Centers for Disease Control and Prevention. https://www.cdc.gov/phlp/docs/menu-pmcr.pdf. Accessed on December 26, 2017.

Merenda, Christine. 2011. "Understanding FDA's Risk Evaluation and Mitigation Strategy." 6(8). https://www .americannursetoday.com/understanding-fdas-risk-evaluation- and-mitigation-strategy/. Accessed on December 22, 2017.

"National Prescription Drug Abuse Prevention Strategy." 2010. Center for Lawful Access and Abuse Deterrence. http://claad.org/wp-content/uploads/2013/10/2010_ National_Strategy.pdf. Accessed on December 21, 2017.

"Neonatal Abstinence Syndrome." 2017. Medline Plus. https:// medlineplus.gov/ency/article/007313.htm. Accessed on December 27, 2017.

Nevius, James. 2016. "The Strange History of Opiates in America: From Morphine for Kids to Heroin for Soldiers." *Guardian.* https://www.theguardian.com/commentis free/2016/mar/15/long-opiate-use-history-america-latest-epidemic. Accessed on December 28, 2017.

"New Vaccine Technology Shows Promise as a Tool to Combat the Opioid Crisis." 2017. *Science Daily.* https://www.sciencedaily.com/releases/2017/12/171218090923 .htm. Accessed on January 3, 2018.

"NFLIS Brief: Fentanyl, 2001–2015." 2017. NFLIS Information System. https://www.deadiversion.usdoj.gov/ nflis/2017fentanyl.pdf. Accessed on December 26, 2017.

"NIH Analysis Shows Americans Are in Pain." 2015. National Center for Complementary and Integrative Health. https://nccih.nih.gov/news/press/08112015. Accessed on December 15, 2017.

Nygaard, E., et al. 2016. "Behavior and Attention Problems in Eight-Year-Old Children with Prenatal Opiate and Poly-Substance Exposure: A Longitudinal Study." 2016. *PLoS One.* 11(6): e0158054. doi: 10.1371. https://www.ncbi .nlm.nih.gov/pmc/articles/PMC4918960/. Accessed on March 19, 2018.

O'Hara, Mary Emily. 2016. "U-47700: Everything You Need to Know about Deadly New Drug." *Rolling Stone.* http:// www.rollingstone.com/culture/news/u-47700-everything-you-need-to-know-about-deadly-new-drug-w443344. Accessed on December 11, 2017.

Ontiveros, Judith. 2012. "Pain. Part I." Nursing 53A. https:// www.slideshare.net/twiggypiggy/pain-part-1. Accessed on December 28, 2017.

"Opioid Abuse Prevention." 2017. Ohio Department of Education. http://education.ohio.gov/Topics/Learning-in-Ohio/Health-Education/Opioid-Abuse-Prevention. Accessed on December 23, 2017.

"Opioid Antagonists." 2017. Medscape. https://reference
.medscape.com/drugs/opioid-antagonists. Accessed on
December 29, 2017.

"The Opioid Crisis in America." 2017. Harvard University
Online Learning. http://online-learning.harvard.edu/
course/opioid-crisis-america. Accessed on December 23,
2017.

"Opioid Education Resources." 2017. Prevention First. https://
www.prevention.org/Professional-Resources/Opioid-
Education-Resources/. Accessed on December 23, 2017.

"Orlaam." 2017. RxList. https://www.rxlist.com/orlaam-drug
.htm#W. Accessed on December 29, 2017.

"Overdose Death Rates." 2017. National Institute on Drug
Abuse. https://www.drugabuse.gov/related-topics/trends-
statistics/overdose-death-rates. Accessed on December 11,
2017.

Payte, J. T., Jeffrey Smith, and Joycelyn Woods. 2001. "Basic
Pharmacology: How Methadone Works? The Pharmacology
of Opioids." National Alliance of Methadone Advocates.
http://www.methadone.org/downloads/namadocuments/
es05basic_pharmacology2.pdf. Accessed on December 29,
2017.

Perry, Samuel, and George Heidrich. 1982. "Management of
Pain during Debridement: A Survey of U.S. Burn Units."
*Pain*. 13(3): 267–280.

Pezalla, Edmund J., et al. 2017. "Secular Trends in Opioid
Prescribing in the USA." *Journal of Pain Research*. 10:
383–387. https://www.ncbi.nlm.nih.gov/pmc/articles/
PMC5319424/#__ref-listidm140188741869408title.
Accessed on December 14, 2017.

"Pill Mill Initiative." 2011. Florida Office of the Attorney
General. http://myfloridalegal.com/pages.nsf/Main/AA7
AAF5CAA22638D8525791B006A30C8. Accessed on
December 24, 2017.

Podolsky, Scott H. 2014. *The Antibiotic Era: Reform, Resistance, and the Pursuit of a Rational Therapeutics*: Baltimore, MD: Johns Hopkins University Press.

Porter, Jane, and Hershel Jick. 1980. "Addiction Rare in Patients Treated with Narcotics." *New England Journal of Medicine*. 302(2): 123. http://www.nejm.org/doi/pdf/10.1056/NEJM198001103020221. Accessed on December 13, 2017.

"Prescription Drug Monitoring Programs." 2017. American Academy of Family Physicians. https://www.aafp.org/dam/AAFP/documents/advocacy/prevention/risk/BKG-PDMPs-103017.pdf. Accessed on December 19, 2017.

"Prescription Drug Safety Network." 2017. EverFi. http://everfi.com/prescription-drug-safety-network/. Accessed on December 23, 2017.

"Preventing Prescription Drug Abuse." 2016. Substance Abuse and Mental Health Services Administration's Center for the Application of Prevention Technologies. https://www.samhsa.gov/capt/sites/default/files/resources/preventing-prescription-drug-misuse-strategies.pdf. Accessed on December 20, 2017.

Public Law 114–255. 114th Congress. 2017. https://www.gpo.gov/fdsys/pkg/PLAW-114publ255/pdf/PLAW-114publ255.pdf. Accessed on December 19, 2017.

Quinn, Mattie. 2017. "The Opioid Files: More Than 100 States and Cities Are Suing Drug Companies." Governing the States and Localities. http://www.governing.com/topics/health-human-services/gov-opioid-lawsuits-companies-states-cities.html. Accessed on December 21, 2017.

Quinones, Sam. 2015. *Dreamland: The True Tale of America's Opiate Epidemic*. New York: Bloomsbury Press.

"Recovery Housing." 2017. Rutgers University. http://rhscaps.rutgers.edu/services/alcohol-and-other-drug-assistance-program-adap/recovery-housing/. Accessed on December 23, 2017.

"Results from the 2012 National Survey on Drug Use and Health: Summary of National Findings." 2013. Substance Abuse and Mental Health Services Administration. https://www.samhsa.gov/data/sites/default/files/NSDUH results2012/NSDUHresults2012.pdf. Accessed on December 14, 2017.

Rudd, Rose A., et al. 2016. "Increases in Drug and Opioid Overdose Deaths—United States, 2000–2015." *Morbidity and Mortality Weekly*. 65(50–51): 1445–1452. https:// www.cdc.gov/mmwr/volumes/65/wr/mm655051e1.htm. Accessed on November 9, 2017.

"Rules—2016." 2016. U.S. Drug Enforcement Administration. https://www.deadiversion.usdoj.gov/fed_regs/rules/2016/ fr0907.htm. Accessed on December 11, 2017.

Rutkow, Lainie, et al. 2015. "Effect of Florida's Prescription Drug Monitoring Program and Pill Mill Laws on Opioid Prescribing and Use." *JAMA Internal Medicine*. 175(10): 1642–1649.

Sacco, Lisa N., and Erin Bagalman. 2017. "The Opioid Epidemic and Federal Efforts to Address It: Frequently Asked Questions." Congressional Research Service. https:// fas.org/sgp/crs/misc/R44987.pdf. Accessed on December 19, 2017.

"Safe Drug Disposal: A Guide for Communities Seeking Solutions." 2015. Partnership for Drug-Free Kids. https:// drugfree.org/article/secure-dispose-of-medicine-properly/. Accessed on December 23, 2017.

Schwartzapfel, Beth. 2017. "Guess Who's Tracking Your Prescription Drugs?" The Marshall Project. https://www .themarshallproject.org/2017/08/02/guess-whos-tracking- your-prescription-drugs. Accessed on December 27, 2017.

"Signs of a Pill Mill in Your Community." 2012. Kentucky Law Enforcement. https://docjt.ky.gov/Magazines/Issue%2041/files/assets/downloads/page0019.pdf. Accessed on December 19, 2017.

Smith, Mitch, and Monica Davey. 2017. "With Overdoses on the Rise, Cities and Counties Look for Someone to Blame." *New York Times*. https://www.nytimes.com/2017/12/20/us/opioid-cities-counties-lawsuits.html?_r=0. Accessed on December 23, 2017.

Smith, S. E. 2016. "War on Prescription Drugs: What If You Depend on Opioids to Live a Decent Life?" *Guardian*. https://www.theguardian.com/us-news/2016/jul/12/prescription-drugs-what-if-you-depend-on-opioids-chronic-pain. Accessed on December 15, 2017.

"States Stem Opioid Overdose through Information Sharing." 2016. National Governors Association. https://www.nga.org/cms/news/2016/opioid-overdose-information-sharing. Accessed on December 20, 2017.

Stotts, Angela, Carrie L. Dodrill, and Thomas R. Kosten. 2009. "Opioid Dependence Treatment: Options in Pharmacotherapy." *Expert Opinion in Pharmacotherapy*. 10(11): 1727–1740. https://www.ncbi.nlm.nih.gov/pmc/articles/PMC2874458/. Accessed on December 29, 2017.

Sullum, Jacob. 2016. "'Opioid Epidemic' Myths." Reason.com. http://reason.com/archives/2016/05/18/opioid-epidemic-myths. Accessed on December 14, 2017.

Surrett, Hilary L., et al. 2014. "Reductions in Prescription Opioid Diversion Following Recent Legislative Interventions in Florida." *Pharmacoepidemiology and Drug Safety*. 23(3): 314–320.

Tayeb, B. O., et al. 2016. "Durations of Opioid, Nonopioid Drug, and Behavioral Clinical Trials for Chronic Pain: Adequate or Inadequate?" *Pain Medicine*. 17(11): 2036–2046.

"Timeline of Selected FDA Activities and Significant Events Addressing Opioid Misuse and Abuse." 2017. U.S. Food and Drug Administration. https://www.fda.gov/Drugs/ DrugSafety/InformationbyDrugClass/ucm338566.htm. Accessed on December 13, 2017.

Title 16. Health and Safety. Food and Drugs. Chapter 47. Controlled Substances Act. Subchapter IV. Offenses and Penalties. 2017. State of Delaware. http://www.delcode .delaware.gov/title16/c047/sc04/index.shtml. Accessed on December 27, 2017.

"To: President's Commission on Combating Drug Addiction and the Opioid Crisis." 2017. Child Welfare League of America. https://www.cwla.org/wp-content/ uploads/2017/09/CWLA-Comments-to-Opioid-Commission-Draft.pdf. Accessed on December 31, 2017.

"Top 3 Goals of Drug Detox." 2017. Rehab International. https://rehab-international.org/blog/top-3-goals-of-drug-detox. Accessed on December 28, 2017.

"Transcranial Magnetic Stimulation." 2018. Mayo Clinic. https://www.mayoclinic.org/tests-procedures/transcranial-magnetic-stimulation/about/pac-20384625. Accessed on January 3, 2018.

"The Underestimated Cost of the Opioid Epidemic." 2017. The Council of Economic Advisors. https://www.white house.gov/sites/whitehouse.gov/files/images/The%20 Underestimated%20Cost%20of%20the%20Opioid%20 Crisis.pdf. Accessed on December 11, 2017.

"Uniform Controlled Substances Act (1994)." 1994. National Conference of Commissioners on Uniform State Laws. http://www.uniformlaws.org/shared/docs/controlled%20 substances/UCSA_final%20_94%20with%2095amends .pdf. Accessed on December 19, 2017.

Usichenko, Taras I., et al. 2006. "Low-Intensity Electromagnetic Millimeter Waves for Pain Therapy."

*Evidence Based Complementary and Alternative Medicine.*
3(2): 201–208.

Van Zee, Art. 2009. "The Promotion and Marketing of
OxyContin: Commercial Triumph, Public Health Tragedy."
*American Journal of Public Health.* 99(2): 221–227. https://
www.ncbi.nlm.nih.gov/pmc/articles/PMC2622774/.
Accessed on December 12, 2017.

Villapiano, Nicole L. G., et al. 2017. "Rural and Urban
Differences in Neonatal Abstinence Syndrome and Maternal
Opioid Use, 2004 to 2013." *JAMA Pediatrics.* 171(2):
194–196. https://www.researchgate.net/publication/3115
83697_Rural_and_Urban_Differences_in_Neonatal_
Abstinence_Syndrome_and_Maternal_Opioid_Use_2004_
to_2013. Accessed on December 27, 2017.

Weiss et al. 2017. "Opioid-Related Inpatient Stays and
Emergency Department Visits by State, 2009–2014."
Healthcare Cost and Utilization Project. https://www.hcup-
us.ahrq.gov/reports/statbriefs/sb219-Opioid-Hospital-
Stays-ED-Visits-by-State.jsp. Accessed on December 11,
2017.

Weissman, David E., and David J. Haddox. 1989. "Opioid
Pseudoaddiction—An Iatrogenic Syndrome." *Pain.* 36(3):
363–366.

Whitaker, Bill. 2017. "Whistleblowers: DEA Attorneys
Went Easy on Mckesson, the Country's Largest Drug
Distributor." *60 Minutes.* https://www.cbsnews.com/
news/whistleblowers-dea-attorneys-went-easy-on-mckesson-
the-countrys-largest-drug-distributor/. Accessed on
December 20, 2017.

Wichmann, Thomas, and Mahlon R. DeLong. 2006. "Deep
Brain Stimulation for Neurologic and Neuropsychiatric
Disorders." *Neuron.* 52: 197–204. https://ac.els-cdn.com/
S089662730600729X/1-s2.0-S089662730600729X-main
.pdf?_tid=35194720-f0d9-11e7-bcf5-00000aab0f02&acd

nat=1515020315_3488623380f6fdc11ea9b504dfe33dd1. Accessed on January 3, 2018.

Yan, Jun. 2010. "Opioid-Addiction Treatment: Maintenance or Abstinence Better?" Psychiatric News. https://psychnews .psychiatryonline.org/doi/10.1176/pn.45.14.psychnews_ 45_14_024. Accessed on December 28, 2017.

Yang, Y. Tony, Marc R. Larochelle, and Rebecca L. Haffajee. 2017. "Managing Increasing Liability Risks Related to Opioid Prescribing." *The American Journal of Medicine.* 130(3): 249–250. http://www.amjmed.com/article/S0002-9343(16)30932-9/pdf. Accessed on December 16, 2017.

A temptation may exist from time to time to think of the opioid epidemic in the abstract, counting deaths and discussing medications for treatment of the disorder. But the crisis also has very concrete and painful effects on parents, children, siblings, best friends, and others, effects that can give a face to the problem of opioid addiction. This chapter focuses on some of those stories, ways in which the epidemic has changed the lives of others or oneself, for example, of describing approaches for preventing others from falling under the spell of illicit drugs. Each of the following essays has a special and meaningful story to tell about the current opioid crisis.

## It's Not My Problem, or Is It?
*Judith Ellsesser*

The opioid crisis has hit our area hard. In fact, the tristate area we live in (southern Ohio, northern Kentucky, and western West Virginia) is regarded as the epicenter of the problem, and our kids know that. Each person sitting in front of me

---

Students from Orchard Gardens K-8 School protest in front of their school in Boston on December 11, 2017, calling attention to the problems associated with opiate addiction. One of the negative impacts has been an increase in the number of discarded needles found on school grounds, or nearby. The most common places are in the grassy areas near the faculty parking lot, the trees behind the school, and the baseball/soccer field adjacent to the school playground. (Dina Rudick/The Boston Globe via Getty Images)

in the classroom has or personally knows a family member or friend who is a victim of this plague. I teach in the high school, but the elementary school is just across the parking lot from us, and the principal of that school has talked to these kids about how they are affected by the problem. She tells of children climbing up the steps of the school bus in the morning and greeting their driver with something like, "My mommy wouldn't wake up this morning. I had to get myself dressed, and there was nothing I could fix for breakfast." In an extreme case, one little girl got on saying "I think my mommy is dead." And it turns out she was right.

Not all our students are in such dire straits, but until this year, they did not realize that whether they had direct contact with drugs or not, they were, indeed, part of the collateral damage. The book *Dreamland*, by Sam Quinones, tells in graphic and gripping detail exactly how all of us are affected by the opioid crisis. After reading it for part of my summer reading, I knew I had found the perfect vehicle for meeting the standards we are required to teach, as well as addressing the pressing concerns of my own students. I immediately contacted my colleague who teaches government and history, and we began to plan the first semester for the juniors we jointly teach.

The field of education has changed in monumental ways in the past 35 years, and one of the most intriguing developments is problem-based learning (PBL). This is a method of teaching that begins by suggesting that students develop a solution to a problem—a problem that matters to them. It intersects quite effectively with the standards, with 21st-century learning, and with students' interests. Our project began to unfold in the late summer, and we soon found ourselves nearly sprinting to keep up with it as it developed into the first of the new school year.

The first step, naturally, was to introduce the book and start the conversation about the opioid crisis. The book mentions many places that are familiar to our kids, but it spans the continent following the development of the drug trade that incudes opiates, black tar heroin, fentanyl, and carfentanil, so the text is easily adapted to many locations. Then we started with the steps of PBL.

Here are the most commonly accepted steps of PBL:

**Steps to a PBL Approach**

Step 1: Explore the issue. Gather necessary information; learn new concepts, principles, and skills about the proposed topic.

Step 2: State what is known. Individual students and groups list what they already know about the scenario and list areas where they are lacking information.

Step 3: Define the issues. Frame the problem in a context of what is already known and information the students expect to learn.

Step 4: Research the knowledge. Find resources and information that will help create a compelling argument.

Step 5: Investigate solutions. List possible actions and solutions to the problem, and formulate and test potential hypotheses.

Step 6: Present and support the chosen solution. Clearly state and support your conclusion with relevant information and evidence.

Step 7: Review your performance. Often forgotten, this is a crucial step in improving your problem-solving skills. Students must evaluate their performance (including a statement of how they feel they have been changed by the experience) and plan improvements for the next problem.

Together my colleague and I began to brainstorm outside resources we could line up for our kids. We began with a local judge who presides over the drug court; he came in and talked about the overload created on foster care because so many children are being removed from homes of drug-addicted parents. He also discussed the problem of drug-addicted babies born in the local hospital. Next, we asked our elementary school principal to share some of her stories, and then a fellow teacher whose brother came out on the positive side of the problem shared a personal perspective on the way addiction impacts families. We listened to representatives of our local politicians (local and state levels) and the fire chief who talked about responding to overdose calls and administering Narcan. We were especially fortunate to be able to skype with the author of the book *Dreamland*, and through networking, we connected with Marty Blank, director of the Institute for Educational Leadership in Washington, D.C. He was most helpful in providing an authentic audience for our students' thoughts, plans, ideas, and writing.

After much discussion of the ideas presented in these sessions, our students began to formulate plans for what they could do to address the problem. Since so many of them were struck by the stories from the elementary school principal, many of them came up with the idea of volunteering their time after school in a Big Buddies program. Their goal was to provide marginalized students with positive role models, spend time with them after school in the enrichment program helping them with homework, and, finally, getting them started in intramural sports programs to give them a sense of belonging to a group. The project was and continues to be a success. The elementary school teachers have been a tremendous source of encouragement to our students, as have the elementary students themselves. The benefits have ranged far beyond original intent. The sixth graders who enter the high school building will have "built-in" connections. The fact that students volunteer their time in the after-school program is a boon to our district as it tries to self-sustain the after-school program. But perhaps the biggest impact we have seen is the effect on our students. Another group decided to establish a Drug Free Clubs of America chapter at our school. This is a national organization that helps schools administer voluntary drug tests to the student body. Students who test and remain drug free can win awards and participate in fun activities, rallies, and events. This project required students to contact medical personnel from the local area to agree to administer the tests, local businesses to provide donations to pay for the tests and for the benefits, and students to negotiate with school administration to establish and maintain the club in the school. These students had to write up proposals, write letters, make phone calls, and write and respond to e-mails to align all of these entities.

The overall effect of this project on our students has been extraordinary. They no longer feel helpless or hopeless in the face of such an overwhelming problem. They have developed the skills of collaboration, communication, creativity, and critical thinking. Not only have they come to understand the importance of community in attacking such issues, but also they have been given the chance to read informational texts about the problem; learn how to construct e-mails and letters to ask local, state, and national officials for help; write informational, narrative, and reflective essays about their work, and learn the importance of working together, which includes listening to and valuing others' opinions.

*Judith Ellsesser has taught English in grades 5 through college level for 35 years in Ohio, North Carolina, and Japan. She completed her graduate work at Bread Loaf School of English in Vermont. Her interests include writing, blended and online education, and problem-based learning. She is the proud daughter and a proud mother of an English teacher.*

## Education Fosters Prevention
### *Heather Kulp*

America has been battling problems with addiction for decades. Addiction is real and certainly does not discriminate. It can happen to anyone from all walks of life. Unfortunately, over the past several years opioid addiction has been on the rise, and today's young adults are battling an opioid crisis. The

Brandywine Heights Area, a small rural community, in Berks County, Pennsylvania, struggles to fight this battle. The small school district, consisting of about 1,400 students, has lost several graduates to heroin overdoses, and a significant number of students have been referred to drug rehabilitation programs and residential treatment centers.

The Brandywine Heights Area School District utilizes its Student Assistance Program (SAP) in helping identify students at risk and in need of assistance. The state of Pennsylvania requires every school district to have a plan for identifying and helping students who experience barriers to their learning. The school's SAP team consists of trained school personnel and a staff member from the Caron Foundation. It also receives assistance from the Council on Chemical Abuse. The school district has also partnered with the community in forming a task force, to help fight the increase of heroin use and overdoses within the area. Based on interviews with students who had drug abuse problems, it was discovered that in almost every case, the first time the students used was in a "peer pressure" situation. Looking at the problem through an educational lens, this tells us that there needs to be more of a focus on teaching the skills and providing the tools that our students need in order to resist peer pressure. Teaching these resiliency skills as early as possible is crucial. As a school counselor, at the Brandywine Heights Area Intermediate/Middle School, it is imperative that I help kids develop the skills and provide them with the tools that they need to make good decisions and be successful contributors to today's society. At the Brandywine Heights Area Intermediate/Middle level, we emphasize being a person of "good character." The students are being taught about the traits and skills that a person of good character possesses. Each month the students are introduced to a different positive character trait. The monthly trait is explained to the students, and they are educated on how a person who possesses that trait thinks and acts. Students who display good character are recognized and awarded throughout the school year. Along with our

school-wide character counts initiative, we have implemented
the Too Good for Drugs curriculum (http://www.toogoodpro
grams.org) created by the Mendez Foundation.

The Too Good for Drugs program consists of 10 lessons that
teach healthy social and emotional skills with a focus on positive character traits. Throughout the lessons the students are
engaged in whole-group and small-group instruction, as well as
being able to participate in skits and role-play scenarios. They
learn how to set obtainable goals, work through the decision-
making model, learn and rehearse effective communication
skills, and practice identifying emotions in themselves and others, as well as learning healthy strategies to help them manage
their own emotions. The students also have a chance to explore
friendships and what classifies someone as a "good" friend. My
belief is that a young person who has developed these skills
and can apply them with confidence will be less likely to turn
to drugs and/or alcohol. The program spends time introducing information to the students about tobacco, alcohol, and
other drugs and the effects of their use on the body. The information being delivered is factual and relates the effects of
drugs and alcohol to something that the students are familiar
with; it's brought to their level of understanding. I find the
program's focus on peer pressure refusal strategies to be one of
the most beneficial aspects. The students learn nine different
peer pressure refusal strategies. These strategies are "steer clear,"
"say no," "walk away," "ignore," "broken record," "make an ex-
cuse," "reverse the pressure," "better idea," and "state the facts."
The students have several opportunities to identify and practice
using these strategies in a variety of exercises. I believe these
strategies can be used in different types of circumstances, not
just in a situation that deals with drugs and/or alcohol. It's been
encouraging to have students report to me that they have used
a refusal strategy that they learned in class, in their interactions
with classmates, friends, and siblings. Another valuable component of the program is the promotion of communication at
home. Each lesson is followed up with a homework assignment

designed for parents and their children to do together. These assignments help open the lines of communication between kids and their parents about this difficult topic, which is a vital piece of drug/alcohol awareness and education.

I had the opportunity to sit down and talk with some fifth-grade students, who have been exposed to the program for about two years. It was rather refreshing to hear that they are learning and applying aspects from the program. All of the students were able to tell me about something they learned, as well as a tool or strategy that they will use or have already used. Some of the comments that the students shared are as follows: "I learned that doing drugs is bad for you and what effects alcohol has on younger people." "I learned about the importance of being a person with good character." "I learned many ways to refuse peer pressure and handle bullying." "I have learned better ways to take care of myself." "I have learned different ways of handling my anger and how to make healthy choices." The overall results of our focus on character education coupled with the Too Good for Drugs curriculum are promising. As a school district coupled with community support, we will continue to support our youth and help them develop the skills they need to make good decisions that lead to being productive, healthy adults.

*Heather Kulp has been a school counselor in the Brandywine Heights Area School District for 13 years. She has a bachelor's degree in social work and a master's degree of education in school counseling. She absolutely loves her job and strives to make a difference in children's lives every single day. Her focus is to help students grow socially and emotionally while in the academic setting to become successful contributors to today's society.*

## Epidemic in Asheville
### *Heather Pack*

July 3, 2017, changed the face of how Asheville-Buncombe Technical Community College (A-B Tech) viewed the opioid epidemic. Stuart Moseley was doing well in his classes and had been drug free for nine months. As per his habit, he took a break during class for a period of time. By the end of class, his instructor called campus police to give them his bookbag as Stuart had not returned. At this same time, it was discovered that a single-stalled bathroom door was locked with nobody responding. Shortly thereafter, Stuart's body was discovered.

It was determined that Stuart was a victim of heroin poisoning, possibly fentanyl.

Stuart had struggled for many years with the disease of addiction, according to his mother, Anne Seaman. He had been doing well though for nine months. It is believed this was his first use since being in recovery.

While Stuart's drug poisoning was the first fatal overdose on A-B Tech's campus, it was not the first overdose. Two other students had previously overdosed on campus but were able to be revived with the use of Narcan. Near campus, another student was found dead in his vehicle and several others overdosed.

Stuart's death brought to life the reality of the opioid epidemic in our area. While we were already doing things to help bring awareness and support to our student population, efforts to support those in treatment and recovery have dramatically increased.

Asheville is a city nestled in the mountains in western North Carolina. With approximately 250,000 residents, a booming hospitality industry, and growing beer and craft beverage businesses, tourists flock to Asheville to enjoy all the outdoor activities, downtown, and restaurant experiences. A-B Tech serves approximately 23,000 students through curriculum, continuing education, and basic skill classes (including high school equivalency and English-language learners).

An informal count from the spring semester of 2017 showed about 90 percent of the students who sought counseling through Support Services were either in active addiction or in recovery. While this is a small subset from the rest of the student body, it's still a significant revelation. How can we provide ongoing support for these students and for all the ones we do not know about?

For the past several years, the Support Services division of A-B Tech had held a Substance Abuse Awareness Event. In the spring of 2017, the focus and title of the event changed to Addiction, Recovery, and Coping (ARC). Being aware of substances is not the issue; how we manage life during recovery from our addictions is. We brought in professionals from the community to speak about the neuroscience of addiction and ways to reduce the stigma. There was also a drum circle and panel discussion. Attendance for this event was the highest it had been in many years.

We knew that was not enough, though. One event a year with sporadic mention the rest of the time is not going to stay in anyone's mind long enough to make a difference. There has to be ongoing support. The idea of having a Collegiate Recovery Group was taking shape during the spring semester of 2017. When Stuart died, the idea started to become a reality.

The first thing accomplished was making a video with Anne Seaman, Stuart's mother. Anne shared her experience with Stuart's addiction and gave a warning to those viewing how devastating this disease is. This video is shown to all new students in our Academic Study Skills classes, which act like a freshman seminar. All students must complete this course. We quickly realized that Anne's voice impacted students, with many opening about their own addiction or that of friends and family. The video and Anne's story also were shared in a page dedicated to opioid information on our website and in the college magazine, the *A-B Tech Education Journal*.

A monthly article also goes out in our student newsletter, *The Inbox*, regarding ARC. The articles are short reminders to keep the issue and offer of support in the foreground. During our Wellness Fair held in the fall of 2017, addiction information and resources also were included.

With the administration's support, we are moving forward to implement a Collegiate Recovery Group. This will include not only some type of supportive weekly meeting but also a room on campus that will serve as a refuge for those in recovery. Currently, we are conducting focus groups with students who have identified in recovery and desiring more support as well as a way to give back to others. We are working with these focus groups to develop our mission and vision. The goal is to make this group sustaining. In a community college, the population tends to be more transient in nature. There are many reasons why the population does not sustain for two to three years. Having a core group that will be involved from semester to semester can be difficult, especially as the group forms and determines its identity.

There is not one set way for recovery to be successful. Everyone is different. Being mindful of the various options is also important. Typically, there needs to be a combination of recovery efforts, such as support groups, therapy, and medication assistive therapy. When stress returns, as it inevitably does, how a person in recovery responds can make the difference between life and death. The brain's instinct is to return to the path that worked before, the drug that instantly took away the discomfort. Students know this is not the best path to take, so shame develops. With shame comes the need to isolate. In isolation, there is not a voice of reason. Also, the same dosage used before may be too powerful or the drugs could likely be laced with something, like fentanyl.

For our institution, having the Collegiate Recovery Group is the key. Students and volunteers support each other in their recovery efforts. Our hope is to have a place where students can come that would have someone readily available to listen, support, and redirect the urge to use again. The situation is too critical not to do all we can.

*Heather Pack has been a licensed professional counselor for eight years. She's worked for the North Carolina Community College*

*System for 14 years in various capacities. Currently she serves as the director of Student Support Services at Asheville-Buncombe Technical Community College in Asheville, North Carolina. She lives there with her husband and two children.*

## Confessions of an Opioid User
### *Bob Roehr*

I've used an opioid drug—hydrocodone—for a decade, every day, about every six hours. For me, it is a very effective medicine. I have a lot of company. The latest research, a large government survey of over 50,000 people, suggests that 92 million Americans used a prescription opioid in 2015, 38 percent of the adult population. Only a very small portion, 0.8 percent, had what was broadly defined as a use disorder (Han et al. 2017).

My medical problems started in high school when I tried to be a jock, screwed up some cartilage in my foot and a doctor took it out. The incision became infected and I was on crutches for about six months. That was also my last growth spurt and the left foot grew a bit longer and narrower than the right just hanging there without any weight on it. The difference between them isn't real obvious, but if you look closely enough you can see it. Then after recovery I walked a little bit different, more on the outside of the foot, to minimize blisters that would form under the less-flexible scar tissue. My body was out of alignment.

Flash forward through 40 years of uneven wear and tear and my left knee was shot while the right was fine. The effects soon became apparent further up in my spine. Over the past 10 years I've had a total knee replacement and five spinal surgeries.

Nerve damage was part of each insult to my body. Doctors, and the insurers who pay them, are reluctant to cut into you at the first sign of a problem; they want to wait until it becomes severe enough. The surgeries often helped, but as the late actor Christopher "Superman" Reeve could attest, nerves seldom grow back or repair themselves.

Because of that I have a variety of nerve-associated chronic aches, pain, numbness, and tingling from the waist down. It affects walking, the time I can spend on my feet, and just overall quality of life.

A drug seldom works equally well with all patients, and meds that work in the black box of the brain—pain relief, antidepressants, psychiatric drugs—have the most variable effect on people who take them. In my twenties I was given the opioid percodan, which took away the pain but left me really spaced out, in a stupor for the few hours a day it didn't put me to sleep, which was fine immediately following surgery but not later on in recovery. Ten years ago another doctor tried gabapentin, a drug that targets nerves, which had little effect at all.

I've been fortunate that hydrocodone works for my problems. It simply takes away the pain and pretty much stops there. I started out at 40 milligrams a day, and as tolerance grew, my doctor increased the dose in steps over the years to a peak of 80 milligrams a day.

Morning begins with juice and a larger dose of the drug to build up blood concentrations that have fallen from when the last pill was taken seven to nine hours earlier. For the next hour or so, I do some stretching and self-massage while sitting reading e-mails and other online tasks. Once the drug kicks in and the pain eases, I fix breakfast.

While the drug is primarily meant to treat lower body pain, it has the added benefit of addressing headaches (which used to be frequent), arthritis and carpal tunnel pain, and even the ringing in my left ear known as tinnitus (hearing in my right has deteriorated so much that tinnitus is not an issue there). In fact, I can tell when the drug level in my body is heading down because some of those symptoms start coming back.

I've worked with a physical therapist, but the exercises didn't seem to help much and certainly didn't justify the hours of effort. I used to walk a lot but can't do it much anymore. Surprisingly, I still can get on a bicycle, and I try to get in at least 50 miles a week. Often it allows me to reduce my dose of hydrocodone a bit. Ironically, my heaviest use of the drug comes when I cover scientific or medical meetings as a reporter, am on my feet more, and cannot get enough exercise.

As for side effects, constipation can be an issue at the highest doses but mainly when I exercise and forget to drink enough water. Hydrocodone may have contributed to decreased libido and sexual function, but it is difficult to tell how much of that is because of the drug, the underlying medical condition, and just getting older.

A few years back I thought I might need to increase the dose again, which I wanted to avoid because the cycle might never end. I was able to cut back from 80 milligrams to 60 milligrams a day, sometimes a bit lower. I did it mainly with a change in attitude from seeking to eliminate pain to helping to manage that pain. I put up with less relief, rather than try to more completely stop pain 24/7.

When I started taking hydrocodone I had to show an identification at the pharmacy and sign for the pills. I could get a 90-day supply, just like any other prescription. Now the rules have tightened up and I can get only a 30-day supply, with no refills; the doctor has to write a new prescription every month. He offered to prescribe a longer-acting version of the drug that could be taken twice a day. But I prefer the basic pill because it gives me the best way to reduce the total amount of drug I take and still provide the relief I need.

I am as dependent on hydrocodone as I am on the pills that help manage my blood pressure or a diabetic would be on insulin to regulate blood sugar. It has allowed me to remain productive rather than be consumed with pain. I am reminded of that fact four times a day as its effects wear off.

If all of this sounds a bit tedious, that's because it is. When used properly, opioids don't add anything to life, like a high; they can help reduce pain and restore living to something closer to normal.

My fear is that in this crisis atmosphere people will lose sight of the good that opioids can do when used properly, that they will focus too much on their very real potential for harm. That would be a mistake.

## Reference

Han, Beth, et al. 2017. "Prescription Opioid Use, Misuse, and Use Disorders in U.S. Adults: 2015 National Survey on Drug Use and Health." *Annals of Internal Medicine.* 167(5): 293–301. doi:10.7326/M17-0865.

*Bob Roehr is a biomedical journalist based in Washington, D.C., and a regular contributor to* The BMJ, Scientific American, *and other publications.*

## Rationale for Cannabis-Based Interventions in the Opioid Overdose Crisis
### Anjali A. Sarkar

Licit and illicit use of opioid painkillers has North America in the throes of a crisis. At the root of this crisis lie the prevalence of chronic pain and a tug-of-war among health care organizations, patients, and policy makers. Arguments in favor of opioids are largely based on a long tradition of the use of opioids to curb pain. Liberalization of health care laws on prescribing opioids, a heightened awareness of the right to pain relief, and aggressive marketing on the part of pharmaceutical companies have been pivotal in increasing the use of opioids. Partially the rampant use of opioids has also increased due to misconceptions and assumptions that the use of opioids is effective, safe, and devoid of adverse side effects, whereas the truth is that opioid painkillers are responsible for more deaths than the number of deaths from suicides and motor vehicle crashes put together (Manchikanti et al. 2012; Nelson and Perrone 2012).

The majority of opioid-related deaths occur in patients receiving a low or regulated dose of morphine and the remainder in individuals abusing the opioid drugs illicitly. This demonstrates that the obstacles that must be surmounted are inappropriate prescriptions, lack of correct knowledge on the side effects of opioids, erroneous notions on undertreatment of pain, and inadequate research on alternatives to opioid analgesics. Research into novel therapeutic strategies and interventions to check the harmful effects of opioids reveals evidence that cannabis may play a role in reducing some of the ills of opioids.

Recent research supports the implementation of cannabis interventions to manage the opioid crisis. Reports present evidence for three windows of opportunity for cannabis intervention in progressive stages of the opioid crisis, including before the introduction of opioids to manage chronic pain, in patients already on opioids, and as an adjunct to drugs like methadone to increase rates of success.

Just as electronic cigarettes and nicotine patches have helped smokers curb or even quit smoking, researchers postulate an evidence-based rationale for cannabis interventions in the management of the opioid overdose crisis. The notion of replacing a more harmful substance by a less harmful substance is popularly known as the substitution effect theory and is a derivative of behavioral economics. The substitution effect, in the context of substance abuse, proposes the substitution of an illicit drug or its replacement with one of reduced potency.

Growing population-level evidence in regimes of legalized cannabis shows increasing adult access to medical and recreational cannabis precedes reduction in homicides, violent crimes, suicides, and automobile fatalities (Morris et al. 2014). More relevant to the context, U.S. states with legalized medical cannabis show a 24.8 percent lower average annual opioid-related death rate than states without medical cannabis laws (Bachhuber et al. 2014). In a retrospective study on patients from Michigan, medical use of cannabis was associated with a 64 percent decrease in opioid use and a significant improvement in quality of life (Boehnke, Litinas, and Clauw 2016). Senior citizens in medical cannabis states show reduction in

Medicare prescriptions filled for pain, depression, anxiety, nausea, psychoses, seizure, and insomnia (Bradford and Bradford 2016). In a survey study on 890 patients from California on opioid painkillers, 97 percent reported that they "agreed" or "strongly agreed" that using medical cannabis has reduced their opioid use (Reiman, Welty, and Solomon 2017).

Why is it possible to substitute cannabis and cannabinoids for opioids? The biological mechanism of action and biological function of cannabinoids and opioids overlap (Abrams et al. 2011). Both cannabinoids and opioids share analgesic properties, together with the ability to lower body temperature, promote sleep, lower blood pressure, and reduce intestinal and skeletal movements. Molecular studies show that cellular receptor molecules that bind opioids and lead to pain reduction also bind cannabinoids. Moreover, both classes of drugs are coupled to similar secondary and tertiary signaling pathways inside the cell. In addition, research shows that cannabinoids stimulate the synthesis of opioids in the body.

The majority of opioid dependence begins with the use of prescribed pharmaceutical opioids. Medical use of the relatively safe, less-addictive, and equally effective alternative, cannabis, can stop the risk of opioid dependence at inception. National and international prohibitionist policies against cannabis no longer reflect the current state of research and evidence on cannabis, opioids, and chronic pain management.

For individuals already on opioids, it is imperative to ensure pain management without dependence of abuse of opioids. The use of cannabis together with opioids, in such cases, can help bring about the desired outcome. Cannabis increases the pain-relieving capacity of opioids and reduces the need to increase opioid dosage in patients suffering from chronic pain. Studies show using cannabis as an adjunct therapy in the care continuum can lead to stopping opioid use completely. For individuals already dependent on opioids, the use of cannabis offers a credible success rate of recovering from opioid cravings and warrants inclusion in opioid replacement therapy.

Some limitations do exist in the implementation of cannabis intervention to curb the opioid crisis. Smoking cannabis has raised concerns regarding bronchial issues, although no causative link has been established between cannabis smoking and lung or upper respiratory tract malaise. However, alternatives to smoking, such as inhaling and ingesting, are equally viable and effective. High-quality, oil-based extracts are also available in the form of drops or capsules. Preexisting medical conditions certainly do preclude the use of cannabis intervention, including a history of psychotic disorders or a genetic risk for such disorders and pregnancy. Considering vulnerable populations, it is important to organize outreach and education campaigns to inform individuals of possible cannabis-related harms, rather than withhold the treatment option of cannabis intervention.

In conclusion, multilayered obstacles still exist in the implementation of cannabis-based interventions to overcome the current opioid crisis; however, support for cannabis intervention to meet the opioid crisis continues to grow. The National Institute on Drug Abuse recently acknowledged the potential use of cannabis in reducing the dose of opioids required for pain relief (Lucas 2017). Cannabis intervention alone will not stall the opioid epidemic, yet a growing body of evidence indicates that judicious use of cannabis as an alternative or adjunct to opioids can go a long way in curbing the harmful effects of opioid overdose.

## References

Abrams, D. I., et al. 2011. "Cannabinoid-Opioid Interaction in Chronic Pain." *Clinical Pharmacology and Therapeutics.* 90(6): 844–851.

Bachhuber, M. A., et al. 2014. "Medical Cannabis Laws and Opioid Analgesic Overdose Mortality in the United States, 1999–2010." *JAMA Internal Medicine.* 174(10): 1668–1673.

Boehnke, K. F., E. Litinas, and D. J. Clauw. 2016. "Medical Cannabis Use Is Associated with Decreased Opiate

Medication Use in a Retrospective Cross-Sectional Survey of Patients with Chronic Pain." *Journal of Pain.* 17(6): 739–744.

Bradford, A. C., and W. D. Bradford. 2016. "Medical Marijuana Laws Reduce Prescription Medication Use in Medicare Part D." *Health Affairs.* 35(7): 1230–1236.

Lucas, P. 2017. "Rationale for Cannabis-Based Interventions in the Opioid Overdose Crisis." *Harm Reduction Journal.* 14(1): 58. https://doi.org/10.1186/s12954-017-0183-9. Accessed on March 20, 2018.

Manchikanti, L., et al. 2012. "Opioid Epidemic in the United States." *Pain Physician.* 15(3 Suppl.): ES9–ES38.

Morris, R. G., et al. 2014. "The Effect of Medical Marijuana Laws on Crime: Evidence from State Panel Data, 1990–2006." *PLoS One.* 9(3): e92816. https://doi.org/10.1371/journal.pone.0092816. Accessed on March 20, 2018.

Nelson, L. S., and J. Perrone. 2012 "Curbing the Opioid Epidemic in the United States: The Risk Evaluation and Mitigation Strategy (REMS)." *JAMA.* 308(5): 457–458.

Reiman, A., M. Welty, and P. Solomon. 2017. "Cannabis as a Substitute for Opioid-Based Pain Medication: Patient Self-Report." *Cannabis and Cannabinoid Research.* 2(1): 160–166.

*Anjali A. Sarkar is a scientist with MindSpec Inc., Virginia, and is working on neurobehavioral disorders. She holds a PhD in molecular biology and a master's degree in physiology. Dr. Sarkar has worked in the field of neurodevelopmental disorders for over 10 years. She is also a certified yoga teacher.*

## The U.S. Opioid Crisis—A Personal Perspective
*William G. Schulz*

Most people remember 2001 because of the horrific terrorist attacks launched against the United States by Al Qaeda, events that touched off what has become nearly two decades of global terror unleashed by a multiplying number of extremist groups.

I lived through the attack on Washington, D.C., on September 11, 2001, and, of course, I can never forget that awful day. But another event, just two months later on November 2, also hit with a devastating impact. My brother, Thomas Patrick Schulz, at age 39, was found dead on the cold, basement floor of an antiques store in Cambridge, Ohio.

The events of that late-autumn day, of course, are now also seared in memory. As I was packing to board a plane early the next morning for a long-awaited, sea-kayaking trip in Mexico, the phone rang late at night in my downtown D.C. apartment. I answered, greeted by the calm, practiced voice of a police officer in Cambridge—a small, rural town of farmers and blue-collar workers—who said he had pulled a scrap of paper with my phone number on it from the jeans pocket of a young man's lifeless body.

Did I know who the young man might be, the detective asked?

And, of course, I knew—he was describing my kid brother, Tom.

I sank into a chair at my kitchen table, head in hand, and listened to details of the awful death scene being documented by the Cambridge police department. Tom's death, the investigator said, was undoubtedly caused by an overdose of prescription narcotics. Near his body lay a bottle of the prescription pain medication, OxyContin, the child-safety cap screwed off, empty.

But the word *overdose* had flashed through my mind even before the detective spoke the word. My brother had struggled with opioid addiction for several years, his physical and mental health in ever more-rapid decline as time, and his multiple, sincere efforts to get and stay clean, passed by. To family and friends, Tom's death, tragically, was not a surprise.

Police at the scene knew that the phone number they found on Tom's body might belong to someone next of kin. But a local family member, the officer who called me explained, would have to formally identify his body at the morgue. Because I live several hundred miles from Cambridge, that meant I would first have to call and deliver the gut-wrenching news to my parents, who lived in nearby Dayton, Ohio, where Tom and I grew up, the only boys among five sisters.

But Tom's death by prescription narcotics overdose, I soon learned, was also not something out of the ordinary for a small-town Ohio police department. The investigator, when I spoke to him some months later, explained to me that police and paramedics were responding to an increasing number of overdose deaths and emergencies by legally prescribed opioid drugs.

In hindsight, in 2001, large swaths of working-class Ohio—including the Dayton area, where I grew up—were in fact emerging hotspots in an opioid addiction epidemic that has metastasized wildly and now grips the entire nation.

On October 26, 2017, President Donald J. Trump—noting that more than 11.5 million Americans have reported abusing prescription drugs in the past year and that U.S. drug overdose deaths are likely this year to exceed 64,000—declared the crisis to be a public health emergency.

"The United States is by far the largest consumer of these drugs, using more opioid pills per person than any other country by far in the world," President Trump said. "Opioid overdose deaths have quadrupled since 1999 and now account for the majority of fatal drug overdoses. Who would have thought? No part of our society—not young or old, rich or poor, urban or rural—has been spared this plague of drug addiction and this horrible, horrible situation that's taken place with opioids" ("Remarks by President Trump on Combatting Drug Demand and the Opioid Crisis" 2017).

In part because of President Trump's declaration, the federal government is responding with greater force to the opioid crisis. The Centers for Disease Control and Prevention (CDC), one of the lead agencies for this effort, is awarding more than $28.6 million in additional funding to 44 states and the District of Columbia to support their responses to the opioid overdose epidemic. The funds will be used to strengthen prevention efforts and better track opioid-related overdoses. This builds on a July 2017 announcement that CDC would provide $12 million to states to support overdose prevention activities.

Purdue Pharma, the makers of OxyContin and one of the nation's leading suppliers of pain management narcotic drugs, has acknowledged the tragedy of the opioid crisis but also tried to clarify the value of its products:

> We focused our talented research scientists and applied our innovative thinking to making opioids with abuse-deterrent properties, making them harder to crush and, therefore, harder to be abused by snorting or injection. With this investment, we pioneered the pharmaceutical industry's movement toward developing opioids with abuse-deterrent properties when we were the first to receive FDA approval. Developing new formulations is risky and there are never any guarantees, but we did it anyway. Our company also took the initiative to distribute the CDC Guideline for Prescribing Opioids to thousands of prescribers and pharmacists shortly after it was released. ("We Manufacture Prescription Opioids. How Could We Not Help Fight the Prescription and Illicit Opioid Abuse Crisis?" 2017)

Of President Trump's declaration and other action by the federal government to combat the opioid crisis, Purdue says, "There are too many prescription opioid pills in people's medicine cabinets. We support initiatives to limit the length of first opioid prescriptions. Reducing the number of excess tablets won't end the epidemic, but we believe it will help rein in the problem."

The last time I saw my brother alive—about a year before his death—we sat by a stream, ablaze in the autumn colors of Ohio. He spoke directly about his addiction because that was also something we shared. I had abused drugs for many years but had finally found my way back to health and abstinence from drugs. He told me about the hopelessness he sometimes felt in the struggle to kick narcotics for good. But we also talked about the hope that exists every day for any addict who wants to get clean.

My brother is gone, and I miss him every day of my life. But hope remains. As Americans face the reality of drug abuse of every kind and reach for new solutions, a lifeline back to health can be in reach of any person struggling in the grip of opioid addiction.

## References

"Remarks by President Trump on Combatting Drug Demand and the Opioid Crisis." 2017. Healthcare. https://www .whitehouse.gov/briefings-statements/remarks-president-trump-combatting-drug-demand-opioid-crisis/. Accessed on March 20, 2018.

"We Manufacture Prescription Opioids. How Could We Not Help Fight the Prescription and Illicit Opioid Abuse Crisis?" 2017. Purdue Pharmaceutical. http://www.purduepharma .com/wp-content/pdfs/Purdue_Pharma_Strong_Track_ Record_of_Addressing_Prescription_Drug_Abuse_and_ Diversion.pdf. Accessed on January 13, 2018.

*William G. Schulz is a freelance writer in Washington, D.C. He specializes in investigative reporting, particularly in the areas of scientific misconduct, research fraud, and science policy. He is an avid scuba diver and scuba instructor with experience in technical and cave diving, a board member of the Bead Society of Greater Washington, a jewelry artist, and a world traveler.*

## Citing History: The Need for Genuine Context
### *John Galbraith Simmons*

Frequently missing or buried in discussions over the agony of addiction and its multiple distressing consequences for individuals and communities is recognition of historical context and its basic role in imagining and implementing solutions. Addiction to opioids, as to other narcotics and mind-altering substances, owes to both biological and biosocial features of human societies that resist accurate articulation. Contending with this epidemic, as with others, would benefit from instilling in policy decisions the specific sociopolitical background, character, and chemistry of the substance itself—and its history.

With the onset of the current opioid epidemic, a brief communication from 1980 in a prestigious medical journal encapsulates the problem of context (Porter and Jick 1980). The letter under the heading "Addiction Rare in Patients Treated with Narcotics" appeared in the *New England Journal of Medicine* (*NEJM*). It reported that from a cohort of 11,882 patients in hospital who received at least one prescription for a narcotic, there were only 4 documented cases of addiction. The authors, from Boston University Medical Center, concluded that "despite widespread use of narcotic drugs in hospitals, the development of addiction is rare in medical patients with no history of addiction."

Statistics from the current opioid epidemic, of course, belie this conclusion, with drug overdose deaths tripling between 1991 and 2015 and an estimated 2 million cases of opiate-related addiction currently in the United States (Rudd, Seth, et al. 2016). This five-sentence letter in *NEJM* became a bibliographic touchstone, eventually with toxic results. It was subsequently often cited in medical journals as evidence to bolster the notion that opiates, for the vast majority of patients, would not result in addiction. They could therefore be widely and readily prescribed to treat not just acute pain but also chronic pain—the distress of arthritis, for example. The letter was cited in various medical journals no fewer than 608 times, with a notable spike after Purdue Pharma launched a campaign, about 2000, to help promote its branded opiate OxyContin. The marketing program was abetted by major stakeholders such as the American Medical Association, concerned about the genuine problem of treating pain in an aging population (Chapman 2013).

In 2017, long after the epidemic began, an important corrective in the same journal (Leung, Macdonald, et al. 2017) analyzed the way in which the 1980 letter was used in the medical literature, which effectively served as an aspect of the drug maker's marketing strategy. It noted that authors of medical papers designed to spread information about OxyContin often misused the letter when citing it, not noting its narrow patient base of hospitalized patients. The brief letter helped to "shape a narrative that allayed prescribers' concerns about the risk of addiction associated with long-term opioid therapy" (Leung, Macdonald, et al. 2017, 2194).

Purdue Pharma's efforts to promote OxyContin for chronic pain eventually ran afoul of Food and Drug Administration rules, and in 2007 the company admitted to "misbranding" the drug and encouraging false advertising; three executives paid millions in fines but escaped prison (Meier 2007). The prescription practices Purdue had pursued fueled abuse of all the branded opiates, and eventually a black market developed for related drugs such as heroin. The current situation, in 2018, underscores the scene envisioned more than half a century ago by surgeon Warren Cole in an early textbook on cancer pain: "[Physicians] are often loathe to give liberal amounts of narcotics because the drug addiction itself may become a hideous spectacle" (quoted in Meldrum 2016). What could happen to an individual patient could well happen to whole communities, and so it has.

Historical context keyed to both the recent and distant past helps explain why a short letter in a distinguished medical journal could help ignite and spread today's opioid abuse epidemic. The letter's conclusion—that addiction is a rare outcome of taking prescribed drugs—emerges from and tends to support a whole current of thought in the 20th century concerning drugs of all kinds. Any number of honest efforts have attempted to reset the conversation around drugs, to legalize some psychoactive substances, such as marijuana, and to decriminalize others such as cocaine and heroin. This viewpoint has directly competed with law-and-order efforts to criminalize and penalize. An influential 1965 study by sociologist Alfred Lindesmith, for example, recommended a medical model (Lindesmith 1965) that ran counter to the "war on drugs" that would soon be proclaimed, in 1971, by President Richard Nixon. Efforts to legalize and ameliorate stand as a constant alternative to the view that punishment and incarceration are the only ways to tame the individual and allay the social ills of illicit drug use.

Today, although harsh drug laws have consistently failed as policy prescriptions, the fact remains that medicalization of drug abuse, at least for the foreseeable future, will be subject to substantial limitations. Demographics (an aging population), poverty, family distress, and mental illness represent just a few of the variables not easy to control in a globalized world in which communications can foster illegal transactions and chemical secrets are hard to keep. The most accurate message from both contemporary biochemistry and neuroscience is that the biology of pain and pleasure invoke fundamental processes that cannot be controlled, at least on a macro-societal scale (Leknes and Tracey 2008). The risk of addiction may well be an essentially unalterable feature of civilized human life.

History writ large would tend to agree with science on a neurologic and molecular scale. Humans from the Neolithic era used plant-based psychoactive substances (Vetulani 2001). Societies shaped their economies around spices and peppers. Alcohol use, ancient in origin, spiked in Europe in the 16th century; then came coffee, tea, sugar, and tobacco. The historian who chronicled the rise of capitalist economies and the dense weave of European history, Fernand Braudel, took note of this ever-present factor, writing that the 19th and 20th centuries "were destined to have new luxuries of their own, their good and evil drugs." He concluded, with authority that surpasses common wisdom, that "humanity has need of compensation, according to a constant rule of life" (Braudel 1981, 261).

For today's opioid crisis, how those words and that "rule of life" should best apply to both policy prescriptions and the shape of treatments to come should not be ignored but, rather, explicitly acknowledged, accepted, and embraced.

## References

Braudel, F. 1981. *Civilization and Capitalism, 15th–18th Century*. London: Collins.

Chapman, C. R. 2013. "Opioid Pharmacotherapy for Chronic Noncancer Pain: The American Experience." *Korean Journal of Pain*. 26(1): 3–13.

Leknes, S., and I. Tracey 2008. "A Common Neurobiology for Pain and Pleasure." *Nature Reviews Neuroscience*. 9: 314, 314–319. doi: 10.1038/nrn2333. Accessed on March 20, 2018.

Leung, P. T. M., et al. 2017. "A 1980 Letter on the Risk of Opioid Addiction." *New England Journal of Medicine*. 376(22): 2194–2195.

Lindesmith, A. R. 1965. *The Addict and the Law*. Bloomington: Indiana University Press.

Meier, B. 2007. "3 Executives Spared Prison in OxyContin Case." *New York Times*. http://www.nytimes. com/2007/07/21/business/21pharma.html. Accessed on January 3, 2018.

Meldrum, M. L. 2016. "The Ongoing Opioid Prescription Epidemic: Historical Context." *American Journal of Public Health*. 106(8): 1365–1366.

Porter, J., and H. Jick. 1980. "Addiction Rare in Patients Treated with Narcotics." *New England Journal of Medicine*. 302(2): 123.

Rudd, R. A., et al. 2016. "Increases in Drug and Opioid-Involved Overdose Deaths—United States, 2010–2015."

*Morbidity and Mortality Weekly Reports.* 65(5051): 1445–1452.

Vetulani, J. 2001. "Drug Addiction. Part I. Psychoactive Substances in the Past and Presence." *Polish Journal of Pharmacology.* 53(3): 201–214.

*A science and medical writer and nonfiction author, John Galbraith Simmons's most recent book, in collaboration with Justin A. Zivin, MD, PhD, is* tPA for Stroke: The Story of a Controversial Drug *(Oxford University Press, 2011). His other nonfiction titles include* The Scientific 100 *(Carol, 1996) and* Doctors and Discoveries: Lives That Created Today's Medicine *(Houghton Mifflin, 2002). He is the author of more than 300 articles and 4 published novels.*

## I'm High as I Write This
*Rebecca Smith*

I don't know a lot of statistics or facts, I only know what I've seen in my life—and that is, that opiates have destroyed me. I am 33 years old, college educated, from a strong and tight-knit family. A fairly unremarkable background. Looking back, I cannot really pinpoint a time or place where this descent into lunacy began. I was always the party girl, up for a good time. I drank and smoked too much, did some cocaine on weekends, and then went to school and/or work the next day, so I never thought there was a problem. And then, someone introduced me to little white, oval, love letters to feeling good. I do remember that the first pill I ever took—probably hydrocodone, I cannot imagine starting out with what I ended up with (oxycodone, and a *lot* of it)—was like stepping out of Kansas, into Oz. You mean to tell me that with these, I can feel this good, all the time? I knew nothing of withdrawals, the massive amounts of money (most of it not actually mine) I would end up spending, or the absolute hell I would rain down on myself and the lives of those around me.

The best word I have come up with to describe opiates and the addiction to them is *insidious*. Generally defined as meaning "treacherous" or "seemingly harmless but with grave results," it is a perfect term for the way that actual addiction sneaks up on you. It isn't like getting drunk, where you can and will have a hangover the first time you ever overindulge. It creeps up on you, the way kudzu creeps into a yard—it's only here and there at first but before you know it, it has absolutely overtaken everything lush and green, replacing it instead with a vine that slowly strangles the life out of everything. The first time, or even the second, third, and fourth, there is no comedown. None of the flu-like symptoms classically associated with opiate withdrawal—aching body, feverish, runny nose, constant sneezing, inability to sleep coupled with a total lack of energy, nausea. Those come after you've decided that this drug is safe enough to take on an extended basis, daily. Then you run out that first time and realize it's far too late to go back—you're totally dependent.

At the point that I incurred a prison sentence, I was no longer stealing money and property in order to get high. I was stealing in order to keep myself from getting dope sick. Not only was it intensely uncomfortable, to put it mildly, but it was nigh impossible to hide the fact that I was going through withdrawal. If I was unable to find opiates or the money to buy any, I would stay in bed for days on end. I couldn't eat, couldn't sleep, and didn't have the energy to move; the thought of water hitting my skin from a shower was enough to make me cringe in pain, and anyone who approached me was more likely than not to get their head bitten entirely off because even talking made me hurt. There were times when my parents literally threw money at me, money they couldn't afford to spend, and told me to get up out of bed and go buy a pill; they just couldn't deal with my behavior. And as most addicts do, every time this happened, I swore I was going to wean myself off. It would never happen again. Instead, I found a doctor willing to write me prescriptions for morphine and oxycodone. If it was under a doctor's orders no one could say anything about it, right? That way

I knew I would have a steady supply each month. Except having them so readily available only made me take more, and before too long I was running out just days after my doctor's visit.

Meanwhile I had also been pilfering pills anywhere I could—friends' houses, family members' medicine cabinets, along with absolutely anything of any value I could get my hands on. (I also had a full-time job at the time and spent every cent feeding the monkey on my back.) Thus, my first felony charge after an uneventful 28 years: verifying false information to a pawn broker. I was offered either 6 months in jail or 18 months of probation. Having spent 24 hours going through withdrawal in a stinking, dirty, overcrowded jail medical ward, I decided 6 months of that was definitely not for me. I took the probation. No worries, I had a prescription—my officer couldn't say anything about an opiate-positive drug test.

The next two years brought 15 or so more arrests for various probation violations, all resulting in jail time until the state stopped giving me chances. I had no choice but to accept a prison sentence. It was and is sometimes hard to believe that I went to prison. I tried to make the best of it—there's no other choice. I made friends, worked, and tried not to think about home. Twenty-six months later I walked out a free woman and got high that night. It's said that nothing changes if nothing changes. It's also said that the spirit is willing but the flesh is weak. Both apply. I have destroyed my life, my family will never trust me again, and everything that I ever worked for crumbled like chalk under a hammer; and still I cannot escape this disease.

What I can say now is that I fight a lot harder than I used to. Weeks pass without even thinking about pills, but then the opportunity appears and it's as if the hell I've been through never happened. But, I don't steal anymore, and I am working hard to regain even a modicum of trust and respect from my loved ones. I'd like to be able to say that I've come through to the other side of addiction. In so many ways, I have, but it is a light at the end of a long, perilous tunnel, and for every 10 steps closer I get to it, it moves 15 farther away.

I am high as I write this. But tomorrow is a new day, with a new chance to be a new, better me. There is *always* a chance to be a new, better you—no matter how far you've spiraled. The chances stop only when you die; if you're still breathing, hope is there. It is elusive and fleeting, but it does, in fact, spring eternal. When it crosses your path, latch onto it; don't let go no matter how hard addiction tries to buck you off. Take it for everything it has to offer, and use that to hold you over until the next ray of light comes along. I am not perfect, and neither is my life, but I know that as long as I have the strength to fight it, I will continue to do so. And that is all I ask of myself—nothing more, nothing less.

*Rebecca Smith is working and attempting to rebuild her life and her credit score, as well as saving money to go back to school to pursue a master of arts degree in substance abuse counseling. She also volunteers with community organizations dedicated to helping convicted felons readjust to life after prison and finding the assistance they need to become productive members of society—housing, job placement, financial assistance, and mental health care.*

## Opioid Drugs Provide Pain Relief but with Serious Risks
### Stephani Sutherland

Opioid drugs—whether derived from the opium poppy or synthesized in a laboratory—have long been held up as the "gold standard" when it comes to pain medications. After surgery or a serious injury, these powerful drugs stop pain in its tracks like no other tool available today. But the drugs also have serious, potentially life-threatening side effects, including addiction and death by overdose. The pain-stopping power and the hazards of opioids all stem from their molecular structure, which mimics opium-like molecules produced in our own brains, called endogenous opioids.

Our brains contain a complex signaling network made up of endogenous opioids and their receptors. Like all signaling molecules found in our bodies, opioids bind to specific receptors, which they fit into like a key in a lock. Once bound, the receptors become activated and in turn pass along messages to other parts of the cell. Researchers long postulated that opioids worked at specialized receptors in the brain, but the main opioid receptor, called the mu opioid receptor, was finally isolated in 1973 by researchers Candace Pert and Solomon Snyder at Johns Hopkins University in Baltimore.

Opioid receptors are the cornerstone of the brain's ability to dampen incoming pain signals. Researchers call that ability "descending modulation" of pain, because higher brain centers send endogenous opioids down to the spinal cord to stop pain signals from entering the brain, thereby preventing us from feeling them. Descending modulation constantly affects our perception of pain, but in some instances, it can dramatically drown out pain—for example, in times of stress when pain might endanger our survival, or during childbirth.

Pain circuits, however, are not the only place in the brain and body that opioid receptors are found. If they were, opioid drugs could reduce pain without side effects. But as it is, opioid receptors are also found in the gut and throughout the brain. And opioid drugs can't be directed specifically at the pain-modulating receptors. Like all drugs, once opioids are in the circulatory system and in the brain, they will activate any opioid receptors they encounter. In the gut, opioid receptor activation results in constipation. Opioid receptors are also found in the brainstem, which controls breathing. Overactivation of those receptors can lead to respiratory depression—or stopping breathing—which is why opioid drug overdoses can be deadly. (Over 64,000 people died of drug overdoses in the United States in 2016, about half from opioids.) And opioids activate receptors in the brain's reward system—which produces feelings of euphoria and well-being—making the drugs very addictive.

Because opioid drugs are so addictive, researchers correctly presumed that endogenous opioids play an important role in how we perceive highly rewarding experiences. But recently, endogenous opioids have also been implicated in human behaviors ranging from social bonding to energy metabolism. All of those functions could be potentially disrupted by opioid drugs.

While opioids are highly addictive, not everyone who takes them—even for long periods of time—becomes addicted. For example, some people with severe chronic pain may take opioids for months or even years, at high yet stable doses, and not be addicted. There is no evidence that opioid drugs improve chronic pain—and in fact research shows that they can worsen pain conditions—but for some people, the pain relief the drugs provide allows them to maintain higher function than they would be able to achieve without them.

It's important to distinguish between different ways that the drugs act in our brains. Everyone who takes an opioid drug—say a pain medication prescribed after surgery—for more than a week or so will become physically dependent. That means that your brain has gotten used to the drug, and when you stop taking it, you will go through "withdrawals," which can include sweating, shaking, nausea, and paranoia. Withdrawals are your body's physical reaction to not having the drug, and they have nothing to do with one's personality, nor do they on their own indicate addiction. Patients can avoid withdrawals by tapering off or gradually reducing the amount of drug they take each day.

Another phenomenon associated with opioid drugs is tolerance; that is, the pain-relieving effect of the drugs diminishes with time, so that higher doses of drug are required to achieve the same benefits. Tolerance is also separate from addiction, but it can contribute to escalating drug doses.

The term *addiction* describes a complex behavioral pattern that some adults will succumb to with use of opioid drugs.

Babies may be born dependent on opioids, but they cannot be "born addicted." Although addiction was once thought to arise from "moral weakness," today researchers understand that addiction—now officially called substance use disorder—is a brain disease and that certain people are more susceptible due to their genes or their life experiences. The behaviors include compulsively seeking drugs and taking drugs even when doing so causes harm to one's self or others.

How can researchers develop opioid drugs that can relieve pain without dangerous side effects? One strategy has been to create "abuse-deterrent" formulas, which are basically time-release formulations that avoid the "high" that normally accompanies a dose of opioids—one that has met with limited success.

Another strategy may be on the horizon, though—one that centers on how drugs activate opioid receptors in brain cells. When opioids bind the mu opioid receptor, two separate signaling pathways can be triggered. Activation of the G-protein pathway results in pain relief, whereas activation of another messenger protein, called beta-arrestin 2, leads to some side effects, including respiratory depression. Tiny tweaks in a drug's molecular structure can bias it to activate one pathway over the other. Researchers are now working to develop drugs biased toward G-protein activation to relieve pain without the danger of overdose.

Perhaps more important, researchers have realized that better treatments are needed to safely treat chronic pain. The best strategy might be to activate the endogenous opioid system without drugs, using treatments like behavioral therapy, exercise, and mind-body practices like yoga.

*Stephani Sutherland is a neuroscientist and freelance journalist in Southern California. Stephani earned her PhD in 2001 studying the nerve cells that sense pain and has been writing ever since. For the past five years, she has focused on covering chronic pain and opioid research for publications, including* Scientific American *and* RELIEF.news. *Follow Stephani @SutherlandPhD.*

NEW YORK

## Nasal Naloxone Kit ☐ Injection Naloxone K

① remove caps / remueva tapas

① draw contents of vial into s
extraiga el contenido del fr
llene la jeringuilla

② assemble / ensamble

② inject into
large musc
inyecte al
músculo

③ spray into nose
½ in each side

rocee en la nariz
½ en cada orificio

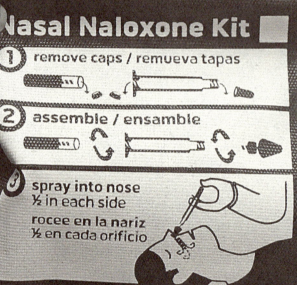

1cc

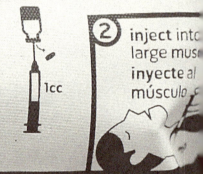

# Overdose Rescue Kit
## Equipo de Rescate para Sobredosis

## Introduction

To a large extent, the story of today's opioid crisis is also the story of individuals and organizations that have made important contributions to the study of opium and its chemical analogs, the effects they have on humans, the diseases that can result from these effects, and methods for preventing and treating such conditions. This chapter contains brief biographical sketches of some of those individuals and organizations throughout history.

## Academy of Integrative Pain Management

The Academy of Integrative Pain Management (AIPM) was founded in 1988 by pain specialist Richard S. Weiner. The organization's original name was the American Academy of Pain Management, a name that was changed in 2016 to its current name. The change was adopted in order to better reflect the way pain is treated today. The term *integrative medicine* has been adopted to describe a new approach to medicine that focuses on "a state of complete physical, mental, and social well-being and not merely the absence of disease or infirmity." (This definition

---

A typical opioid overdose rescue kit, like the one shown here, contains vials of naloxone and syringes for injection. They may also contain other materials needed for rescue efforts, such as alcohol pads, rescue breathing masks, rubber gloves, prescription cards, and/or educational materials for the patient. (Spencer Platt/Getty Images)

comes from the preamble to the Constitution of the World Health Organization, as adopted by the International Health Conference held in New York City between June 19 and 22, 1946.) Integrative medicine differs from traditional medicine largely in its willingness to consider virtually any form of therapy for which there is evidence of efficacy for any particular medical condition. AIPM's own definition of integrative medicine is "a model of care that is patient-centered; considers the whole person; encourages healthful lifestyle changes as part of the first line of treatment to restore wellness; is evidence-based and brings together all appropriate therapeutic approaches and clinicians to reduce pain and achieve optimal health and healing; and encourages a team approach" ("Academy of Integrative Pain Medicine" 2015).

AIPM policies are established by an 11-member board of directors that includes physicians, dentists, osteopaths, nurses, and physical therapists. Policies are carried out on a day-by-day process by specialists in the field of education, legislative and regulatory affairs, professional development, and state pain policy. The last of these individuals is also director of the organization's State Pain Policy Advocacy Network (SPPAN). SPPAN is the arm of the organization that advocates for, monitors, and reports on actions of individual states on topics of interest to AIPM. Among the topics in which SPPAN is interested are prior authorization, prescription monitoring programs, access to integrative pain care, pain clinic regulation, clinician pain education, step therapy/specialty tier, pain medication prescribing and dispensing, abuse-deterrent formulations, palliative care/quality of life, scope of practice and licensing, overdose prevention and safe disposal, and rescheduling hydrocodone.

AIPM has three primary fields of action: policy and advocacy, education, and information. The first of these functions is carried out through SPPAN, whose activities are described in more detail on its website, http://www.integrativepainmanage ment.org/page/policyandadvocacy. Its education arm also consists of three primary offerings: its annual meeting, a collection of more than 70 online courses in integrative pain medicine, and a number of resources through which it provides information to the general public, legislators and administrators in pain management programs, and practitioners in the field. The list of online courses provides a feel for the type of work being done by the organization:

- Who Is at Risk for Opioid Addiction: How Do I Know?
- Yoga, Mindfulness, and Hypnosis: An Exploration of the Science and Art of Healing
- An Evidence-Based Review of Dietary Supplements Used to Treat Pain
- The Pain in the Brain Is Primarily Migraine
- Neuroimaging of Central Pain
- The Emerging Role of the Microbiome in Pain Medicine: Why It Matters to You
- Opioid-Induced Hyperalgesia
- Hormones and Pain Care
- Pharmacology: Non-Opioid and Opioid Medications for Chronic Pain
- Regulatory Issues in Pain Management

Another aspect of the AIPM educational objective is the opportunity to earn the association's Advanced Pain Management Practitioner certificate. In order to earn the certificate, a person must answer 70 percent of 200 questions asked on the examination for the certificate, training for which is available on the organization's website.

Among the resources available through the organization's website are special social media sites on Twitter, Facebook, Google Plus, and YouTube, along with the AIPM blog at http:// blog.aapainmanage.org/, the *Pain Practitioner Magazine*, and a biweekly electronic newsletter, *Currents*.

## Advocates for Opioid Recovery

Advocates for Opioid Recovery (AOR) was founded in 2016 by three well-known political figures: Newt Gingrich, former Speaker of the U.S. House of Representatives; former congressman Patrick Kennedy of Massachusetts; and long-time civil rights advocate Van Jones. The organization's mission is "to advance a science-based, evidence-based treatment system that can reduce death and suffering from opioid addiction, and produce more long-term opioid addiction survivors who are positively engaged in their families and communities" ("Our Mission" 2018). The underlying assumption by founders of the group is that opioid prevention and treatment programs are based on outdated and/or incorrect concepts about the nature of opioid dependence and addiction and that greater attention needs to be paid to scientific evidence for dealing with the opioid epidemic.

The program developed by AOR consists of six fundamental objectives:

- Extending Medicare coverage to include all types of medication that has been shown to be effective in the treatment of opioid dependence and addition
- Expanding the capacity of treatment programs to include all evidence-based options
- Developing ways to achieve parity in opioid treatment programs and overcoming barriers to insurance coverage
- Changing the mind-set of individuals and organizations about the nature of opioid dependence and addiction by focusing on the conditions as diseases rather than moral failings and criminal behavior
- Providing more extensive and wider-ranging educational programs for the general public and the medical profession
- Accelerating the rate of innovation in medication development by changing the mechanisms by which the FDA grants approval for new drugs

On its website, AOR provides a more detailed discussion of each of these general principles. In the area of Medicare coverage, for example, the organization argues that methadone has been shown to be the only medication which is both safe and effective for treating heroin addiction, and it is both "unbelievable and unacceptable" that such treatment is not routinely covered by Medicare. The reason for this problem, AOR claims, is that methadone treatment has "fallen through the cracks" of permitted reimbursable treatments under existing Medicare rules.

Changing attitudes toward the fundamental character of opioid addiction, AOR suggests, means, in practice, taking actions, such as directing individuals identified as dependent on or addicted to opioids to evidence-based community treatment centers, increasing federal funding for drug courts, expanding treatment options for those already in jail or prison, and supporting a reentry program for individuals who are released from incarceration.

AOR attempts to achieve its objectives through a number of activities, such as appearing before congressional groups, issuing reports on the status of opioid treatment programs, making presentations on television and in the print media, and commenting on federal and other position statements and programs on the opioid epidemic, such as the 2017 report by the President's Commission on Combating Drug Addiction and the Opioid Crisis.

The organization's website also contains an abundance of information on many aspects of the opioid crisis, such as information on medication-assisted treatment (MAT) from the Substance Abuse and Mental Health Services Administration; evidence about the efficacy of MAT from the National Council for Behavioral Health; programs, benefits, and controversy surrounding the use of MAT in opioid treatment programs; opioid treatment and buprenorphine programs locators; resources about the opioid crisis from the National Institute on Drug Abuse; an MAT video from the Pew Charitable Trust; a patient guide and list of resources from the American Society of Addiction Medicine; a list of treatment and recovery resources from the U.S. Department of Health and Human Resources; suggestions for talking to kids about opioid issues; and suggestions for assisting employees who have just returned from drug rehabilitation programs.

## Alliance for Safe Online Pharmacies

Opioid abusers and addicts have access to the drugs they want and need through a number of avenues. One such source of drugs is the Internet. According to some estimates, there may be anywhere between 35,000 and 50,000 online pharmacies worldwide willing to sell opioids and other drugs to individuals of any age. When the U.S. Department of Justice closed down just one site in 2017, it found that the company involved, AlphaBay, had a list of more than 200,000 customers and an inventory of more than 250,000 illegal and/or toxic drugs for sale. In response to this problem, the Alliance for Safe Online Pharmacies (ASOP) was established in 2009 to monitor online websites that maintain such operations. ASOP estimates that 97 percent of active online sellers of drugs and medications do not comply with relevant national and international laws and regulations dealing with patient safety. Without guidance from some reliable source, such as the ASOP, the average consumer has virtually no way of knowing which Internet sites are legitimate sources of safe drugs and which are not.

The mission of ASOP, therefore, is to protect patient safety in the purchase of drugs online. The organization is an international association with headquarters in Washington, D.C. It is classified as a 501(c)(4) social welfare organization that is supported financially by contributions from companies, nonprofit organizations, and trade associations, along with voluntary donations and contributions from interested individuals.

ASOP has two categories of participants, members and observers. Membership, in turn, is divided into two classes: board members and general members. Board members establish policy and carry out the organization's day-to-day operations. General members advise the board and participate equally in all policy decisions. Those decisions are not voted upon but are made by consensus of all members participating in the discussion. Current members of the organization come from a variety of fields and include organizations such as the American Pharmacists Association, Amgen, Eli Lilly & Company, European Alliance for Safe Access to Medicines, Generic Pharmaceutical Association, Italian Medicines Agency, Johnson & Johnson, Partnership for Drug-Free Kids, Takeda Pharmaceuticals, and U.S. Pharmacopeial Convention.

The observers group consists of organizations to whom ASOP turns for specialized advice on specific topics or that provide information to the organization on a volunteer basis. Observers do not vote on ASOP policies or practices. Some organizations currently serving as observers are the American Association of Colleges of Pharmacy, Federation of State Medical Boards, National Health Council, Partnership for Safe Medicines, and Rx-360.

ASOP's activities focus on the collection of information about the sale of medications on the Internet, information that is then used to educate health care providers, policy makers, drug manufacturers and suppliers, and the general public. In collaboration with its members and observers, the organization develops policy solutions for issues related to online pharmaceutical marketing that it recommends to legislative and administrative agencies at all levels of government.

ASOP uses primarily two methods in its educational efforts: direct (usually video) presentations and electronic publications. Examples of the former are presentations made by ASOP staff at the Asia-Pacific Economic Cooperation Life Sciences Innovation Forum Workshop on Medical Products Safety and Public Awareness and Establishing of a Single Point of Contact System in Seoul, Korea; at the Partnership for Safe Medicines' Interchange 2011; and at the PDA/FDA

Pharmaceutical Supply Chain Conference: Patients Impacted by Supply Chain Dangers.

Some of the many electronic publications on Internet pharmacies available on ASOP's website are "How to Protect Yourself and Your Loved Ones Online," "Infographic about the Origin of Counterfeit Drugs in G8 Member Countries," "LegitScript's Legitimate Online Pharmacy List," "Legitscript's Website Url Verification Tool," "Making the Internet Safe for Patients," "National Association of Boards of Pharmacy's VIPPS List," "Online Pharmacy 101: What You Need to Know," and the U.S. Food and Drug Administration's "Know Your Online Pharmacy" tool.

ASOP's website is also a valuable resource for reports, news items, and other documents about the availability of medications online. Some of these resources come from ASOP itself, others from government sources, others from academic sources, and still others from partner resources. The types of documents that one might find in this section of the website are articles on "Vaccine Shortages and Suspect Online Pharmacy Sellers," "ASOP One-Pager on the Online Pharmacy Safety Act," "Consumer Fact Sheet: FDA Online Medicine Buying Guide," "The Japanese Rogue Internet Pharmacy Market," and "Assessing the Problem of Counterfeit Medications in the United Kingdom."

## American Society of Addiction Medicine

The American Society of Addiction Medicine (ASAM) had its origins in the early 1950s, largely through the efforts of Dr. Ruth Fox. Fox was a psychoanalyst who, in 1959, became the first medical director of the National Council on Alcoholism, an agency devoted to alcoholism prevention. Even before this period, Fox had initiated a series of meetings with fellow physicians interested in the research and clinical aspects of alcoholism and its treatment. In 1954, this group formalized its existence by creating the New York Medical Society on Alcoholism (NYMSA). The organization's work was funded primarily by the U.S. Alcohol, Drug Abuse, and Mental Health Administration, predecessor of today's Substance Abuse and Mental Health Services Administration. In 1967, NYMSA decided to extend its work nationwide and changed its name to the American Medical Society on Alcoholism (AMSA).

As interest in medical aspects of drug abuse and addiction grew in the 1970s, a second organization began operation in California, the California Society for the Treatment of Alcoholism and Other Drug Dependencies (CSTAODD), expanding traditional alcohol treatment programs to include those dependent on or addicted to drugs. Over time, the two groups at opposite ends of the country, AMSA and CSTAODD, began to collaborate with each other, eventually leading to their union in 1983 under the name AMSA. In 1988, AMSA was accepted by the American Medical Association as a national medical specialty society and adopted its present name American Society of Addiction Medicine. Today, the organization consists of more than 5,000 physicians and related health providers interested primarily in issues of substance abuse. It has state chapters in 37 states, organized into 10 regions, one of which covers Canada and other parts of the world.

The mission of ASAM consists of five major elements:

- to increase access to and improve the quality of addiction treatment;
- to educate physicians (including medical and osteopathic students), other health care providers, and the public;
- to support research and prevention;
- to promote the appropriate role of the physician in the care of patients with addiction;
- and to establish addiction medicine as a specialty recognized by professional organizations, governments, physicians, purchasers, and consumers of health care services, and the general public.

The work carried out by ASAM can be divided into four major categories: education, advocacy, research and treatment, and practice support. The organization's education component is designed to provide physicians and other health care workers with the most up-to-date information on basic issues in addiction treatment. In 2017, for example, ASAM offered courses on Combatting the Opioid Epidemic by Expanding Medication Assisted Treatments; Interventional Pain Management: A Pain Control Strategy for the Patient in Treatment; Methadone and Long QTc: Clinical Prediction, 5-Year Prevalence, and Causes-Interventions; Complex Addiction Medicine Clinical Cases Discussion; and Drug Testing: Special Populations and Additional Considerations in Addiction Treatment. The advocacy element in ASAM's program is aimed at influencing state and federal policies involving substance abuse to reflect the organization's goals and objectives. Some examples of the types of actions it has taken include pushing for insurance coverage of mental health and addiction disorders, working for the repeal of alcoholism exclusions in insurance policies, expanding treatment for substance abuse among veterans, and regulating the sale of tobacco and alcohol to minors.

The research and treatment feature of ASAM's work aims to provide health care providers with a wide range of informational materials on all aspects of addiction and substance abuse. Some of the materials it provides are a Common Threads Conference on Pain and Addiction; clinical updates from the International Association for the Study of Pain; a joint statement on pain and addiction from the American Pain Society, the American Academy of Pain Medicine, and the American Society of Addiction Medicine; and a variety of publications on prescription drug abuse from federal agencies. The area of practice support is designed to provide materials that will help addiction physicians and other providers with the best-available information about best practices in the field of addiction medicine. These materials include guidelines and consensus documents, such as the National

Practice Guideline for Medications for the Treatment of Opioid Use Disorder; "how to's" and practice resources, such as the Drug Enforcement Agency document "How to Prepare for a DEA Office Inspection"; standards and performance measures, such as the ASAM Standards of Care for the Addiction Specialist Physician Document; and "ASAM Criteria," a comprehensive set of guidelines for placement, continued stay, and transfer/discharge of patients with addiction and co-occurring conditions.

ASAM produces and provides a wide variety of print and electronic publications for the addiction physician and health care worker, such as the books *Principle of Addiction Medicine* and *The ASAM Essentials of Addiction Medicine*; *Journal of Addiction Medicine*, the association's official peer-reviewed journal; *ASAMagazine*, a publication containing news and commentary; and *ASAM Weekly*, an online publication intended for both members and nonmembers who are interested in issues of addiction medicine.

Information about the opioid epidemic is available throughout the association's website in a number of different locations. It can best be found by using the site's search function by looking for "opioids." One of the most useful publications is a position statement by the association on the issue, found at https://www.asam.org/docs/default-source/advocacy/letters-and-comments/opioid-epidemic-recommendations_secy-burwell_2014-07-31.pdf?sfvrsn=4#search="opioids".

## Center for Lawful Access and Abuse Deterrence

The Center for Lawful Access and Abuse Deterrence (CLAAD) was founded in 2009 "to prevent prescription drug fraud, diversion, misuse, and abuse while advancing consumer access to high-quality health care" (Center for Lawful Access and Abuse Deterrence 2018). Funding for the organization is provided by a coalition of about a dozen commercial members (pharmaceutical companies) such as Allergan, Mallinckrodt

Pharmaceuticals, Millennium Laboratories, Purdue Pharmaceuticals, and Zogenix. In addition to its commercial members, the organization includes a number of governmental and nonprofit organizations, including the Alliance for Safe Online Pharmacies, Allies in Recovery, American Pharmacists Association, American Society for Pain Management Nursing, American Society of Addiction Medicine, American Society of Anesthesiologists, Community Anti-Drug Coalitions of America, Drug Free America Foundation, Healthcare Distribution Management Association, International Nurses Society on Addictions, Johns Hopkins Bloomberg School of Public Health, National Alliance for Model State Drug Laws, National Association of Attorneys General, National District Attorneys Association, National Family Partnership, National Governors Association, National Sheriffs' Association, Northeastern University, and the 15th Judicial Circuit of Florida.

CLAAD activities fall into three major categories: policy leadership, information and analysis, and coalition building. Policy leadership involves the development of laws, regulations, and other provisions that ensure that efforts to prevent the abuse and misuse of opioids and other prescription drugs are effective without impeding the access of individuals to the medication they need for dealing with their own real medical problems. Some examples of actions taken within this context include the preparation of a document called National Prescription Drug Abuse Prevention Strategy, which lays out a plan for acting on the abuse of and addiction to opioids and other prescription drugs. Other examples of work within this category include a proposed draft legislation offered to the state of Florida as an aid for dealing with its prescription drug abuse problems and letters to various federal and state legislators and agencies on specific bills under consideration at both levels for ways of preventing prescription drug abuse.

CLAAD has also made presentations or attended dozens of meetings at which prescription drug abuse was being considered, such as the 25th annual meeting of the National

Association of Drug Diversion Investigators, the U.S. Food and Drug Administration Public Meeting on the Development and Regulation of Abuse-Deterrent Opioid Medications, the Partnership for Safe Medicines Interchange, the Generation Rx University Conference, the National Rx Drug Abuse Summit, and the National Sheriffs' Association 2014 Winter Conference. All policy decisions and positions made by CLAAD are required to be approved by at least 80 percent of nonprofit members of the organization.

Coalition building has also been a field of active interest for CLAAD. In 2014 alone, for example, the organization reached out to form coalitions with a variety of nonprofit organizations, including Trust for America's Health, National Governors Association, U.S. Conference of Mayors, Pew Charitable Trusts, Clinton Foundation, Transforming Youth Recovery, Arthritis Foundation, National Collegiate Athletic Association, The Jed Foundation, Johns Hopkins Bloomberg School of Public Health, Legal Action Center, National Association of Counties, Network for Public Health Law, and State Association of Addiction Services. It also worked with a network of organizations in the state of Missouri in an attempt to assist in the adoption of prescription drug monitoring program legislature in that state, the last one in the country not to have such a program.

The area of information and analysis refers to the process of monitoring scientific research, legislation, policy recommendations and making, and other events related to the prescription drug abuse issue. Information obtained from such sources is then analyzed, and summaries and trends are made available to relevant stakeholders in the field through the organization's website, social media, mass media, and other sources. Probably the most important single document developed for this purpose was its "National Prescription Drug Abuse Prevention Strategy," first produced in 2008 and updated regularly ever since. All versions of the document are available at http://claad .org/national strategy/.

The CLAAD website is a goldmine of resources and general information on virtually every imaginable aspect of the prescription drug abuse issue. One section classifies news articles relating to six specific categories of topics: abuse-deterrent medication, access to quality care, counterfeit and black market drugs, prescriber education and standards, prescription monitoring programs, and prosecutions. Another section provides a wealth of resources on prescription drug abuse, including a summary of policy activities, prescription drug abuse statistics, medication safety A to Z, myths versus facts of drug abuse, a list of acronyms, and additional print and visual resources on the topic. Some of the special features on opioid abuse and addiction are articles on the targeting of opioid traffic through U.S. mails, how opioids enter the United States from foreign countries by way of the U.S. Postal Service, the increasing threat of illicit opioids for first-responders, current rates of newborns addicted to opioids, collateral risks to teenagers posed by their exposure to opioids, and risks of combining alcohol consumption and opioid misuse, especially among seniors.

## Coalition to Stop Opioid Overdose

The Coalition to Stop Opioid Overdose was formed in May 2016 for the purpose of ensuring that state and federal legislatures would take the actions necessary to reduce the rate of opioid misuse, dependence, and overdose in the United States. Current members include the American Academy of Family Physicians, American Academy of Neurology, American Academy of Pediatrics, American Association of Nurse Practitioners, American College of Emergency Physicians, American College of Osteopathic Emergency Physicians, American Congress of Obstetricians and Gynecologists, American Medical Student Association, American Psychiatric Association, American Society of Addiction Medicine, Association for Behavioral Health and Wellness, California Consortium of Addiction Programs and Professionals, Central City Concern (Portland, Oregon), Children and Family Futures, Facing Addiction, HIV Medicine

Association, International Certification & Reciprocity Consortium, Illinois Alcohol and Drug Dependence Association, National Alliance to End Homelessness, National Association of Clinical Nurse Specialists, The National Center on Addiction and Substance Abuse, National Health Care for the Homeless Council, National Safety Council, Treatment Communities of America, Valley Hope, and Young People in Recovery.

The organization has identified five "key strategies" that will direct its efforts in the future:

- Improving access to medication-assisted treatment for those with opioid addiction
- Expanding availability of naloxone in health care settings and beyond
- Implementing enhanced prescription drug monitoring programs that track the dispensing and prescribing of controlled substances
- Raising the level of opioid prescriber education
- Enacting the Comprehensive Addiction and Recovery Act

The primary actions taken by the coalition include writing letters to legislators and administrators of health care policy in support of specific actions, such as passage of the Comprehensive Addiction and Recovery Act, and publishing statements about the group's position on specific bills and pending actions. The organization is also committed to involving members of the general public in its efforts by providing form letters and tweets for interested individuals to send to their own representatives and suggesting questions that a citizen can ask of his or her representative and/or candidate for office.

## Thomas De Quincey (1785–1859)

De Quincey was an English author best known for his autobiographical work, *Confessions of an Opium Eater*. He also wrote a number of other works, including novels, essays, critical reviews, and additional autobiographical sketches.

Thomas De Quincey was born on August 15, 1785, in Manchester, England. After his father died in 1796, De Quincey's mother moved the family to Bath, where he was enrolled in King Edward's School. He was an outstanding scholar, able to read Greek and compose poems in the language as a teenager. His home life was difficult, however, and he ran away to Wales at the age of 17, with the blessings and minimal financial support of his mother and uncle. Eventually he found his way to London, where he nearly died of starvation and survived only because of the kindness of a 15-year-old prostitute whom we now know of only as "Anne of Oxford Street."

In 1804, De Quincey was found by friends in London and returned to his family, who arranged for him to enroll at Worcester College, Oxford. It was at Oxford that he first took opium, in the form of laudanum, for a painful and persistent toothache. He soon became addicted to the drug, an addiction that persisted to a greater or lesser degree for the rest of his life. He describes his years of addition in *Confessions*, as well as its effects on his life and writing and his efforts to overcome his addiction. From time to time, he was able to withdraw from use of the drug but, a point noted by some of his biographers, the quantity and quality of his literary work suffered significantly during these periods of abstinence.

In 1816, De Quincey married Margaret Simpson, who was eventually to bear him eight children. She has been described as the "anchor" in his life, and after her death in 1837, De Quincey's use of opium increased significantly.

De Quincey survived for most of his life after about 1820 partially through the financial support of his family and partially through his own literary efforts. In the early 1820s, he moved to London where he worked as a novelist, essayist, translator, reporter, and critic. Publication of *Confessions* in 1821 essentially made his career as a writer, although he never again produced a work with such wide popularity. In addition to his opium addiction, De Quincey spent most of his life battling financial problems, and he was convicted and imprisoned on five occasions for nonpayment of his debts.

Biographers have noted De Quincey's substantial influence on later writers and artists, including Edgar Allan Poe, Charles Baudelaire, Nikolai Gogol, Aldous Huxley, William Burroughs, and Hector Berlioz, whose "Symphonie Fantastique" is reputedly loosely based on *Confessions*. The most recent collection of De Quincey's works was published in 21 volumes between 2000 and 2003. De Quincey died in Glasgow on December 8, 1859.

## Drug Enforcement Administration

The U.S. Drug Enforcement Administration (DEA) has a long bureaucratic history. Its original predecessors were the Bureau of Narcotics, created within the Department of the Treasury in 1930, and the Bureau of Drug Abuse Control, established as a part of the Food and Drug Administration in 1966. The two agencies were then combined in 1968 with the creation of the Bureau of Narcotics and Dangerous Drugs (BNDD) by Reorganization Plan No. 1 and placed within the Department of Justice. Five years later, another reorganization plan created the DEA in the merger of the BNDD with four other drug-related agencies, the Office of National Narcotics Intelligence in the Department of Justice; the drug investigation arm of the U.S. Customs Services, in the Department of the Treasury; the Narcotics Advance Research Management Team, in the Executive Office of the President; and the Office of Drug Abuse Law Enforcement, also in the Department of Justice. At the time it was created, DEA had 1,470 special agents and a budget of less than $75 million. Today it employs more than 9,200 men and women, including over 4,600 special agents, over 600 diversion investigators, nearly 800 intelligence research specialists, and close to 300 chemists. It has a FY 2017 budget of $2.103 billion and maintains 21 district offices in the United States and 86 overseas offices in 67 countries.

The mission of the DEA is to enforce the controlled substances laws and regulations of the U.S. government and to bring to justice those individuals and organizations that violate those laws and regulations. In achieving this objective, the agency carries out a number of specific activities, such as

- investigating and preparing for prosecution violators of controlled substance laws operating at interstate and international levels;
- investigating and preparing for prosecution individuals and gangs who use violence to terrorize individuals and communities in their sale and trafficking of drugs;
- managing a national drug intelligence program, in cooperation with other federal agencies, as well as state, local, and international agencies, to collect, analyze, and distribute information on drug activities;
- seizing assets that can be shown to be associated with illicit drug activities;
- enforcing, in particular, the provisions of the Controlled Substances Act of 1970 and its later amendments pertaining to the manufacture and distribution of substances listed under that act;
- working with state and local agencies to deal with interstate and international illicit drug activities;
- working with the United Nations, Interpol, and other organizations on matters related to international drug control programs.

DEA activities are organized under 16 distinct programs: Asset Forfeiture, Aviation, Cannabis Eradication, Clandestine Drug Laboratory Cleanup, DEA Museum, Diversion Control/ Prescription Drug Abuse, Drug Prevention/Demand Reduction, Foreign Cooperative Investigations, Forensic Sciences, High-Intensity Drug Trafficking Areas, Money Laundering, Office of the Administrative Law Judges, Organized Crime and

Drug Enforcement Task Force, State and Local Task Forces, Southwest Border Initiative, and Victim Witness Assistance Program. Specific opioid activities are a part of a number of these programs. For example, DEA agents in the Diversion Control/Prescription Drug Abuse program are involved in the monitoring of physicians and pharmacists who provide prescription drugs to those not qualified to receive such drugs or who falsify their records about such transactions and identifying employees who steal such drugs or falsify records to cover illegal sales, individuals who steal or forge prescriptions, and criminals who rob pharmacies or other facilities to obtain prescription drugs. In addition, agents in the program have a variety of other nonfield work, such as coordinating major investigations, fulfilling U.S. obligations under international drug treaties and agreements, advising state and local policy makers, controlling the import and export of controlled substances, and liaising with industry representatives.

In addition to its investigative, enforcement, advisory, and other functions, the DEA has an active program of prevention, housed within its Demand Reduction Section. As its title suggests, the goal of this department is to reduce the demand of drugs among existing and potential drug users and addicts by providing good education about the nature of drugs for populations thought to be most at risk for drug problems. The section has created and maintains two major Internet programs in this area, Just Think Twice (www.justthinktwice.com) and Get Smart about Drugs (www.getsmartaboutdrugs.com), the former designed primarily for teenagers and the latter for parents, educators, and other adults.

The DEA website is also a useful source of information about all aspects of drug use and abuse. Its Drug Information page contains documents on Drug Scheduling, the Controlled Substances Act, and Federal Trafficking Penalties, as well as fact sheets with information about more than two dozen commonly abused drugs, such as various opioids, stimulants, and depressants, as well as certain over-the-counter products, such as inhalants and bath salts. The fact sheets are sections taken from the agency's 2011 publication "Drugs of Abuse," which provides basic information about all forms of illegal drugs presented in a clear and understandable format.

## Jack Fishman (1930–2013)

One of the great dreams of opioid researchers has long been to find some type of chemical that can counteract the effects of opioids on the human body. The search for such a compound might be thought of as similar to the search for a vaccine that can prevent a disease or a drug that can cure the disease. The availability of such a compound would provide health care workers with a mechanism for treating people who have overdosed on an opioid drug, often saving their lives. That research has thus far produced meager results, probably the most important of which was the invention of the compound (N-allyl-14-hydroxydtiydro-nor-morphinone), 17-allyl-4,5a-epoxy-3,14-dihydroxymorphinan-6-one, or much better known (thankfully) by its generic name naloxone or one of its trade names, such as Evzio, Narcan, Narcanti, Narcotan, Nalone, or Prenoxad.

The breakthrough in this search for a drug with which to battle opioids occurred in the late 1950s when researchers Jack Fishman and Mozes J. Lewenstein found that naloxone is an opioid receptor antagonist, a substance that can attach to an opioid receptor in the same way as an endogenous or exogenous opioid attaches to the receptor. If naloxone is introduced into the human body, then it attaches to those receptors, blocks other opioids from doing so, and ameliorates the effects those opioids would otherwise have on the brain. In 1961, Fishman, Lewenstein, and the Japanese pharmaceutical company Sankyo received a patent for the synthesis of naloxone. At the time, the researches had little understanding of the profound effects that naloxone would eventually have on the treatment of opioid overdoses in the coming years.

One of the great ironies of Jack Fishman's life was that his stepson, Jonathan Stampler, died of heroin overdose in 2004. At the time, the drug was not readily available in some states, and even Fishman's wife, Jonathan's mother, was not aware of the fact that naloxone kits were available that could have saved her son.

Jack Fishman was born Jacob Fiszman in Krakow, Poland, on September 30, 1930. World War II was looming on the horizon at the time and, in fact, the Fishman family was forced to flee their home a day after Jack's eighth birthday. They traveled to China, where Fisher attended the Jewish School in Shanghai. At the age of 18, Jack and his family moved to the United States, and Jack enrolled at Yeshiva University in New York City, from which he received his BS in chemistry in 1950. He then continued his studies at Columbia University, from which he earned his MA in chemistry in 1952, and Wayne State University, in Detroit, from which he received his PhD in chemistry in 1955.

For his postdoctoral work, Fishman spent a year (1955–1956) at Oxford University. He then accepted an appointment at the Sloan-Kettering Institute for Cancer Research, where he served as a research associate and assistant from 1956 to 1962. He then moved to the Montefiore Hospital and Medical Center in the Bronx, New York, where he worked in the Institute for Steroid Research (ISR) from 1962 to 1974. It was during this period of his career that his research was focused on the role of estrogen in the development of breast cancer, a subject for which, during his lifetime, he gained greater fame than from his work on naloxone. In 1967, Fishman also accepted an appointment as associate professor of biochemistry at the Albert Einstein College of Medicine at Yeshiva. He was later promoted to full professor and remained at Yeshiva until 1978. Fishman also served as director of ISR from 1974 to 1978. In 1978, Fishman was named professor of biochemistry and director of the Laboratory for Biochemical Endocrinology at the Rockefeller University in New York City. He also served as director of research at the Strang-Cornell Institute for Cancer Research (now the Strang Cancer Prevention Institute) until shortly before his death on December 7, 2013, at his home in Remsenburg, New York. In 1987, Fishman moved to Florida, where he became director of IVAX Corporation, a pharmaceutical research company. He later served with the company as chief scientific officer, from 1991 to 1995, and as vice chairman of the board, from 1991 to 1997. Fishman also held the position of research professor of biochemistry and molecular biology at the University of Miami, where he remained until his retirement in 1992.

Among Fishman's awards and honors were the Norman E. Zinberg Award for Achievement in the Field of Medicine and the John Scott Award, given annually since 1818 by the city of Philadelphia in recognition of "the most deserving men and women whose inventions have contributed in some outstanding way to the comfort, welfare and happiness of mankind" ("The John Scott Award" 2018).

### Francis B. Harrison (1873–1957)

Harrison is probably best known today as author of the Harrison Narcotics Tax Act of 1914, an act that was passed, somewhat ironically, only after Harrison himself had left office. The act did not specifically prohibit any illegal substance, but it provided for the registration and taxation of "all persons who produce, import, manufacture, compound, deal in, dispense, sell, distribute, or give away opium or coca leaves, their salts, derivatives, or preparations, and for other purposes" (Public Acts of the Sixty-Third Congress of the United States. 1915. https://www.loc.gov/law/help/statutes-at-large/63rd-congress/session-3/c63s3ch1.pdf. Accessed on March 20, 2018). Law enforcement officers and the courts immediately began to interpret the law as restricting physicians from writing prescriptions for the nonmedical use of opiates, and they began arresting, prosecuting, and convicting individuals for such activities. To a significant extent, then, the Harrison Act marked the beginning of a national campaign against the use of certain substances for other than medical uses.

Francis Burton Harrison was born in New York City on December 18, 1873, to Burton Harrison, an attorney and private secretary to Jefferson Davis, president of the Confederate States, and Constance Cary Harrison, a novelist and social activist. He attended the Cutler School, in New York City, and Yale University, from which he received his BA in 1895. He then earned his LLB at New York Law School in 1897. Harrison was elected to the U.S. Congress from New York 13th district but resigned after one term to run (unsuccessfully) for lieutenant governor of New York. After a brief hiatus in the private practice of law, he ran for Congress again in 1907, this time from New York 20th district, and was elected. He served for three terms in Congress before accepting appointment as governor general of the Philippine islands, where he remained until 1921. Following his service in the Philippines, Harrison essentially retired from public life, spending extended periods of time in Scotland and Spain. He returned to the Philippines on a number of occasions, however, as consultant and advisor, especially when the islands were granted their independence in 1934. Harrison was married six times, with five of those marriages ending in divorce. He died in Flemington, New Jersey, on November 21, 1957.

## Heroin Epidemic Relief Organization

The Heroin Epidemic Relief Organization (HERO) was founded in 2010 by two fathers, each of whom had lost a son to heroin overdose. The organization saw as its purpose to "stop the growing heroin/opioid epidemic that has rapidly swept across our nation through our own programs and by supporting strategic pieces of legislation all while providing comfort and support to those who have lost a loved one to heroin/opioid or are currently helping a loved one who is struggling with this deadly disease" ("About Us" 2018). The organization is currently working on heroin-related issues in the Chicago area.

HERO's program consists of a five-pronged approach: activism, grief support, family support, prevention, and intervention. The activism element of the program involves efforts to reach out to legislators and other decision makers to offer needed information about and suggestions for ways of dealing with the heroin epidemic in the Chicago areas. The grief and family support elements consist of meetings in the Chicago area run by licensed and qualified professionals in these fields. The meetings are held weekly and are open to the public free of charges. The prevention and intervention elements of the program are currently under development.

Perhaps the most useful aspect of the program's work for the general public is the information about the heroin epidemic provided on its web page. That section consists of four sections: the law, heroin, naloxone training, and how to cope. The section on law discusses and explains Illinois legal actions relating to the abuse of heroin. The section on heroin provides a good background on the opioid, how one can become addicted to the drug, and what a treatment process entails. The naloxone section is an excellent resource on the drug that has proved to be most effective in the treatment of overdose, including when and how it should be used. The section on coping contains suggestions for individuals who have lost a son, daughter, other relative, or loved one to a heroin overdose. The education section also contains links to three videos helpful in further understanding the heroin epidemic and its impact on families and the general public: "There Is a Hole in My Sidewalk," "Restless Streets," and "I Thought I Knew."

One of the resources most in demand from HERO is the HERO trailer. The trailer is an eight-wheel vehicle carrying the organization's name and the slogan "Hidden in Plain Sight," whose interior has been made up to resemble a teenager's bedroom. The facility includes many of the signs with which a heroin addiction might be associated.

## Felix Hoffmann (1868–1946)

Hoffmann was a German chemist who worked at Bayer pharmaceutical company (then known as Farbenfabriken vorm. Friedr. Bayer & Company) from 1894 to 1928. He is best known as the discoverer of two of the company's most successful products, aspirin and heroin, both within a two-week period in 1897. Hoffmann's research was based on his interest in a chemical process known as *acetylation*, a chemical reaction in which an acetyl group is added to some other substances to make a derivative of that substance.

That reaction had been used successfully by Bayer researchers in synthesizing the antipyretic phenacetin from the medically useless compound p-nitrophenol and the antidiarrheal medication Tannig, from tannic acid, whose main use was in the tanning of leather.

In his own research, Hoffmann first attempted to acetylate salicylic acid, a compound extracted from willow bark that had long been used as an analgesic and antipyretic but which tended to cause gastrointestinal distress. Hoffmann called the product of this reaction *acetylsalicylic acid*, which became better known as *aspirin*. Although first rejected by Hoffmann's superiors as having no marketable value, the product went on to become by far the best known and best-selling of the company's pharmaceutical products in the form of Bayer aspirin.

Less than two weeks after his success with aspirin, Hoffmann studied the results of acetylating morphine, a reaction that resulted in the formation of the product *diacetylmorphine*, later better known as *heroin*. This reaction had been studied earlier by the English chemist C. R. Wright, who had, however, never pursued the practical medical applications of the product. As with aspirin, heroin eventually became one of the best-selling products of Bayer.

Felix Hoffmann was born in Ludwigsburg, Germany, on January 21, 1868. His father, Jakob, was a successful industrialist in the city, who suffered from arthritis. Legend has it that Felix Hoffmann became interested in the development of a pain medication at least to some extent as a way of helping his father to deal with this painful condition. He entered the Ludwig Maximilian University of Munich in 1889 to study chemistry, with an ultimate objective of becoming a pharmacist. He completed his studies a year later and passed the state examination in pharmacy. In 1891, he graduated from Munich and then stayed on to study for his doctorate, which he received in 1893. He then accepted a post as research chemist at Bayer, a company with which he remained for the rest of his working life. After completing his historic studies on aspirin and heroin, he left research to work in the company's marketing department. He retired from the company in 1928 and lived as a bachelor in Switzerland until his death on February 8, 1946. The details of his post-Bayer life are largely lost to a world which, until recently, knew little about his contributions to the development of two essential medical compounds.

## Paul Janssen (1926–2003)

In a biographical sketch about Janssen's life on the Scientific American blog, Janssen is described as "the most prolific drug inventor of all time." He and the research teams that worked at his company, Janssen Pharmaceutica, have been credited with the synthesis of at least 80 new drugs. At the time of his death in 2003, Janssen himself held more than 100 patents on new bioactive compounds. Among the most important of his many discoveries was the opioid fentanyl, sold under a number of brand names, best known of which is Sublimaze. Sublimaze is most widely used as an anesthetic for surgical and other medical procedures. In the early 2000s, fentanyl became very popular among drug abusers and addicts. It gained this popularity because it is much more potent than many other opioids, about 100 times more potent than an equal quantity of morphine, for example. It also tends to act more quickly than other popular opioids. In some cases, fentanyl is also easier to obtain on the streets than are heroin, morphine, or other opioids. In the United States, fentanyl is classified as a Schedule II drug, a drug with a high potential for abuse, potentially leading to severe psychological or physical dependence.

Paul Adriaan Jan Janssen was born on September 12, 1926, in Turnhout, Belgium. His father was Jan Constant Janssen, a physician, and his mother was Margriet Fleerackers Janssen. Biographers note that Janssen's later career as a drug innovator was strongly influenced by two events early in his life. First, his father, already interested in developing his own business, obtained the rights to the sale of Hungarian-produced drugs into the Belgian Congo. That experience is thought to have made Paul Janssen aware of the possible economic benefits of drug research. The second event was the death of his younger sister of tubercular meningitis when she was only four years of age. That event appears to have convinced Janssen that he wanted to devote his life to the discovery of substances that could be used in the treatment of disease.

Janssen attended secondary school at the Jesuit-run St Jozef College in Turnhout, where he decided to pursue a medical career. On graduation, he matriculated at the Faculté Universitaire Notre Dame de la Paix in Namur, no small accomplishment in and of itself given the wartime conditions then existing in Western Europe. At Notre Dame, he continued his premedical curriculum, concentrating in chemistry, biology, and physics. After receiving his BS in natural sciences in 1945, Janssen continued his studies at the Catholic University of Louvain, from where he earned his MD in 1951. His studies there were interrupted briefly when he traveled to the United States for six months to visit a number of pharmaceutical companies.

Over the next two years, Janssen served his required term of service in the Belgian army while simultaneously working in the Institute of Pharmacology at the University of Cologne, in Germany. In 1953, Janssen decided that it was time to strike out on his own and found a pharmaceutical research company. He and his first four employees established a laboratory on the third floor of his father's business in Turnhout and began a remarkable career of drug creation. Within the first year of operation, the Janssen team had synthesized about 500 new compounds and, two years later, more than 1,100 new substances. Obviously, not every new discovery turned out to have a medical application (the vast majority of them did not). But one of his earliest discoveries, ambucetamide, was found to have significant antispasmodic effects and was put to use for the treatment of menstrual pain. The new drug established Janssen's company as a serious organization to be reckoned with in the drug market. Some of the other drugs discovered during the company's early years were isopropamide, used for the treatment of peptic ulcers and gastrointestinal pain; diphenoxylate, used in the treatment of diarrhea; and the painkiller dextromoramide.

In 1957, Janssen's company, now called N.V. Research Laboratorium Dr. C. Janssen, had outgrown its Turnhout location and had been moved to a former military camp at Beerse, less than five miles from Turnhout. There, research continued at an impressive rate, with the discovery of more than a dozen important drugs over the next five years. In 1961, Janssen agreed to sell his company to the giant pharmaceutical firm Johnson & Johnson, with the understanding that Janssen's own laboratory would be allowed to continue its own line of research independent from the parent company's control. The list of drugs eventually discovered by the Janssen research team includes important compounds such as disopromine, cinnarizine, moperone, trifluperidol, pipamperone, benperidol, dehydrobenzperidol, spiperone, fluspirilene, pimozide, bromperidol, penfluridol, bromperidol decanoate, risperodone, haloperidol, levamisole, miconazole, and mebendazole. The last four of these compounds is currently included on the World Health Organization's List of Essential Medicines. Janssen died in Rome, Italy, on November 11, 2003, while attending the celebration of the 400th anniversary of the founding of the Pontifical Academy of Sciences, of which he had been a member since 1990. His work has been recognized by a number of honors and awards, including the Canada Gairdner Award, one of the highest honors given to researchers in the field of medicine and health. In 2005, he was chosen the second "greatest Belgian" of all time (after Father Damien) in a poll conducted by Belgian public TV broadcaster Canvas, public radio broadcaster Radio 1, and newspaper *De Standaard*.

## The National Alliance of Advocates for Buprenorphine Treatment

The National Alliance of Advocates for Buprenorphine Treatment (NAABT) was founded on April 1, 2005, by three individuals, Timothy Lepak, Kathleen Gargano, and Nancy Barmashi, who believed that the semisynthetic opioid buprenorphine holds the potential for helping people addicted to other opioids recover from their addiction. The drug had been approved for use by the U.S. Food and Drug Administration three years earlier, but the three individuals felt that information about its potential value for opioid drug addiction was being ignored, that insufficient numbers of doctors were trained to use buprenorphine therapy, and that addicts themselves knew little or nothing about the procedure. They incorporated NAABT as a 501(c)(3) charitable foundation to work toward solving these problems and making the drug more widely used in the treatment of drug addictions.

NAABT says that its primary source of finances is donations from individuals in the organization's work. It also, however, asks for "unrestricted grants" from pharmaceutical companies to carry on its work. An *unrestricted grant* is one that a company provides an organization with "no strings attached," that is, that can be used by the organization for any purpose whatsoever. NAABT emphasizes the role of unrestricted grants in its work to avoid the impression that it is beholden to any of the companies that provide it with financial support.

NAABT makes use of a number of methods for advancing its core objective of promoting the use of buprenorphine for the treatment of opioid addictions. One of its primary approaches is a registry service that allows a person who wants assistance with his or her addiction to find a physician who is willing to treat him or her. The service also provides a place where physicians can also register so that their contact information can be provided to prospective patients. This matching system can be found at http://www.treatmentmatch.org/. NAABT reports that, as of late 2017, 110,078 patients had used the TreatmentMatch® website and 4,656 providers had signed on for the program.

The NAABT website is also a valuable source of information on the basics of buprenorphine treatment. It includes a "frequently asked questions" section, a number of educational essays that provide information about various aspects of the drug and its use in the treatment of addiction, information on the "30–100 patient limit" that restricts the number of patients that can be treated by a single provider, patient stories about the use of buprenorphine therapy, laws dealing with buprenorphine, print and electronic resources, and links to other online sources of information and assistance. Of particular value to those who need further information about buprenorphine treatment is the organization's free resource kit, which contains a collection of NAABT materials about the issue.

Other publications available from NAABT include a patient discussion guide and physician discussion guide about buprenorphine and its use in treating addictions; online peer support forums on a number of specific issues, such as starting treatment, side effects, cost and insurance, tapering off and post-taper, and friends and family; a list of local resources; and a large number of publications on specific issues relating to buprenorphine treatment. Examples of these publications are a brochure on buprenorphine basics, a pamphlet about "precipitated withdrawal," a brochure on the ways in which peer support works, an emergency contact card, a counter-display card explaining how the NAABT matching system works, and the National Institute on Drug Abuse booklet on "The Science of Addiction." The website also has a section that provides detailed information about treatment programs specifically for physicians, counselors, pharmacists, and nurses.

## National Association of State Controlled Substances Authorities

The National Association of State Controlled Substances Authorities (NASCSA) is a 501(c)(3) nonprofit, educational organization established in 1985. Its primary objective is to provide a mechanism through which state and federal agencies can work together to increase the effectiveness of efforts to monitor and prevent the diversion of controlled substances to nonmedical purposes for which they are not intended. The organization consists of representatives from all 50 states, the District of Columbia, and Guam. Representatives come from a variety of agencies within each state, such as the Board of Pharmacy, Office of the Attorney General, Bureau of Drug Control, Consumer and Industry Services, Division of Professional Licensing, and Department of Health. A number of associate members come from organizations interested in issues surrounding controlled substances, such as AbbVie Pharmaceuticals, Associated Pharmacies Incorporated, Cardinal Health, CVS Pharmacy, Express Scripts, GW Pharmaceuticals, Healthcare Distribution Management Association, Janssen Pharmaceuticals, Inc., Mallinckrodt, National Association of Chain Drug Stores, Optimum Technology, Omnicare, Purdue Pharma L.P., Quarles & Brady, LLP, Rite Aid, Walgreens, and Walmart.

The organization's two main activities are an annual conference at which new information on drug diversion and related topics is shared and a variety of educational programs on legislation, regulation, and enforcement of laws relating to controlled substances. The 2017 conference, for example, featured sessions on topics such as Responding to the Prescription Opioid and Heroin Crisis, Abuse-Deterrent Opioid Formulations, Case Studies: Diversion Trends and Investigations, the Ongoing War against Drugs by the U.S. Customs and Border Protection, and Deployments in Technology Relating to Diversion Detection.

NASCSA makes use of resolutions to express its views on a variety of prescription drug-related issues. Some topics of resolutions adopted in 2017 are support for the Synthetics Trafficking and Overdose Prevention Act of 2017, support for the dispensation of controlled substances to state prescription monitoring programs (PMPs), and continued support for PMPs.

An important feature of the organization's website is an interactive map that provides information about prescription drug monitoring programs in all member states and territories. One can click on any one of the states or territories and receive a detailed description of that state's program, contact information for the responsible official, and relevant legislation. Access is also available through the website to surveys that NASCSA has conducted in the past on topics such as issues of importance and information and opinion surveys of state and territory representatives on PMPD issues.

NASCSA publishes an online newsletter that is available for general viewing. It contains information about the organization's activities and events occurring in member states and territories.

## National Institute on Drug Abuse

The National Institute on Drug Abuse (NIDA) is the nation's primary governmental organization for dealing with drug-related issues. Its history dates back to 1935 with the creation of a facility known as the United States Narcotic Farm, in Lexington, Kentucky. The stated purpose of the facility was to provide drug abusers with a setting in which they could receive the assistance they needed to overcome their drug habit. It was the third of three related institutions established by the U.S. Public Health Service in a research effort to find a substitute for morphine that was medically effective and nonaddictive. The other two facilities focused on drug development and animal testing, while the Lexington facility was assigned the task of testing promising new drugs on addicts. In some respects, the farm was just that, a large, open program that allowed patients to work in the fields, at least partially as a step toward their own recovery. But it also had the characteristics of a prison, with armed guards and barred windows. The farm continued in operation until 1974, with a name change to the Addiction Research Center in 1948.

NIDA was created in September 1973 through an executive order issued by President Richard M. Nixon. The organization was an amalgam of the White House Special Action Office for Drug Abuse Prevention and the Division of Narcotic Abuse and Drug Addiction within the National Institute of Mental Health. Among its responsibilities was operation of the Drug Abuse Warning Network, the National Household Survey on Drug Abuse (now the National Survey on Drug Use and Health), and Monitoring the Future, a research program that tracks drug use patterns among 8th-, 10th-, and 12th-grade students in the United States. In 1992, NIDA became part of the National Institutes of Health of the U.S. Department of Health and Human Services. At that time, responsibility for the Drug Abuse Warning Network (DAWN) and National Household Survey on Drug Abuse (NHSDA) programs was transferred to the newly created Substance Abuse and Mental Health Services Administration. A detailed chronology and timeline of the organization's history is available at https://www.nih.gov/about-nih/what-we-do/nih-almanac/national-institute-drug-abuse-nida#legislation.

NIDA today has a two-pronged mission involving research on and dissemination of information about drug abuse in the United States. More specifically, its goals are to support and conduct basic and clinical research on drug use (including nicotine), its consequences, and the underlying neurobiological, behavioral, and social mechanisms involved and to ensure the effective translation, implementation, and dissemination of scientific research findings to improve the prevention and treatment of substance use disorders and enhance public awareness of addiction as a brain disorder. The four stated goals of NIDA's research to achieve these goals are to

- identify the biological, environmental, behavioral, and social causes and consequences,
- develop new and improved strategies,
- develop new and improved treatments, and
- increase the public health impact of NIDA research.

To achieve these objectives, NIDA is organized into several offices, divisions, centers, cross-cutting research teams, workgroups, interest groups, and consortia. Some of these groups are the Office of Diversity and Health Disparities; Office of Translational Initiatives and Program Innovations; AIDS Research Program; International Program; Office of Science Policy and Communications; Intramural Research Program; Center for Clinical Trials Network; Division of Epidemiology, Services and Prevention Research; Division of Neuroscience and Behavior; Division of Therapeutics and Medical Consequences; Brain Development Research Consortium; Cannabis Science Interest Group; Genetics and Epigenetics Cross-Cutting Research Team; Nicotine and Tobacco Research Team; Prescription Opioid and Pain Workgroup; and Women & Sex/Gender Differences Research Group.

A record of the organization's specific legislative activities and accomplishments is available on its website where its budgetary records and director's reports are available. This resource also provides detailed information about NIDA's efforts related to opioid abuse and the current opioid epidemic. Among the specific legislative actions that it has sponsored or participated in recent congressional sessions are Stem the Tide of Overdose Prevalence from Opiate Drugs Act of 2017, Expanding Opportunities for Recovery Act of 2017, Opioid Abuse Prevention and Treatment Act of 2017, Examining Opioid Treatment Infrastructure Act of 2017, Comprehensive Fentanyl Control Act, Prescription Drug Monitoring Act of 2017, Abuse-Deterrent Opioids Plan for Tomorrow Act of 2017, Opioid Preventing Abuse through Continuing Education Act of 2017, and Student and Student Athlete Opioid Misuse Prevention Act.

Current director of NIDA is Dr. Nora D. Volkow, who has held that post since 2003. Volkow is very active in a number of legislative settings focusing on opioid and other drug abuse issues. She has met with specific members of the Congress and small groups of members, testified before legislative committees, provided specialized briefings to congressional members on specific topics of interest, and written and spoken extensively to professional groups and the general public.

## Office of National Drug Control Policy

The Office of National Drug Control Policy (ONDCP) was established in 1989 as a provision of the Anti-Drug Abuse Act of 1988. The organization is the primary mechanism for providing advice to the president and for laying out the nation's approach for dealing with drug abuse. As is to be expected, the objectives and activities of the office change considerably from one administration to another. Under President Barack Obama, the office was assigned widespread and innovative approaches for dealing with drug abuse in the nation. President Donald Trump, by contrast, has, as of early 2018, taken a somewhat less-aggressive approach to the problem. During his campaign for the presidency, Trump listed ONDCP as one of the federal agencies he intended to abolish if he were elected. Thus far, President Trump has not carried out this promise, although, shortly after his inauguration, he suggested reducing funding for ONDCP by about 95 percent, from $388 million to $24 million. The direction of ONDCP's work should become more clear as President Trump's tenure develops.

ONDCP's primary responsibility is development of a National Drug Control Strategy, which outlines the federal government's efforts to reduce illicit drug use and its consequences in the United States. As of early 2018, no such strategy had been announced by the Trump administration, but a sense of the type of document that might be produced can be seen in a review of the documents produced under the administration of President Barack Obama. See, for example, the strategies produced for 2009–2016 at https://obamawhitehouse.archives .gov/ondcp/policy-and-research/ndcs.

The two main features of ONDCP's activities currently are the High Intensity Drug Trafficking Areas (HIDTA) and Drug-Free Communities (DFC) Support programs. Both programs consist of federal grants for the purpose of reducing the use of illicit drugs. HIDTA was created by the Anti-Drug Abuse Act of 1988 to focus on certain specific regions in which problems of drug abuse were particularly serious. There are currently 28 HIDTA programs that cover just over 18 percent of all counties in the United States with a population equal to 65.5 percent of the total population of the country. They cover 49 states (Alaska not included), Washington, D.C., Puerto Rico, and the Virgin Islands. (A map of the programs and regions covered is available at https://www.whitehouse.gov/sites/whitehouse.gov/ files/ondcp/Fact_Sheets/hidta_2017_letter_oct2016.pdf.)

ONDCP currently funds 752 HIDTA programs that consist of federal, state, and local agencies that carry out investigation, interdiction, and prosecution of drug-related activities. Most of these programs fall into one of three major categories: domestic highway enforcement, national emerging threats initiative, and prevention. As indicated by the last of these categories, the major purpose of HIDTA programs is law enforcement and reduction of supply of drugs; some efforts are also being made to reduce the use of illegal drugs by individuals.

The Drug Free Communities program was authorized by the Drug Free Communities Act of 1997. That act authorized the ONDCP to carry out a national initiative that awards federal grants directly to community coalitions in the United States. These coalitions work "to reduce substance abuse among adolescents, strengthen collaboration among organizations and agencies in both the private and public sectors, and serve as catalysts for increased citizen participation in strategic planning to reduce drug use over time" ("Authorizing Legislation" 2018). The program has grown from an initial group of 92 grants that shared a budget of $10 million to a total in 2016 of more than 2,000 grants and a budget of $95 million. One of the requirements that must be satisfied in order to receive a DFC grant is that the requesting organization must include members of every part of a community, including youth; parents; businesses; media; schools; youth-serving organizations; religious or fraternal organizations; law enforcement; civic and volunteer groups; health care professionals; state, local, or tribal agencies; and other organizations involved in reducing substance abuse.

## Pain Therapy Access Physicians Working Group

The Pain Therapy Access Physicians Working Group (PTAPWG) is a group within the Alliance of Patient Access, a national network of physicians who work to ensure that patients are able to receive access to approved therapies and appropriate clinical care. PTAPWG was formed in 2013, at least partly in response to governmental efforts to gain greater control over the misuse and abuse of opioid pain medications, in order to work for policies and practices that make it possible for patients who are in legitimate need of pain medications to obtain adequate types of forms of those drugs. The organization focuses on developing educational resources that will help inform the general public as well as provide the basis for informed policy making.

Among the white papers and policy briefings prepared by the group are the health policy briefings, "Access to Integrated Care for Chronic Pain" and "Abuse-Deterrent Opioid Formulations: Promising Technology, Unique Challenges," and a white paper, "Prescription Pain Medication: Preserving Patient Access while Curbing Abuse." A variety of educational resources are also available from the group, including an infographic, "Integrated Care Addresses the Multiple Issues of Chronic Pain"; a policy briefing, "The Pain Debate: Treatment, Abuse, and Deterrence"; a video presentation, "Prescription Pain Medication: Preserving Access While Curing Abuse"; a radio presentation, "Aches and Gains"; information on state prescription drug policies; and a call to action, "Curbing Prescription Drug Abuse while Safeguarding Patient Access." The PTAPWG website, http://allianceforpatientaccess.org/, also provides a wealth of articles on the subject of prescription drug abuse and medications for legitimate pain needs from newspapers, magazines, Internet, and other sources. Resources on the topic of opioids is available at http://allianceforpatientaccess .org/?s=opioids.

## Candace Pert (1946–2013)

Pert is the person probably most responsible for the identification of opiate receptors in the human brain. Opiate receptors are molecules whose physical structure closely matches that of opioids, such as heroin and morphine. When these opioids are introduced into the body, they migrate to the brain where they form a type of lock-and-key structure that allows opioid molecules to exert their effects on the brain. Credit for the discovery of these receptors was formally given to Pert's supervisor in the research, Solomon Snyder, with little specific recognition going to Pert herself. This result prompted Pert to write to Snyder about her strong feelings about having been left off appropriate awards and honors lists. Some years later, the two reconciled after Snyder pointed out to Pert that "that's just the way it is" in scientific research. Informally, Pert has sometimes been referred to as the mother of psychoneuroimmunology or the goddess of neuroscience.

Candace Beebe was born in Manhattan on June 26, 1946, to Robert Beebe, a commercial artist, and Mildred Beebe, a court typist. She attended General Douglas MacArthur High School in Levittown, New York, from which she graduated in 1964. She then matriculated at Hofstra University but dropped out two years later to marry Agu Pert. After moving to Philadelphia and bearing three children, Pert decided to return to college, entering Bryn Mawr College to major in biology. She received her BS degree in 1970 and then continued her studies in pharmacology at the Johns Hopkins University School of Medicine under Snyder. As part of her graduate studies, she carried out the research that allowed her to identify the specific structures in the brain that act as receptors for opioids. That work is described in a now-historic paper published by Snyder and Pert entitled "Opiate Receptor: Demonstration in Nervous Tissue" (*Science*. 179(4077): 1011–1014).

For her postdoctoral studies, Pert worked at Johns Hopkins under a National Institutes of Health Fellowship from 1974 to 1975. She then accepted an appointment at the National Institute of Mental Health (NIMH), where she remained until 1987. In 1983 she was appointed chief of the Section on Brain Biochemistry of the Clinical Neuroscience, the first woman ever to hold that position. After Pert left NIMH in 1987, she held a number of research positions in a variety of organizations: guest researcher in her previous department at NIMH (1987–1990), scientific director at Peptide Design L.P. in Germantown, Maryland (1987–1990), chairman of the board of the Integra Institute in Bethesda, Maryland (1987–1991), visiting professor at the Center for Molecular and Behavioral Neuroscience at Rutgers University (1992–1994), research director at Advanced Peptides and Biotechnology Sciences (1991–1994), research professor in the Department of Physiology and Biophysics at Georgetown University School of Medicine (1994–2006), and cofounder and chief scientific officer of RAPID Pharmaceuticals, AG (2007–2013).

In addition to her scientific research, Pert became interested in the relationship between mind and body in humans. She became convinced that a large part of disease and illness was a result of faulty brain activity. She laid out her beliefs in probably her most famous work, *Molecules of Emotion: The Science between Mind-Body Medicine* (Scribner, 1999), and its successor, *Everything You Need to Know to Feel Go(o)d* (with Nancy Marriott; Hay House, 2006). Pert died in Potomac, Maryland, on September 12, 2013. Among her major awards and honors were the Arthur S. Fleming Award (1979); Musser Burch Lecture, Tulane University (1979); Harrington Lecture, State University of New York at Buffalo (1980); Ethel Mae Wilson Visiting Scientist Lecture, University of Vanderbilt (1981); Hahnemann University Honorary Lecturer (1982); Kilby Award of the Kilby International Awards Foundation (1993); Scientist of the Year of the Nurse Healers Association (1996); American Foundation for Alternative Medicine, Excellence in Research (2002); and the Theophrastus Paracelsus Prize for Holistic Medicine (2008).

## President's Commission on Combating Drug Addiction and the Opioid Crisis

The President's Commission on Combating Drug Addiction and the Opioid Crisis was created in Executive Order 13784, issued by President Donald Trump on March 29, 2017. Trump took the action at least partially in order to fulfill a campaign promise he had made a number of times during the 2016 presidential campaign. Over time, Trump had enumerated a number of elements that he expected to include in his efforts to bring the opioid epidemic to a conclusion, including building a wall on the southern border of the United States to eliminate the importation of opioids, bring an end to so-called sanctuary cities that refused to work with the federal government in arresting illegal immigrants, expelling gangs that are a source of illegal opioids from the country, insist that the FDA approve addiction-deterring drugs more quickly, and reduce the amount of Schedule II drugs that can be sold in the United States.

Trump's executive order did not address any of these issues specifically but focused instead on the creation of the committee, its memberships, and its responsibilities. The committee members were five politicians—Governors Chris Christie (chair), Charlie Baker, and Roy Cooper; Congressman Patrick J. Kennedy; and Florida attorney general Pam Bondi, along with one specialist in opioid issues, Professor Bertha Madras. The committee's job was to

(a) identify and describe existing Federal funding used to combat drug addiction and the opioid crisis;

(b) assess the availability and accessibility of drug addiction treatment services and overdose reversal throughout the country and identify areas that are underserved;

(c) identify and report on best practices for addiction prevention, including healthcare provider education and evaluation of prescription practices, and the use and effectiveness of State prescription drug monitoring programs;

(d) review the literature evaluating the effectiveness of educational messages for youth and adults with respect to prescription and illicit opioids;

(e) identify and evaluate existing Federal programs to prevent and treat drug addiction for their scope and effectiveness, and make recommendations for improving these programs; and

(f) make recommendations to the President for improving the Federal response to drug addiction and the opioid crisis ("Office of National Drug Control Policy Mission" 2017).

The committee eventually met five times before releasing both an interim report on July 31, 2017, and a final report on November 1, 2017. The final report contained several recommendations for ways of dealing with the opioid epidemic, such as

- disrupting the supply of illicit fentanyl,
- increasing screenings and referrals for treatment, using Medicare and Medicaid resources,
- improving treatment options, using evidence-based approaches,
- removing financial barriers to the extended use of medication-assisted treatment (MAT),
- extending the use of MAT within the criminal justice system,
- providing greater assistance for drug courts and diversion programs,
- providing expanded access to and administration of naloxone treatments,
- providing expanded services to families of those who become dependent upon or addicted to opioids,
- expanding and accelerating research on pain, overdose, and MAT medications.

As of early 2018, it is not clear which of these recommendations will be acted on and, if so, what those actions will be. At that point, no funds had actually been allocated to carry out the committee's recommendations. The reader should refer to current news on the steps taken by the Trump administration in following up on these recommendations and any further work of the presidential commission.

### Friedrich Sertürner (1783–1841)

While still a young pharmacist's apprentice, Sertürner isolated the psychoactive agent morphine from the opium plant. His accomplishment is especially important because it was not only the first such agent extracted from opium but also the first alkaloid obtained from any plant. Sertürner named his new discovery after the Greek god of dreams, Morpheus, for its powerful analgesic and sedative properties.

Friedrich Wilhelm Adam Ferdinand Sertürner was born in Neuhaus, Prussia, on June 19, 1783. His parents were in service to Prince Friedrich Wilhelm, who was also his godfather. When both his father and the prince died in 1794, he was left without means of support and, therefore, was apprenticed to a court apothecary by the name of Cramer. One of the topics in which he became interested in his new job was the chemical composition of opium, a plant that had long been known for its powerful analgesic and sedative properties. By 1803, he had extracted from opium seeds a white crystalline powder clearly responsible for the pharmacological properties of the plant. He named the new substance *morphine* and proceeded to test its properties, first on stray animals available at the castle and later on his friends and himself. His friends soon withdrew from the experiments because, while pleasurable enough in its initial moderate doses, the compound ultimately caused unpleasant physical effects, including nausea and vomiting. Sertürner continued, however, to test the drug on himself, unaware of its ultimate addictive properties.

Sertürner was awarded his apothecary license in 1806 and established his own pharmacy in the Prussian town of Einbeck. In addition to operating his business, he continued to study the chemical and pharmacological properties of morphine for a number of years. His work drew little attention from professional scientists, however, and he eventually turned his attention to other topics, including the development of improved firearms and ammunition. During the last few years of his life, he became increasingly depressed about his failure to interest the scientific community in his research on opium. He withdrew into his own world and turned to morphine for comfort against his disillusionment with what he saw as the failure of his life. He did receive some comfort in 1831 when he was awarded a Montyon Prize by the Académie Française, sometimes described as the forerunner of the Nobel Prizes, with its cash award of 2,000 francs. By the time of his death in Hamelin, Prussia, on February 20, 1841, however, the scientific world, in general, had still not appreciated the enormous significance of his research on morphine.

## Solomon H. Snyder (1938–)

Although the biological and psychological effects of opioids have been known for centuries, almost nothing was known about the mechanisms by which they operated in the brain. Neuroscientists had a general notion that the effects of opioids are the consequence of certain naturally occurring compounds in the body that act in some way on the brain. As late as the early 1970s, however, no one really knew what those compounds were or how they acted in the brain. In one series of experiments conducted at about that time, researchers identified the first of those "brain chemicals" responsible for the narcotic effects of the opiates. Those compounds were given the name *endorphins*, a combination of the prefix *endo-*, from "growing within" or "naturally occurring," and *morphine*, that is naturally occurring substances that have morphine-like effects on the brain.

The first concrete step in unraveling the actions of endorphins and other brain chemicals found at about the same time came in 1973 when American neuroscientist Candace Pert, working under the direction of her PhD advisor, Solomon Snyder, discovered the mechanism by which those compounds produce their biological and psychological effects. Pert and Snyder identified certain structures in the brain whose physical shape closely matched the shape of endorphin molecules. When an endorphin molecule enters the brain, it searches for a complementary structure to which it can attach, like a key fitting perfectly into a lock. The endorphin molecule then activates a series of chemical changes that, among other effects, reduces pain signals occurring in the brain. For his part in this discovery, Snyder was awarded the Albert Lasker Award for Basic Medical Research in 1978. That award is often regarded as the second most prestigious award in the biological sciences after the Nobel Prize in medicine or physiology.

Solomon Halbert Snyder was born on December 26, 1938, in Washington, D.C. His father was employed at what was then a small governmental agency that later became the National Security Agency. In his autobiographical sketch for the book *The History of Neuroscience in Autobiography* (Larry R. Squire, Oxford University Press, 1996), Snyder notes that his father held high regard for science and regarded it as "the highest activity of mankind." His mother, whom he described as "complex," opened her own real estate company that eventually employed 15 agents.

Snyder attended Calvin Coolidge High School, in Washington, D.C., from which he graduated in 1955. He then attended Georgetown College, in Washington, for three years, prior to entering the Georgetown Medical School in 1958. (At the time, a bachelor's degree was not needed to enter medical school.) He was awarded his MD, cum laude, from Georgetown in 1962. Following graduation, Snyder worked as an intern at the Kaiser Foundation Hospital in San Francisco, from 1962 to 1963, as a research associate at the National Institute of Mental Health from 1963 to 1965, and as an assistant resident in the Department of Psychiatry at the Johns Hopkins Hospital in Baltimore from 1965 to 1968. In 1968, Snyder continued his long association with the Johns Hopkins Hospital by accepting an appointment as assistant professor of pharmacology and experimental therapeutics at the hospital. He was then promoted to full professor in 1970 and, in 1980, was named distinguished service professor of pharmacology and psychiatry at Johns Hopkins. From 1980 to 2006, Snyder also served as director of the hospital's Department of Neuroscience.

Snyder's work has been recognized by a host of honors and awards that include honorary doctorates from Northwestern

University; Georgetown University; Ben Gurion University, Israel; Albany Medical College; Technion University, Israel; Mount Sinai Medical School; University of Maryland; Charles University, Prague; and Ohio State University. He has also been invited to give honorary lectures at nearly 100 universities such as the universities of Wisconsin, Michigan, California at Davis, Yale, Minnesota, Duke, Harvard, and Pittsburgh. In addition to the Lasker Award, he has received nearly four dozen awards and prizes that include the 1983 Wolf Prize in medicine of the Wolf Foundation, Israel; 1992 Bower Award, from the Franklin Institute; 2005 National Medal of Science and 2007 Albany Prize in Medicine; 2013 U.S. National Academy of Science Award in Neuroscience; 1970 John Jacob Abel Award of the American Society for Pharmacology and Experimental Therapeutics; 1970 A.E. Bennett Award of the Society for Biological Psychiatry; 1972 Hofheimer Award of the American Psychiatric Association; 1974 Daniel H. Efron Award of the American College of Neuropsychopharmacology; 1979 Anna Monica Award in Biological Psychiatry; 1980 Goodman and Gilman Award of the American Society for Pharmacology and Experimental Therapeutics; 1984 Einstein Award for Research in Psychiatry and Related Disciplines of the Albert Einstein College of Medicine of Yeshiva University; 1985 Ciba-Geigy Drew Award in Biomedical Research; 1990 Vittorio Erspamer Award of the FIDIA Research Foundation; 1991 Pasarow Foundation Award for Biomedical Research; 1995 Baxter Award of the American Association of Medical Colleges; 1996 Bristol-Myers Squibb Award for Distinguished Achievement in Neuroscience Research; 2000 Society for Biomolecular Screening Achievement Award; 2001 Lieber Prize of the National Alliance for Research on Schizophrenia and Depression; 2001 Salmon Prize of the New York Academy of Medicine; 2002 Goldman-Rakic Award of the National Alliance for Research on Schizophrenia and Depression; and the 2005 Julius Axelrod Mentorship Award of the American College of Neuropsychopharmacology. Snyder has also been active outside the field of research serving as secretary, vice president, and president of the Beth Am Synagogue, on various committees of the Baltimore Symphony Orchestra, and on the board of directors of Nova Pharmaceuticals, Guildord Pharmaceuticals, Scios, the Shriver Hall Concert Series, and the Peabody Conservatory. In 2006, Johns Hopkins Department of Neurosciences, which Snyder founded in 1980, was renamed in his honor as The Solomon H. Snyder Department of Neuroscience.

## Substance Abuse and Mental Health Services Administration

The Substance Abuse and Mental Health Services Administration (SAMHSA) was created in 1992 during the reorganization of the federal government's agencies responsible for mental health services. It assumed most of the responsibilities of the Alcohol, Drug Abuse, and Mental Health Administration, which was disbanded in the reorganization. The organization is charged with developing and supporting programs that improve the quality and availability of prevention, treatment, and rehabilitation for abusers of both legal and illegal drugs. As of 2018, it had more than 600 employees and a budget of about $3.7 billion. Its headquarters is in Rockville, Maryland, and it maintains four primary research centers there, the Center for Behavioral Health Statistics and Quality, Center for Mental Health Services, Center for Substance Abuse Prevention, and Center for Substance Abuse Treatment.

From time to time, SAMHSA selects a small number of strategic initiatives on which it focuses its efforts over a specific and limited period of time. Currently, those initiatives are as follows:

- Prevention of substance abuse and mental health, the current form of an ongoing effort to make use of existing research knowledge to reduce the risk of substance abuse and mental health among Americans, especially high-risk populations of transition-age youth; college students; American Indian/ Alaska Natives; ethnic minorities experiencing health and behavioral health disparities; service members, veterans, and their families; and lesbian, gay, bisexual, and transgender individuals

- Health care and health systems integration, designed to make the best therapies available to all individuals in the areas of both substance abuse and mental health
- Trauma and justice, an effort to increase the availability of mental health and substance abuse services to individuals in the criminal justice and juvenile justice systems
- Recovery support, which focuses on providing assistance to individuals who are in recovery from both mental health and substance abuse disorders
- Health information technology, designed to promote the use of existing technology, such as electronic health records, to transform the fundamental nature of behavioral health care
- Workforce development, an effort to train more workers in methods for using modern technology to address the behavioral health needs of the nation

More detailed information about these initiatives is available at https://www.samhsa.gov/about-us/strategic-initiatives.

In addition to its specialized strategic initiatives, SAMHSA maintains a large number of ongoing programs and campaigns on specific issues within the areas of substance abuse and mental health. Some of these topics are Behavioral Health Equity, the Buprenorphine Information Center, the Center for Application of Prevention Technologies, National Prevention Week, the Partners for Recovery Initiative, the Recovery to Practice program, the Safe Schools/Healthy Students Initiative, the Disaster Technical Assistance Center, the Division of Workplace Programs, the Fetal Alcohol Spectrum Disorders Center, the Homelessness Resource Center, the SAMHSA Knowledge

Applications Project, and the Tribal Training and Technical Assistance Center.

SAMHSA website is one of the best resources for information on virtually all aspects of substance abuse. This information is organized under about two dozen rubrics, including alcohol, tobacco, and other drugs; behavioral health treatments and services; criminal and juvenile justice; data, outcomes, and quality; disaster preparedness, response, and recovery; health care and health systems integration; health disparities; health financing; health information technology; HIV, AIDS, and viral hepatitis; homelessness and housing; laws, regulations, and guidelines; mental and substance use disorders; prescription drug misuse and abuse; prevention of substance abuse and mental illness; recovery and recovery support; school and campus health; specific populations; state and local government partnerships; suicide prevention; trauma and violence; tribal affairs; underage drinking; veterans and military families; wellness; and workforce. A list of relevant articles and web pages on the current opioid crisis is available at https://search.samhsa .gov/search?q=opioids&sort=date%3AD%3AL%3Ad1&out put=xml_no_dtd&ie=UTF-8&oe=UTF-8&client=beta_fron tend_drupal&proxystylesheet=beta_frontend_drupal&filter= 1&site=data%7CSAMHSA_Beta_Drupal%7Cdefault_colle ction%7CNewsletter&collectionator=data%7CSAMHSA_ Beta_Drupal%7Cdefault_collection%7CNewsletter.

## Thomas Sydenham (1624–1689)

Sydenham was an English physician, sometimes known as "the English Hippocrates" because of his profound influence on the development of modern medicine in that country. He remains well known today because of one of his inventions, commonly known as *Sydenham's laudanum*. Although laudanum had been prepared and used prior to Sydenham's invention, he is thought to be the individual most responsible for its rapid growth in popularity and widespread use as a painkiller in the

17th and succeeding centuries. He expressed his views on the virtues of his laudanum on a number of occasions. He once wrote, for example, that "none of us [the medical profession] would be calloused enough to practise our profession without it" (Hamilton and Baskett 2000). The drug was available in the United States and other developed nations even into the 20th century. The recipe Sydenham provided for his laudanum, as published in a 1669 work on dysentery, called for "1 pound sherry wine, 2 ounces opium, 1 ounce saffron, 1 ounce powder of cinnamon, and 1 ounce powder of cloves" (Stefano et al. 2017). Sydenham praised the value of his invention, saying that "I cannot but break out in praise of God, the giver of all good things, who hath granted to the human race, as a comfort in their afflictions, no medicine of the value of opium, either in regard to the number of diseases it can control, or the efficiency in extirpating them" (Reynolds 1871).

Thomas Sydenham was born on September 10, 1624, at Wynford Eagle in Dorsetshire, England. He grew up in a well-to-do family whose status dated back to the days of Henry VIII. Little information is available on Sydenham's early life, although one biographer has speculated that he without doubt had followed a "regular pattern of field sports, schooling, and religious devotion" (Dewhurst 1966). He and his siblings were probably home-schooled by a tutor before attending the Dorchester Grammar School, where they obtained the background needed for further education at a prestigious college, such as Oxford. Indeed, at the age of 18, Sydenham entered Magdalen College, Oxford University, although he was to remain there for only a short period of time. When a civil war broke out between supporters of King Charles I and the British parliament, Sydenham enlisted on the side of the latter. He is reputed to have survived wounds gained in battle, in one case being left on the field for dead.

At the conclusion of the war, Sydenham returned to Oxford, where he began his medical studies. He obtained his degree in just over a year through an unusual procedure then known as a

Pembrokian Creation, named after the Earl of Pembroke who first introduced the idea. The war had created a shortage of eligible students for the university, and it (and much of the country) was still disorganized by the event. As a way of helping to solve these problems, certain particularly loyal students at the college were granted their degree by a vote of the fellows. As a result, on April 14, 1648, Sydenham was awarded his bachelor of medicine degree and named a fellow at All Saints College, Oxford. He did not actually complete a course of medical studies until 30 years later, at that point from Pembroke Hall, Cambridge. (In a bit of irony, one of his sons was also studying medicine at Pembroke at the time.)

Sydenham continued in his position at All Souls until 1655, when he resigned his appointment to continue his medical practice. According to some reports, he spent a year (1659) at Montpelier University in France, although the evidence for this event is weak. In 1659, Sydenham stood for a seat in Parliament, but was not chosen for the post. Instead, he received an appointment as comptroller of the pipe, an office having no connection with medicine but, instead, being responsible for the collection of rents and leases on royal lands.

In 1663, Sydenham passed the examinations required for a license to practice medicine in the City of London (Central London) and the whole region seven miles around. During his years of practice, Sydenham developed an approach to medicine that had not been seen since the time of Hippocrates, namely a focus on careful direct observation of a patient's condition, rather than adopting some theoretical position about the causes of disease. He collected his views on this approach in his most famous book, *Observationes Medicae* (*Observations on Medicine*), published in 1676. The book was an expanded version of two earlier editions, *Methodus curandi febres* (*The Method of Curing Fevers*), published in 1666, and an expanded version of that text that included a chapter on the plague in 1668. *Observationes* contains chapters on a host of medical conditions, including gout, fever, smallpox measles, scarlet fever, whooping cough, plague, and epidemics. His views on the use of laudanum to treat a variety of medical conditions are also included in the text.

Sydenham died at his home at Pall Mall, London, on December 29, 1689.

## Charles E. Terry (1878–1945)

Terry is perhaps best known for his monumental work on opium, *The Opium Problem*, which he wrote in 1928 with his then associate executive, Mildred Pellens, who was later to become his third wife. Terry was one of the most outspoken advocates of his time for the position that drug addiction was primarily a medical problem, rather than a crime, a philosophy that put him largely at odds with many physicians, law enforcement officers, government officials, and others of the period.

Charles Edward Terry was born in Hartford, Connecticut, on February 14, 1878. His family moved to Florida while he was still a young boy in hopes that warmer weather there would aid in his father's recovery from tuberculosis. When the move failed to achieve that result, his father died of the disease, an event that motivated Terry to consider becoming a physician so that he could contribute to the solution of medical problems such as the one that disrupted his own family's life. He enrolled at the University of Maryland Medical School in 1899, from which he earned his medical degree in 1903. He then returned to Florida, where he joined his brother-in-law in private practice in Jacksonville. In 1910 he was elected president of the Duval County Medical Society and, in the same year, was invited to become the city's first full-time medical officer, a post he held until 1917.

During his tenure as medical officer in Jacksonville, Terry instituted a number of progressive policies concerning the city's drug abuse and addiction problems. For example, he established a drug clinic at which drug addicts could receive free prescriptions for the narcotic drugs they needed, largely in hopes of weaning them off their addiction. The clinic was, in a way, a forerunner of modern methadone clinics that also aim to wean users away from heroin or other opioids by offering them treatment with a milder narcotic, methadone.

Terry also introduced the concept of multiple prescription copies, an early form of the duplicate and triplicate prescription forms that later became routine in most parts of the country. This practice allowed Terry to track physicians and pharmacists who wrote and filled prescriptions for larger quantities of drugs than would normally be required for medical purposes. Possession of such large quantities of a drug by an individual became a misdemeanor, but the city health office was allowed to contact anyone accused of such an act in order to offer them access to the health department drug clinic and its services.

Beyond his work with drug addiction, Terry introduced a number of other reforms in the city health program, including a more aggressive program of smallpox vaccinations, a rat-eradication project, improvements in the city's sewage disposal system, and creation of midwifery and visiting nurse programs.

Terry was also active in public health issues on a national level, which led to his election in 1914 as president of the American Public Health Association (APHA). He also served as chair of the APHA Committee on Habit-Forming Drugs, where he continued to push for a greater acceptance among professionals for the concept of drug addiction as a medical problem and a more compassionate philosophy for dealing with those addicted to drugs.

In 1917, Terry left the Jacksonville health department to become medical editor of *The Delineator*, a woman's magazine that claimed to be "A Journal of Fashion, Culture, and Fine Arts." Four years later, he left Florida to accept a position as executive secretary of the newly formed Committee on Drug Addictions of the Bureau of Social Hygiene in New York, an organization funded by a wealthy group of philanthropists that included John D. Rockefeller Jr. and Paul Warburg. One of the first problems with which Terry had to deal on the committee was the lack of a common understanding as to exactly what the nature of drug addiction was. As a consequence, the committee decided to conduct a comprehensive study on the nature of opium addiction, a study to be led by Terry, assisted by Pellens. The study continued for a number of years, resulting in a report of more than 1,000 pages covering topics such as the development and extent of the problem, its etiology and general nature, its pathology and symptomatology, the nature of users, and national and international laws and regulations about opium use and trafficking. Seldom in the history of drug studies has a research project dealt with such a comprehensive range of topics in so much detail.

As the Terry–Peller study was being completed, a debate was going on within the Committee on Drug Addictions between those who saw addiction as a medical problem and those who viewed it as an issue of crime and punishment. Over time it was the latter view that became predominant, and Terry eventually decided that he could no longer continue his work on the committee. After completing a survey in Detroit that he was conducting in the early 1930s, Terry resigned from the committee and accepted a position at the Harlem Valley Hospital, in Dover, New York, where he remained until his death in 1945. After leaving the Committee on Drug Addictions, he was never again involved in the field of drug addiction.

### Hamilton Wright (1867–1917)

Wright has been described as the father of drug laws in the United States because of his strong objections to the use of illegal drugs and his vigorous efforts to have laws passed against the manufacture, transport, sale, and consumption of illegal substances. Although he was not a member of Congress at the time, he is generally regarded as the author of the Harrison Narcotics Tax Act of 1914, which instituted taxes on opiates for the first time in U.S. history.

Hamilton Wright was born in Cleveland, Ohio, on August 2, 1867. After graduating from high school in Boston, he enlisted in the U.S. Army, where he served in the 7th Fusiliers in the Reale Rebellion, earning a medal for his valor during the war. He then attended McGill University, in Montreal, Canada, from which he received his MD in 1895. From 1895 to 1908, he was engaged in a variety of research projects at a number of sites around the world, studying tropical diseases such as beri-beri, plague, and malaria. His work took him to China, Japan, Malaya, Great Britain, Germany, and France. In 1908, President Teddy Roosevelt appointed Wright the nation's first commissioner on international opium, a capacity in which he represented the United States at the International Opium Conference held at The Hague, the Netherlands, in 1911. He spent the rest of his life campaigning against opium use in the United States, which, as he wrote in a 1911 article for *The New York Times*, had the highest proportion of opium users of any country in the world.

Wright is known today for his willingness to use inflammatory, often inaccurate statements about the dangers posed by opium. He was especially critical of blacks and Chinese Americans for their use of the drug, suggesting at one point that "one of the most unfortunate phases of the habit of smoking opium in this country is the large number of women who have become involved and are living as common law wives or cohabiting with Chinese in the Chinatowns of our various cities" ("Chapter 3: Long Day's Journey into the Night" 2018). He also railed against cocaine use, suggesting at one time that "cocaine is often the direct incentive to the crime of rape by the Negroes of the South and other sections of the country."

Wright was very successful in pushing his anti-opium agenda both domestically and internationally. His greatest achievement at home was adoption of the Harrison Act in 1914 and overseas was adoption of the International Opium Convention in 1912. In both cases, Wright had pushed for even broader, more comprehensive control over drugs other than opium, especially marijuana, but without success. Wright died at his home in Washington, D.C., on January 9, 1917, as a result of complications resulting from an automobile accident in France two years earlier. He was assisting in U.S. relief efforts in that country following the conclusion of World War II.

## References

"About Us." 2018. The HERO Foundation. http://thehero foundation.org/about.php. Accessed on March 20, 2018.

"Academy of Integrative Pain Medicine." 2015. YouTube. https://www.youtube.com/channel/UCBh9l9pQ_ s1Icy0m5ZPtgyg/about?disable_polymer=1. Accessed on March 20, 2018.

"Authorizing Legislation." 2018. Office of National Drug Control Policy. https://www.whitehousedrugpolicy.org/ about/authorizing_legislation.html. Accessed on March 20, 2018.

Center for Lawful Access and Abuse Deterrence (CLAAD)). 2018. The Pain Community. https://paincommunity.org/ resources/center-for-lawful-access-and-abuse-deterence- claad/. Accessed on March 20, 2018.

"Chapter 3: Long Day's Journey into the Night." 2018. Libertary. http://www.libertary.com/books/chapter-3-long- days-journey-into-night/. Accessed on March 20, 2018.

Dewhurst, Kenneth. 1966. *Dr. Thomas Sydenham (1624–1689): His Life and Original Writings*. Berkeley: University of California Press, 4. https://wellcomelibrary.org/item/ b20086313#?c=0&m=0&s=0&cv=19&z=-1.2109%2C- 0.0809%2C3.4218%2C1.6175. Accessed on March 20, 2018.

Hamilton, Gillian R., and Thomas F. Baskett. 2000. *Canadian Journal of Anesthesiology*. 47(4): 372. https://link.springer .com/content/pdf/10.1007%2FBF03020955.pdf. Accessed on March 20, 2018.

"The John Scott Award." 2018. http://www.garfield.library. upenn.edu/johnscottaward.html. Accessed on March 20, 2018.

"Office of National Drug Control Policy Mission. "2017. https://www.whitehouse.gov/ondcp/presidents-commission/ mission/. Accessed on March 20, 2018.

"Our Mission." 2018. Advocates for Opioid Recovery. https:// www.opioidrecovery.org/mission/. Accessed on March 20, 2018.

Reynolds, Sir John Russell. 1871. *A System of Medicine*, 147. https://ia801300.us.archive.org/19/items/b20415126_003/ b20415126_003.pdf. Accessed on March 20, 2018.

Stefano, Geroge B., et al. 2017. "Reciprocal Evolution of Opiate Science from Medical and Cultural Perspectives." *Medical Science Monitor.* https://www.ncbi.nlm.nih.gov/ pmc/articles/PMC5478244/. Accessed on March 20, 2018.

# 5 Data and Documents

One way of having a better understanding of the current opioid epidemic is by examining data and documents relating to that issue. The data provided here all come from federal reporting agencies, such as the National Vital Statistics System and the National Center for Health Statistics. The documents included here are all excerpts from national and state laws, court cases dealing with opioids, and reports on the opioid epidemic.

## Data

Data on opioids provided in this chapter may differ from table to table depending on the definition used for the term. In some cases, the term is used to describe all types of opioids, from natural to semisynthetic to synthetic. In other cases, one or more specific opioids are treated separately, with totals for "opioids" excluding data for those specific opioids. The most common opioids receiving separate attention are methadone, heroin, and fentanyl. For more detailed information on the precise opioids listed in each table, see the original source for the data, listed at the end of each table.

Massachusetts attorney general Maura Healey holds a CVS prescription bottle as she announces, in a first-in-the-nation settlement, that CVS Pharmacy will strengthen its policies and procedures around the dispensing of opioids. (John Tlumacki/The Boston Globe via Getty Images)

Table 5.1 Misuse of Opioids in Past Year and Past Month among Persons Aged 12 or Older, by Detailed Age Category: Numbers in Thousands and Percentages, 2015 and 2016

| Age | Past Year | | | | Past Month | | | |
|---|---|---|---|---|---|---|---|---|
| | 2015 | | 2016 | | 2015 | | 2016 | |
| | Numbers in Thousands | Percentage | Numbers in Thousands | Percentage | Numbers in Thousands | Percentage | Numbers in Thousands | Percentage |
| Total | 12,693 | 4.7 | 11,824 | 4.4 | 3,963 | 1.5 | 3,649 | 1.4 |
| 12–17 | 980 | 3.9 | 891 | 3.6 | 277 | 1.1 | 241 | 1.0 |
| 12 | 66 | 1.7 | 49 | 1.3 | 29 | 0.8 | 20 | 0.5 |
| 13 | 83 | 2.1 | 81 | 2.0 | 34 | 0.9 | 30 | 0.7 |
| 14 | 138 | 3.2 | 112 | 2.7 | 45 | 1.0 | 24 | 0.6 |
| 15 | 169 | 3.9 | 193 | 4.4 | 40 | 0.9 | 53 | 1.2 |
| 16 | 236 | 5.6 | 201 | 4.7 | 60 | 1.4 | 61 | 1.4 |
| 17 | 289 | 6.9 | 255 | 6.1 | 68 | 1.6 | 54 | 1.3 |
| 18 or older | 11,712 | 4.8 | 10,933 | 4.5 | 3,686 | 1.5 | 3,408 | 1.4 |
| 18–25 | 3,029 | 8.7 | 2,516 | 7.3 | 880 | 2.5 | 688 | 2.0 |
| 18 | 293 | 6.4 | 263 | 5.8 | 72 | 1.6 | 76 | 1.7 |
| 19 | 349 | 8.2 | 279 | 7.1 | 79 | 1.9 | 72 | 1.8 |
| 20 | 325 | 7.8 | 309 | 7.3 | 92 | 2.2 | 80 | 1.9 |
| 21 | 413 | 10.0 | 346 | 8.0 | 116 | 2.8 | 100 | 2.3 |

| | | | | | | | | |
|---|---|---|---|---|---|---|---|---|
| 22 | 393 | 9.2 | 315 | 7.4 | 104 | 2.4 | 98 | 2.3 |
| 23 | 413 | 9.2 | 297 | 6.6 | 150 | 3.3 | 86 | 1.9 |
| 24 | 421 | 9.4 | 373 | 8.6 | 158 | 3.5 | 97 | 2.2 |
| 25 | 423 | 9.3 | 333 | 7.5 | 111 | 2.4 | 80 | 1.8 |
| 26 or older | 8,683 | 4.2 | 8,417 | 4.0 | 2,806 | 1.3 | 2,720 | 1.3 |
| 26–29 | 1,434 | 8.4 | 1,329 | 7.6 | 424 | 2.5 | 380 | 2.2 |
| 30–34 | 1,452 | 6.9 | 1,450 | 6.8 | 450 | 2.1 | 448 | 2.1 |
| 35–39 | 1,089 | 5.6 | 1,132 | 5.5 | 326 | 1.7 | 367 | 1.8 |
| 40–44 | 989 | 4.9 | 865 | 4.4 | 354 | 1.8 | 299 | 1.5 |
| 45–49 | 951 | 4.6 | 769 | 3.8 | 390 | 1.9 | 264 | 1.3 |
| 50–54 | 910 | 4.0 | 975 | 4.5 | 315 | 1.4 | 353 | 1.6 |
| 55–59 | 816 | 3.9 | 880 | 4.0 | 246 | 1.2 | 287 | 1.3 |
| 60–64 | 434 | 2.3 | 437 | 2.3 | 182 | 1.0 | 146 | 0.8 |
| 65 or older | 609 | 1.3 | 577 | 1.2 | 119 | 0.3 | 176 | 0.4 |

*Note*: Opioid misuse refers to the use of heroin or the misuse of prescription pain relievers. Misuse of prescription pain relievers is defined as use in any way not directed by a doctor, including use without a prescription of one's own; use in greater amounts, more often, or longer than told; or use in any other way not directed by a doctor.

*Source*: "Results from the 2016 National Survey on Drug Use and Health: Detailed Tables." 2017. Substance Abuse and Mental Health Services Administration. Center for Behavioral Health Statistics and Quality, Tables 1.27A and 1.27B. https://www.samhsa.gov/data/sites/default/files/NSDUH-DetTabs-2016/NSDUH-DetTabs-2016.pdf.

Table 5.2 Any Use of Pain Relievers in Past Year and Misuse of Pain Relievers in Past Year and Past Month among Persons Aged 12 or Older, by Detailed Age Category: Numbers in Thousands and Percentages, 2015 and 2016

| Age | Any Use in Past Year | | | | Misuse in Past Year | | | | Misuse in Past Month | | | |
|---|---|---|---|---|---|---|---|---|---|---|---|---|
| | 2015 | | 2016 | | 2015 | | 2016 | | 2015 | | 2016 | |
| | Numbers in Thousands | Percentage | Numbers in Thousands | Percentage | Numbers in Thousands | Percentage | Numbers in Thousands | Percentage | Numbers in Thousands | Percentage | Numbers in Thousands | Percentage |
| Total | 97,499 | 36.4 | 91,846 | 34.1 | 12,462 | 4.7 | 11,517 | 4.3 | 3,775 | 1.4 | 3,350 | 1.2 |
| 12–17 | 5,650 | 22.7 | 4,732 | 19.0 | 969 | 3.9 | 881 | 3.5 | 276 | 1.1 | 239 | 1.0 |
| 12 | 521 | 13.5 | 456 | 12.2 | 66 | 1.7 | 49 | 1.3 | 29 | 0.8 | 20 | 0.5 |
| 13 | 740 | 18.5 | 588 | 14.4 | 83 | 2.1 | 78 | 1.9 | 34 | 0.9 | 30 | 0.7 |
| 14 | 904 | 20.9 | 710 | 17.0 | 138 | 3.2 | 111 | 2.7 | 45 | 1.0 | 24 | 0.6 |
| 15 | 1,053 | 24.4 | 901 | 20.3 | 166 | 3.8 | 192 | 4.3 | 40 | 0.9 | 52 | 1.2 |
| 16 | 1,155 | 27.3 | 960 | 22.4 | 235 | 5.6 | 196 | 4.6 | 60 | 1.4 | 59 | 1.4 |
| 17 | 1,277 | 30.7 | 1,116 | 26.8 | 281 | 6.8 | 255 | 6.1 | 67 | 1.6 | 54 | 1.3 |
| 18 or older | 91,848 | 37.8 | 87,114 | 35.6 | 11,492 | 4.7 | 10,635 | 4.3 | 3,499 | 1.4 | 3,111 | 1.3 |
| 18–25 | 12,148 | 34.8 | 10,407 | 30.1 | 2,979 | 8.5 | 2,454 | 7.1 | 829 | 2.4 | 631 | 1.8 |
| 18 | 1,487 | 32.6 | 1,176 | 25.7 | 287 | 6.3 | 259 | 5.7 | 71 | 1.6 | 69 | 1.5 |
| 19 | 1,516 | 35.6 | 1,092 | 27.7 | 348 | 8.2 | 272 | 6.9 | 77 | 1.8 | 64 | 1.6 |
| 20 | 1,292 | 31.0 | 1,195 | 28.4 | 319 | 7.6 | 303 | 7.2 | 87 | 2.1 | 80 | 1.9 |
| 21 | 1,466 | 35.5 | 1,251 | 28.9 | 413 | 10.0 | 341 | 7.9 | 116 | 2.8 | 92 | 2.1 |

| | | | | | | | | | | | | |
|---|---|---|---|---|---|---|---|---|---|---|---|---|
| 22 | 1,471 | 34.5 | 1,289 | 30.2 | 385 | 9.0 | 301 | 7.1 | 98 | 2.3 | 92 | 2.2 |
| 23 | 1,647 | 36.8 | 1,417 | 31.6 | 413 | 9.2 | 281 | 6.3 | 150 | 3.3 | 74 | 1.7 |
| 24 | 1,594 | 35.5 | 1,506 | 34.8 | 399 | 8.9 | 369 | 8.5 | 126 | 2.8 | 89 | 2.1 |
| 25 | 1,674 | 36.7 | 1,481 | 33.2 | 415 | 9.1 | 327 | 7.3 | 104 | 2.3 | 70 | 1.6 |
| 26 or older | 79,701 | 38.3 | 76,706 | 36.5 | 8,513 | 4.1 | 8,181 | 3.9 | 2,670 | 1.3 | 2,480 | 1.2 |
| 26–29 | 6,412 | 37.4 | 5,731 | 32.9 | 1,405 | 8.2 | 1,301 | 7.5 | 411 | 2.4 | 341 | 2.0 |
| 30–34 | 7,974 | 37.6 | 7,781 | 36.4 | 1,412 | 6.7 | 1,370 | 6.4 | 409 | 1.9 | 388 | 1.8 |
| 35–39 | 7,245 | 37.2 | 7,612 | 37.0 | 1,065 | 5.5 | 1,100 | 5.3 | 298 | 1.5 | 339 | 1.6 |
| 40–44 | 7,120 | 35.5 | 7,015 | 35.9 | 979 | 4.9 | 842 | 4.3 | 341 | 1.7 | 271 | 1.4 |
| 45–49 | 7,803 | 37.6 | 7,297 | 36.1 | 941 | 4.5 | 756 | 3.7 | 387 | 1.9 | 247 | 1.2 |
| 50–54 | 9,087 | 39.5 | 8,327 | 38.1 | 874 | 3.8 | 967 | 4.4 | 281 | 1.2 | 345 | 1.6 |
| 55–59 | 8,544 | 40.5 | 8,942 | 40.9 | 793 | 3.8 | 841 | 3.8 | 242 | 1.1 | 229 | 1.0 |
| 60–64 | 7,530 | 40.4 | 7,089 | 37.0 | 434 | 2.3 | 427 | 2.2 | 182 | 1.0 | 145 | 0.8 |
| 65 or older | 17,984 | 38.7 | 16,912 | 35.2 | 609 | 1.3 | 577 | 1.2 | 119 | 0.3 | 176 | 0.4 |

*Source:* "Results from the 2016 National Survey on Drug Use and Health: Detailed Tables." 2017. Substance Abuse and Mental Health Services Administration. Center for Behavioral Health Statistics and Quality, Tables 1.23A and 1.23B. https://www.samhsa.gov/data/sites/default/files/NSDUH-DetTabs-2016/NSDUH-DetTabs-2016.pdf.

**Table 5.3   Drug-Poisoning Deaths Involving Opioid Analgesics: United States, 1999–2015**

| Year | Drug Poisoning | | Opioid-Analgesic Poisoning | |
|------|--------|--------------------|--------|--------------------|
|      | Number | Deaths per 100,000 | Number | Deaths per 100,000 |
| 1999 | 16,849 | 6.1  | 4,030  | 1.4  |
| 2000 | 17,415 | 6.2  | 4,400  | 1.5  |
| 2001 | 19,394 | 6.8  | 5,528  | 1.9  |
| 2002 | 23,518 | 8.2  | 7,456  | 2.6  |
| 2003 | 25,785 | 8.9  | 8,517  | 2.9  |
| 2004 | 27,424 | 9.4  | 9,857  | 3.4  |
| 2005 | 29,813 | 10.1 | 10,928 | 3.7  |
| 2006 | 34,425 | 11.5 | 13,723 | 4.6  |
| 2007 | 36,010 | 11.9 | 14,408 | 4.8  |
| 2008 | 36,450 | 11.9 | 14,800 | 4.8  |
| 2009 | 37,004 | 11.9 | 15,597 | 5.0  |
| 2010 | 38,329 | 12.3 | 16,651 | 5.4  |
| 2011 | 41,340 | 13.2 | 16,917 | 5.4  |
| 2012 | 41,502 | 13.1 | 16,007 | 5.1  |
| 2013 | 43,982 | 13.8 | 16,235 | 7.9  |
| 2014 | 47,055 | 14.7 | 16,118 | 9.0  |
| 2015 | 52,404 | 16.3 | 20,101 | 10.4 |

*Sources*: "Data Brief 166: Drug-Poisoning Deaths Involving Opioid Analgesics: United States, 1999–2011." https://www.cdc.gov/nchs/data/databriefs/db166_table.pdf#1. https://www.cdc.gov/nchs/data/databriefs/db273_table.pdf. Accessed on November 9, 2017; Rudd, Rose A., et al. 2016. "Increases in Drug and Opioid Overdose Deaths—United States, 2000–2015." *Morbidity and Mortality Weekly*. 65(50–51): 1445–1452. https://www.cdc.gov/mmwr/volumes/65/wr/mm655051e1.htm. Accessed on November 9, 2017.

Table 5.4 Deaths from Opioid Overdose, 2015

| Characteristic | Synthetic Opioids Other Than Methadone | | | Heroin | | | Total | |
|---|---|---|---|---|---|---|---|---|
| | 2014 | 2015 | Percentage Change 2014/2015 | 2014 | 2015 | Percentage Change 2014/2015 | 2014 | 2015 |
| Overall | 5,544 | 9,580 | 72.2 | 10,574 | 12,989 | 20.6 | 16,118 | 22,569 |
| **Sex** | | | | | | | | |
| Male | 3,465 | 6,560 | 90.9 | 8,160 | 9,881 | 21.2 | 11,625 | 16,441 |
| Female | 2,079 | 3,020 | 46.2 | 2,414 | 3,108 | 25.0 | 4,493 | 6,128 |
| **Age Group (years)** | | | | | | | | |
| 0–14 | 10* | 14* | – | ** | ** | – | ** | ** |
| 15–24 | 514 | 999 | 91.7 | 1,452 | 1,649 | 15.2 | 1,966 | 2,648 |
| 25–34 | 1,474 | 2,896 | 94.1 | 3,493 | 4,292 | 21.3 | 4,967 | 7,188 |
| 35–44 | 1,264 | 2,289 | 80.6 | 2,398 | 3,012 | 25.4 | 3,662 | 5,301 |
| 45–54 | 1,359 | 1,982 | 48.4 | 2,030 | 2,439 | 19.1 | 3,389 | 4,421 |
| 55–64 | 742 | 1,167 | 52.6 | 1,064 | 1,407 | 25.9 | 1,806 | 2,574 |
| ≥65 | 181 | 232 | 25.0 | 136 | 184 | 33.3 | 317 | 416 |

(continued)

Table 5.4 *(continued)*

| Characteristic | Synthetic Opioids Other Than Methadone | | Percentage Change 2014/2015 | Heroin | | Percentage Change 2014/2015 | Total | |
|---|---|---|---|---|---|---|---|---|
| | 2014 | 2015 | | 2014 | 2015 | | 2014 | 2015 |
| **Sex/Age Group** | | | | | | | | |
| **Male** | | | | | | | | |
| 15–24 | 376 | 718 | 88.2 | 1,079 | 1,172 | 8.3 | 1,455 | 1,890 |
| 25–44 | 1,845 | 3,764 | 102.3 | 4,566 | 5,602 | 22.2 | 6,411 | 9,366 |
| 45–64 | 1,176 | 1,948 | 65.5 | 2,397 | 2,953 | 22.0 | 3,573 | 4,901 |
| **Female** | | | | | | | | |
| 15–24 | 138 | 281 | 116.7 | 373 | 477 | 29.4 | 511 | 758 |
| 25–44 | 893 | 1,421 | 61.9 | 1,325 | 1,702 | 25.0 | 2,218 | 3,123 |
| 45–64 | 925 | 1,201 | 27.3 | 697 | 893 | 31.3 | 1,622 | 2,094 |
| **Race/Ethnicity** | | | | | | | | |
| White, non-Hispanic | 4,685 | 7,995 | 75.0 | 8,253 | 10,050 | 22.7 | 12,938 | 18,045 |
| Black, non-Hispanic | 449 | 883 | 90.9 | 1,044 | 1,310 | 24.0 | 1,493 | 2,193 |
| Hispanic | 302 | 524 | 50.0 | 1,049 | 1,299 | 21.1 | 1,351 | 1,823 |

* Estimate.

** No data.

*Source:* Rudd, Rose A., et al. "Increases in Drug and Opioid-Involved Overdose Deaths—United States, 2010–2015." *Morbidity and Mortality Weekly.* 65(50–51): 1445–1452, Table 2. https://www.cdc.gov/mmwr/volumes/65/wr/mm655051e1.htm. Accessed on November 10, 2017.

Table 5.5 Death Rates from Heroin and Opioid Analgesic Poisoning, 2000–2015

| Year | Opioid Analgesics | | Heroin | |
|------|--------|-------------------|--------|-------------------|
| | Deaths | Deaths per 100,000 | Deaths | Deaths per 100,000 |
| 2000 | 4,400 | 1.5 | 1,842 | 0.7 |
| 2001 | 5,528 | 1.9 | 1,779 | 0.6 |
| 2002 | 7,456 | 2.6 | 2,089 | 0.7 |
| 2003 | 8,517 | 2.9 | 2,080 | 0.7 |
| 2004 | 9,857 | 3.4 | 1,878 | 0.6 |
| 2005 | 10,928 | 3.7 | 2,009 | 0.7 |
| 2006 | 13,723 | 4.6 | 2,088 | 0.7 |
| 2007 | 14,408 | 4.8 | 2,399 | 0.8 |
| 2008 | 14,800 | 4.8 | 3,041 | 1.0 |
| 2009 | 15,597 | 5.0 | 3,278 | 1.1 |
| 2010 | 16,651 | 5.4 | 3,036 | 1.0 |
| 2011 | 16,917 | 5.4 | 4,397 | 1.4 |
| 2012 | 16,007 | 5.1 | 5,925 | 1.9 |
| 2013 | 16,235 | 5.1 | 8,257 | 2.7 |
| 2014 | 18,893 | 5.9 | 10,574 | 3.4 |
| 2015 | 22,598 | 7.0 | 12,989 | 4.1 |

*Sources*: "Drug-Poisoning Deaths Involving Heroin: United States, 2000–2013." https://www.cdc.gov/nchs/data/databriefs/db190_table.pdf#1. Accessed on November 10, 2017; "National Overdose Deaths from Select Prescription and Illicit Drugs." "Overdose Death Rates." https://www.drugabuse.gov/related-topics/trends-statistics/overdose-death-rates. Accessed on November 10, 2017.

Table 5.6 Drug Overdose Deaths among Adolescents Aged 15–19, by Type of Opioid Drug Involved in the United States: 1999–2015 (per 100,000)

| Year | Natural and Semisynthetic | Heroin | Synthetic (Excluding Methadone) | Methadone |
|------|-----------|--------|----------------------|-----------|
| 1999 | 0.2 | 0.3 | n/a | 0.1 |
| 2000 | 0.3 | 0.2 | n/a | 0.1 |
| 2001 | 0.6 | 0.2 | n/a | 0.2 |
| 2002 | 0.5 | 0.3 | 0.1 | 0.5 |
| 2003 | 0.6 | 0.3 | 0.2 | 0.7 |

*(continued)*

Table 5.6 (*continued*)

| Year | Natural and Semisynthetic | Heroin | Synthetic (Excluding Methadone) | Methadone |
|------|---------------------------|--------|--------------------------------|-----------|
| 2004 | 0.7 | 0.3 | 0.2 | 0.9 |
| 2005 | 0.7 | 0.3 | 0.1 | 0.8 |
| 2006 | 0.8 | 0.3 | 0.3 | 1.0 |
| 2007 | 0.9 | 0.4 | 0.2 | 1.1 |
| 2008 | 1.1 | 0.5 | 0.3 | 0.9 |
| 2009 | 1.0 | 0.4 | 0.2 | 0.7 |
| 2010 | 1.2 | 0.5 | 0.2 | 0.6 |
| 2011 | 1.1 | 0.6 | 0.3 | 0.6 |
| 2012 | 0.8 | 0.6 | 0.2 | 0.4 |
| 2013 | 0.7 | 0.9 | 0.2 | 0.3 |
| 2014 | 0.6 | 0.9 | 0.3 | 0.2 |
| 2015 | 0.6 | 1.0 | 0.7 | 0.3 |

*n/a*: not applicable.

*Source*: "Drug Overdose Deaths among Adolescents Aged 15–19 in the United States: 1999–2015." National Vital Statistics System. https://www.cdc.gov/nchs/data/databriefs/db282_table.pdf#page=4. Accessed on November 10, 2017.

Table 5.7  Opioid Use in Schools*

| Year/Grade | | Narcotics Other Than Heroin**, *** | Heroin |
|------------|-----|------------------------------------|--------|
| 1991 | 8 | | 0.7 |
| | 10 | | 0.5 |
| | 12 | 3.5 | 0.4 |
| 1992 | 8 | | 0.7 |
| | 10 | | 0.6 |
| | 12 | 3.3 | 0.6 |
| 1993 | 8 | | 0.7 |
| | 10 | | 0.7 |
| | 12 | 3.6 | 0.5 |
| 1994 | 8 | | 1.2 |
| | 10 | | 0.9 |
| | 12 | 3.8 | 0.6 |

| Year/Grade | Narcotics Other Than Heroin**, *** | Heroin |
|---|---|---|
| 1995  8 | | 1.4 |
| 10 | | 1.1 |
| 12 | 4.7 | 1.1 |
| 1996  8 | | 1.6 |
| 10 | | 1.2 |
| 12 | 5.4 | 1.0 |
| 1997  8 | | 1.3 |
| 10 | | 1.4 |
| 12 | 6.2 | 1.2 |
| 1998  8 | | 1.3 |
| 10 | | 1.4 |
| 12 | 6.3 | 1.0 |
| 1999  8 | | 1.4 |
| 10 | | 1.4 |
| 12 | 6.7 | 1.1 |
| 2000  8 | | 1.1 |
| 10 | | 1.4 |
| 12 | 7.0 | 1.5 |
| 2001  8 | | 1.0 |
| 10 | | 0.9 |
| 12 | 6.7 | 0.9 |
| 2002  8 | | 0.9 |
| 10 | | 1.1 |
| 12 | 9.4 | 1.0 |
| 2003  8 | | 0.9 |
| 10 | | 0.7 |
| 12 | 9.3 | 0.8 |
| 2004  8 | | 1.0 |
| 10 | | 0.9 |
| 12 | 9.5 | 0.9 |
| 2005  8 | | 0.8 |
| 10 | | 0.9 |

*(continued)*

Table 5.7   (*continued*)

| Year/Grade | | Narcotics Other Than Heroin**, *** | Heroin |
|---|---|---|---|
| | 12 | 9.0 | 0.8 |
| 2006 | 8 | | 0.8 |
| | 10 | | 0.9 |
| | 12 | 9.0 | 0.8 |
| 2007 | 8 | | 0.8 |
| | 10 | | 0.8 |
| | 12 | 9.2 | 0.9 |
| 2008 | 8 | | 0.9 |
| | 10 | | 0.8 |
| | 12 | 9.1 | 0.7 |
| 2009 | 8 | | 0.7 |
| | 10 | | 0.9 |
| | 12 | 9.2 | 0.7 |
| 2010 | 8 | | 0.8 |
| | 10 | | 0.8 |
| | 12 | 8.7 | 0.9 |
| 2011 | 8 | | 0.7 |
| | 10 | | 0.8 |
| | 12 | 8.7 | 0.8 |
| 2012 | 8 | | 0.5 |
| | 10 | | 0.6 |
| | 12 | 7.9 | 0.6 |
| 2013 | 8 | | 0.5 |
| | 10 | | 0.6 |
| | 12 | 7.1 | 0.6 |
| 2014 | 8 | | 0.5 |
| | 10 | | 0.5 |
| | 12 | 6.1 | 0.6 |
| 2015 | 8 | | 0.3 |
| | 10 | | 0.5 |
| | 12 | 5.4 | 0.5 |
| 2016 | 8 | | 0.3 |

| Year/Grade | Narcotics Other Than Heroin**, *** | Heroin |
|---|---|---|
| 10 | | 0.3 |
| 12 | 4.8 | 0.3 |

\* This table includes data for "previous year use" only. For "ever" and "30 preceding days" use, see report cited in source.

\*\* Term used for opioids in this report.

\*\*\* Data for this variable were never collected for grades 8 and 10.

*Source*: Johnston, Lloyd D., et al. 2017. "Monitoring the Future: National Survey Results on Drug Use." Table 6. http://www.monitoringthefuture.org/pubs/monographs/mtf-overview2016.pdf. Accessed on November 10, 2017.

**Table 5.8 Perceived Availability of Narcotics Other Than Heroin, 1991–2016, Grades 8, 10, and 12\***

| Year/Grade | | Narcotics Other Than Heroin**, *** | Heroin*** |
|---|---|---|---|
| 1991 | 8 | No data | No data |
| | 10 | No data | No data |
| | 12 | 34.6 | 30.6 |
| 1992 | 8 | 19.8 | 19.7 |
| | 10 | 26.9 | 24.3 |
| | 12 | 37.1 | 34.9 |
| 1993 | 8 | 19.0 | 19.8 |
| | 10 | 24.9 | 24.3 |
| | 12 | 37.5 | 33.7 |
| 1994 | 8 | 18.3 | 19.4 |
| | 10 | 26.9 | 24.7 |
| | 12 | 38.0 | 34.1 |
| 1995 | 8 | 20.3 | 21.1 |
| | 10 | 27.8 | 24.6 |
| | 12 | 39.8 | 35.1 |
| 1996 | 8 | 20.0 | 20.6 |
| | 10 | 29.4 | 24.8 |
| | 12 | 40.0 | 32.2 |
| 1997 | 8 | 20.6 | 19.8 |
| | 10 | 29.0 | 24.4 |

(*continued*)

**Table 5.8**   (continued)

| Year/Grade | Narcotics Other Than Heroin**, *** | Heroin*** |
|---|---|---|
| 12 | 38.9 | 33.8 |
| 1998  8 | 17.1 | 18.0 |
| 10 | 26.1 | 23.0 |
| 12 | 42.8 | 35.6 |
| 1999  8 | 16.2 | 17.5 |
| 10 | 26.6 | 23.7 |
| 12 | 40.8 | 32.1 |
| 2000  8 | 15.6 | 16.5 |
| 10 | 27.2 | 22.3 |
| 12 | 43.9 | 33.5 |
| 2001  8 | 15.0 | 16.9 |
| 10 | 25.8 | 20.1 |
| 12 | 40.5 | 32.3 |
| 2002  8 | 14.7 | 16.0 |
| 10 | 25.4 | 19.9 |
| 12 | 44.0 | 29.0 |
| 2003  8 | 15.0 | 15.6 |
| 10 | 23.5 | 18.8 |
| 12 | 39.3 | 27.9 |
| 2004  8 | 12.4 | 14.1 |
| 10 | 23.1 | 18.7 |
| 12 | 40.2 | 29.6 |
| 2005  8 | 12.9 | 13.2 |
| 10 | 23.6 | 19.3 |
| 12 | 39.2 | 27.3 |
| 2006  8 | 13.0 | 13.0 |
| 10 | 22.2 | 17.4 |
| 12 | 39.6 | 27.4 |
| 2007  8 | 11.7 | 12.6 |
| 10 | 21.5 | 17.3 |
| 12 | 37.3 | 29.7 |
| 2008  8 | 12.1 | 13.3 |

| Year/Grade | Narcotics Other Than Heroin**, *** | Heroin*** |
|---|---|---|
| 10 | 20.3 | 17.2 |
| 12 | 34.9 | 25.4 |
| 2009   8 | 11.8 | 12.0 |
| 10 | 18.8 | 15.0 |
| 12 | 36.1 | 27.4 |
| 2010   8 | 14.6 | 11.6 |
| 10 | 28.7 | 14.5 |
| 12 | 54.2 | 24.1 |
| 2011   8 | 12.3 | 9.9 |
| 10 | 25.0 | 13.2 |
| 12 | 50.7 | 20.8 |
| 2012   8 | 10.6 | 9.4 |
| 10 | 24.3 | 11.9 |
| 12 | 50.4 | 19.9 |
| 2013   8 | 9.7 | 10.0 |
| 10 | 22.5 | 11.9 |
| 12 | 46.5 | 22.1 |
| 2014   8 | 9.2 | 8.6 |
| 10 | 18.8 | 10.9 |
| 12 | 42.2 | 20.2 |
| 2015   8 | 8.8 | 7.8 |
| 10 | 19.2 | 11.0 |
| 12 | 39.0 | 20.4 |
| 2016   8 | 8.9 | 8.9 |
| 10 | 16.8 | 10.6 |
| 12 | 39.3 | 20.0 |

* Percentage saying "fairly easy" or "very easy" to get.

** Term used for opioids in this report.

*** Data from 1975 to 1990 for grade 12 are also available. See original report, Table 17.

*Source*: Johnston, Lloyd D., et al. 2017. "Monitoring the Future: National Survey Results on Drug Use." Tables 15, 16, and 17. http://www.monitoringthefuture .org/pubs/monographs/mtf-overview2016.pdf. Accessed on November 10, 2017.

## Documents

### Smoking Opium Exclusion Act of 1909

*In the early 1900s, opium use had become a major cause of concern in the United States. A number of leading officials, including President Theodore Roosevelt, encouraged a number of nations to meet in Shanghai in 1909 to consider this issue. Originally the conference was supposed to be focused on opium issues in China, but it gradually became obvious that other nations, including the United States, had similar problems. Therefore, the conference agenda was expanded to include a more general discussion of opium abuse in other nations. As the United States prepared to send its representatives to the Shanghai Conference, it was in a somewhat awkward position of having no legislation limiting the importation, sale, or use of opium in the country. To remedy that problem, the U.S. Congress adopted the Smoking Opium Exclusion Act of 1909 that was somewhat limited in its coverage of the issue but sufficient to convince other nations at the Shanghai Conference of its commitment to limit the sale and use of opium in other countries. The body of the new law follows.*

AN ACT to prohibit the importation and use of opium for other than medicinal purposes.

Be it enacted by the Senate and House of Representatives of the United States in Congress assembled, That after the first day of April, nineteen hundred and nine, it shall be unlawful to import in the United States opium in any form or any preparation or derivative thereof: Provided, That opium and preparations and derivatives thereof, other than smoking opium or opium prepared for smoking, may be imported for medicinal purposes only, under regulations which the Secretary of the Treasury is hereby authorized to prescribe, and when so imported shall be subject to the duties which are now and may hereafter be imposed by law.

SEC. 2. That if any person shall fraudulently or knowingly import or bring into the United States, or assist in doing so, any opium or any preparation or derivative thereof contrary to law, or shall receive, conceal, buy, sell, or in any manner facilitate the transportation, concealment, or sale of such opium or preparation or derivative thereof after importation, knowing the same to have been imported contrary to law, such opium or preparation or derivative thereof shall be forfeited and shall be destroyed, and the offender shall be fined in any sum not exceeding five thousand dollars nor less than fifty dollars, or by imprisonment for any time not exceeding two years, or both. Whenever, on trial for a violation of this section, the defendant is shown to have, or have had, possession of such opium or preparation or derivative thereof, such possession shall be deemed sufficient evidence to authorize conviction unless the defendant shall explain to the satisfaction of the jury. Approved February 9, 1909.

**Source:** "CHAP. 100.—An Act to Prohibit the Importation and Use of Opium for Other Than Medicinal Purposes." H. R. 27427. Sixtieth Congress. Sess. II. Chs. 100, 109. 1909, page 614.

### Harrison Narcotic Act (1914)

*Probably the first effort by the U.S. government to exert some control over the production, distribution, and consumption of recreational drugs, such as opium, was the Harrison Narcotic Act of 1914. Although this act did not make the drugs with which it dealt—opium, cocaine, and their derivatives—illegal, it did place a tax on their production, distribution, and sale. In retrospect, the Harrison Act was a weak effort to control substance abuse, but it is historically significant because of its being the first attempt to interrupt substance abuse in any way whatsoever by the federal government. The core of the act is expressed in its first section, which is reproduced here.*

Be it enacted by the Senate and House of Representatives of the United States of America in Congress assembled, that on and after the first day of March, nineteen hundred and fifteen, every person who produces, imports, manufactures, compounds, deals in, dispenses, distributes, or gives away opium or coca leaves or any compound, manufacture, salt, derivative, or preparation thereof, shall register with the collector of internal revenue of the district, his name or style, place of business, and place or places where such business is to be carried on: Provided, that the office, or if none, then the residence of any person shall be considered for purposes of this Act to be his place of business. At the time of such registry and on or before the first of July annually thereafter, every person who produces, imports, manufactures, compounds, deals in, dispenses, distributes, or gives away any of the aforesaid drugs shall pay to the said collector a special tax at the rate of $1 per annum: Provided, that no employee of any person who produces, imports, manufactures, compounds, deals in, dispenses, distributes, or gives away any of the aforesaid drugs, acting within the scope of his employment, shall be required to register or to pay the special tax provided by this section: Provided further, That officers of the United States Government who are lawfully engaged in making purchases of the above named drugs for the various departments of the Army and Navy, the Public Health Service, and for Government hospitals and prisons, and officers of State governments or any municipality therein, who are lawfully engaged in making purchases of the above named drugs for State, county, or municipal hospitals or prisons, and officials of any Territory or insular possession, or the District of Columbia or of the United States who are lawfully engaged in making purchases of the above named drugs for hospitals or prisons therein shall not be required to register and pay the special tax as herein required.

**Source:** 63rd Congress. Public Law 223. 38 Stat. 785.

*United States v. Jin Fuey Moy* (1916)

*United States v. Doremus* (1919)

*Webb v. United States* (1919)

*The Harrison Narcotic Tax Act of 1914 was of considerable significance because it was the first piece of federal legislation designed to deal with almost any aspect of opium and other narcotics. But as the first piece of such legislation, it was subject to later interpretation by the court system and was followed by a number of clarifying decisions by the U.S. Supreme Court in succeeding years. One such case involved the interpretation of a provision of the act that "nothing contained in this section shall apply [t]o the dispensing or distribution of any of the aforesaid drugs to a patient by a physician, dentist, or veterinary surgeon registered under this Act in the course of his professional practice only" (Section 2(a)). In a series of three decisions, the Court declared exactly how this phrase was to be interpreted.*

*In* United States v. Jin Fuey Moy *(1916), the Court ruled that a physician could distribute heroin tablets to a known addict under terms of the Harrison Act. Three years later, in* United States v. Doremus *(1919), the Court changed its mind and said that one of the reasons that Congress wrote the Harrison Act as it did was to prevent physicians and others involved in the distribution of prescription drugs from supplying addicts with narcotics. In the same year, the Court confirmed its previous decision in* Webb v. United States *(1919), saying that it was a perversion to think that the Congress would approve of anyone distributing narcotics to a drug addict. The relevant parts of each decision are given here. (Ellipses indicate the omission of text.)*

## *United States v. Jin Fuey Moy*

This is an indictment under §8 of the Act of December 17, 1914, c.1, 38 Stat. 785, 789. It was quashed by the district court on the ground that the statute did not apply to the case. 225 F. 1003. The indictment charges a conspiracy with Willie Martin to have in Martin's possession opium and salts thereof, to-wit, one dram of morphine sulphate. It alleges that Martin was not registered with the collector of internal revenue of the district, and had not paid the special tax required; that the defendant [Jin Fuey Moy], for the purpose of executing the conspiracy, issued to Martin a written prescription for the morphine sulphate, and that he did not issue it in good faith, but knew that the drug was not given for medicinal purposes, but for the purpose of supplying one addicted to the use of opium. The question is whether the possession conspired for is within the prohibitions of the act.

. . .

Approaching the issue from this point of view, we conclude that "any person not registered" in §8 cannot be taken to mean any person in the United States, but must be taken to refer to the class with which the statute undertakes to deal—the persons who are required to register by §1. It is true that the exemption of possession of drugs prescribed in good faith by a physician is a powerful argument, taken by itself, for a broader meaning. But every question of construction is unique, and an argument that would prevail in one case may be inadequate in another. This exemption stands alongside of one that saves employees of registered persons, as do §§1 and 4, and nurses under the supervision of a physician, etc., as does §4, and is so far vague that it may have had in mind other persons carrying out a doctor's orders, rather than the patients. The general purpose seems to be to apply to possession exemptions similar to those applied to registration. Even if for a moment the scope and intent of the act were lost sight of, the proviso is not enough to overcome the dominant considerations that prevail in our mind.

Judgment affirmed.

### *United States v. Doremus*

There are ten counts in the indictment. . . .

The second count charges in substance that Doremus did unlawfully and knowingly sell, dispense, and distribute to one

Ameris five hundred one-sixth grain tablets of heroin not in the course of the regular professional practice of Doremus and not for the treatment of any disease from which Ameris was suffering, but, as was well known by Doremus, Ameris was addicted to the use of the drug as a habit, being a person popularly known as a "dope fiend," and that Doremus did sell, dispense, and distribute the drug heroin to Ameris for the purpose of gratifying his appetite for the drug as an habitual user thereof.

. . .

Considering the full power of Congress over excise taxation, the decisive question here is: have the provisions in question any relation to the raising of revenue? That Congress might levy an excise tax upon such dealers, and others who are named in §1 of the act, cannot be successfully disputed. The provisions of §2 to which we have referred aim to confine sales to registered dealers and to those dispensing the drugs as physicians, and to those who come to dealers with legitimate prescriptions of physicians. Congress, with full power over the subject, short of arbitrary and unreasonable action which is not to be assumed, inserted these provisions in an act specifically providing for the raising of revenue. Considered of themselves, we think they tend to keep the traffic above-board and subject to inspection by those authorized to collect the revenue. They tend to diminish the opportunity of unauthorized persons to obtain the drugs and sell them clandestinely without paying the tax imposed by the federal law. This case well illustrates the possibility which may have induced Congress to insert the provisions limiting sales to registered dealers and requiring patients to obtain these drugs as a medicine from physicians or upon regular prescriptions. Ameris, being, as the indictment charges, an addict, may not have used this great number of doses for himself. He might sell some to others without paying the tax—at least Congress may have deemed it wise to prevent such possible dealings because of their effect upon the collection of the revenue.

We cannot agree with the contention that the provisions of §2, controlling the disposition of these drugs in the ways described, can have nothing to do with facilitating the collection of the revenue, as we should be obliged to do if we were to declare this act beyond the power of Congress acting under its constitutional authority to impose excise taxes. It follows that the judgment of the district court must be reversed.

Reversed.

### *Webb v. United States*

. . . the circuit court of appeals propounds to this Court three questions:

"1. Does the first sentence of §2 of the Harrison Act prohibit retail sales of morphine by druggists to persons who have no physician's prescription, who have no order blank therefor, and who cannot obtain an order blank because not of the class to which such blanks are allowed to be issued?"

"2. If the answer to question one is in the affirmative, does this construction make unconstitutional the prohibition of such sale?"

"3. If a practicing and registered physician issues an order for morphine to an habitual user thereof, the order not being issued by him in the course of professional treatment in the attempted cure of the habit, but being issued for the purpose of providing the user with morphine sufficient to keep him comfortable by maintaining his customary use, is such order a physician's prescription under exception (b) of §2?"

. . .

What we have said of the construction and purpose of the act in No. 367 [*United States v. Doremus*] plainly requires that question one should be answered in the affirmative. Question two should be answered in the negative for the reasons stated in the opinion in No. 367. As to question three, to call such an order for the use of morphine a physician's prescription would be so plain a perversion of meaning that no discussion of the subject is required. That question should be answered in the negative.

**Sources:**
*United States v. Jin Fuey Moy,* 241 U.S. 394 (1916).
*United States v. Doremus,* 249 U.S. 86 (1919).
*Webb v. United States,* 249 U.S. 96 (1919).

**Controlled Substances Act (1970)**

*The cornerstone of the U.S. government's efforts to control substance abuse is the Controlled Substances Act of 1970, now a part of the U.S. Code, Title 21, Chapter 13. That act established the system of "schedules" for various categories of drugs that is still used by agencies of the U.S. government today. It also provides extensive background information about the domestic and international status of drug abuse efforts. Some of the most relevant sections for the domestic portion of the act are reprinted here. (Ellipses indicate the omission of text.)*

*Section 801 of the act presents Congress's findings and declarations about controlled substances, with special mention in Section 801a of psychotropic drugs:*

§ 801. Congressional findings and declarations: controlled substances

The Congress makes the following findings and declarations:

(1) Many of the drugs included within this subchapter have a useful and legitimate medical purpose and are necessary to maintain the health and general welfare of the American people.

(2) The illegal importation, manufacture, distribution, and possession and improper use of controlled substances have a substantial and detrimental effect on the health and general welfare of the American people.

. . .

(7) The United States is a party to the Single Convention on Narcotic Drugs, 1961, and other international conventions designed to establish effective control over international and domestic traffic in controlled substances.

§ 801a. Congressional findings and declarations: psychotropic substances

The Congress makes the following findings and declarations:

(1) The Congress has long recognized the danger involved in the manufacture, distribution, and use of certain psychotropic substances for nonscientific and nonmedical purposes, and has provided strong and effective legislation to control illicit trafficking and to regulate legitimate uses of psychotropic substances in this country. Abuse of psychotropic substances has become a phenomenon common to many countries, however, and is not confined to national borders. It is, therefore, essential that the United States cooperate with other nations in establishing effective controls over international traffic in such substances.

(2) The United States has joined with other countries in executing an international treaty, entitled the Convention on Psycho-tropic Substances and signed at Vienna, Austria, on February 21, 1971, which is designed to establish suitable controls over the manufacture, distribution, transfer, and use of certain psychotropic substances. The Convention is not self executing, and the obligations of the United States thereunder may only be performed pursuant to appropriate legislation. It is the intent of the Congress that the amendments made by this Act, together with existing law, will enable the United States to meet all of its obligations under the Convention and that no further legislation will be necessary for that purpose.

. . .

*Section 802 deals with definitions used in the act, and section 803 deals with a minor housekeeping issue of financing for the act. Section 811 deals with the Attorney General's authority for classifying and declassifying drugs and the manner in which these steps are to be taken. In general:*

§ 811. Authority and criteria for classification of substances

(a)  Rules and regulations of Attorney General; hearing

The Attorney General shall apply the provisions of this subchapter to the controlled substances listed in the schedules established by section 812 of this title and to any other drug or other substance added to such schedules under this subchapter. Except as provided in subsections (d) and (e) of this section, the Attorney General may by rule-

(1)  add to such a schedule or transfer between such schedules any drug or other substance if he-

   (A)  finds that such drug or other substance has a potential for abuse, and

   (B)  makes with respect to such drug or other substance the findings prescribed by subsection (b) of section 812 of this title for the schedule in which such drug is to be placed; or

(2)  remove any drug or other substance from the schedules if he finds that the drug or other substance does not meet the requirements for inclusion in any schedule.

. . .

*Section (b) provides guidelines for the evaluation of drugs and other substances. The next section, (c), is a key element of the act:*

(c)  Factors determinative of control or removal from schedules

In making any finding under subsection (a) of this section or under subsection (b) of section 812 of this title, the Attorney General shall consider the following factors with respect to each drug or other substance proposed to be controlled or removed from the schedules:

(1)  Its actual or relative potential for abuse.

(2)  Scientific evidence of its pharmacological effect, if known.

(3) The state of current scientific knowledge regarding the drug or other substance.

(4) Its history and current pattern of abuse.

(5) The scope, duration, and significance of abuse.

(6) What, if any, risk there is to the public health.

(7) Its psychic or physiological dependence liability.

(8) Whether the substance is an immediate precursor of a substance already controlled under this subchapter.

*Section (d) is a lengthy discussion of international aspects of the nation's efforts to control substance abuse. Section (e) through (h) deal with related, but less important, issues of the control of substance abuse. Section 812 is perhaps of greatest interest to the general reader in that it establishes the system of classifying drugs still used in the United States, along with the criteria for classification and the original list of drugs to be included in each schedule (since greatly expanded):*

§ 812. Schedules of controlled substances

(a) Establishment

There are established five schedules of controlled substances, to be known as schedules I, II, III, IV, and V. Such schedules shall initially consist of the substances listed in this section. The schedules established by this section shall be updated and republished on a semiannual basis during the two year period beginning one year after October 27, 1970, and shall be updated and republished on an annual basis thereafter.

(b) Placement on schedules; findings required

Except where control is required by United States obligations under an international treaty, convention, or protocol, in effect on October 27, 1970, and except in the case of an immediate precursor, a drug or other substance may not be placed in any schedule unless the findings required for such schedule are made with respect to such drug or other substance. The findings required for each of the schedules are as follows:

(1) Schedule I.-

    (A) The drug or other substance has a high potential for abuse.

    (B) The drug or other substance has no currently accepted medical use in treatment in the United States.

    (C) There is a lack of accepted safety for use of the drug or other substance under medical supervision.

(2) Schedule II.-

    (A) The drug or other substance has a high potential for abuse.

    (B) The drug or other substance has a currently accepted medical use in treatment in the United States or a currently accepted medical use with severe restrictions.

    (C) Abuse of the drug or other substances may lead to severe psychological or physical dependence.

(3) Schedule III.-

    (A) The drug or other substance has a potential for abuse less than the drugs or other substances in schedules I and II.

    (B) The drug or other substance has a currently accepted medical use in treatment in the United States.

    (C) Abuse of the drug or other substance may lead to moderate or low physical dependence or high psychological dependence.

(4) Schedule IV.-

    (A) The drug or other substance has a low potential for abuse relative to the drugs or other substances in schedule III.

    (B) The drug or other substance has a currently accepted medical use in treatment in the United States.

    (C) Abuse of the drug or other substance may lead to limited physical dependence or psychological dependence relative to the drugs or other substances in schedule III.

(5) Schedule V.-

(A) The drug or other substance has a low potential for abuse relative to the drugs or other substances in schedule IV.

(B) The drug or other substance has a currently accepted medical use in treatment in the United States.

(C) Abuse of the drug or other substance may lead to limited physical dependence or psychological dependence relative to the drugs or other substances in schedule IV.

(c)  Initial schedules of controlled substances

Schedules I, II, III, IV, and V shall, unless and until amended [1] pursuant to section 811 of this title, consist of the following drugs or other substances, by whatever official name, common or usual name, chemical name, or brand name designated: The initial list of drugs under each schedule follows.

**Source:** "Title 21 United States Code (USC) Controlled Substances Act." Diversion Control Division. Drug Enforcement Administration.

### Children's Health Act of 2000

*The Children's Health Act of 2000 was a large and complex bill designed to deal with a wide variety of health issues, some of which had little or nothing to do with children's health. One such section was Title XXXV, entitled "Waiver Authority for Physicians Who Dispense or Prescribe Certain Narcotic Drugs for Maintenance Treatment or Detoxification Treatment." The section was an amendment to the Controlled Substances Act of 1970 (CSA), allowing private physicians to prescribe and treat, for the first time in history, patients dealing with "narcotic" problems. Included under this rubric were individuals dealing with opioid issues. The major drawback of the new legislation was that it limited to 30 the number of patients whom a doctor could treat under the new regulations. This problem was reduced to some extent in a 2006 legislation that increased the number of patients a doctor could treat to 100, from the original 30. A section of the relevant act is reprinted here.*

(2)(A) Subject to subparagraphs (D) and (J), the requirements of paragraph (1) are waived in the case of the dispensing (including the prescribing), by a practitioner, of narcotic drugs in schedule III, IV, or V or combinations of such drugs if the practitioner meets the conditions specified in subparagraph (B) and the narcotic drugs or combinations of such drugs meet the conditions specified in subparagraph (C).

"(B) For purposes of subparagraph (A), the conditions specified in this subparagraph with respect to a practitioner are that, before the initial dispensing of narcotic drugs in schedule III, IV, or V or combinations of such drugs to patients for maintenance or detoxification treatment, the practitioner submit to the Secretary a notification of the intent of the practitioner to begin dispensing the drugs or combinations for such purpose, and that the notification contain the following certifications by the practitioner:

"(i) The practitioner is a qualifying physician (as defined in subparagraph (G)).

"(ii) With respect to patients to whom the practitioner will provide such drugs or combinations of drugs, the practitioner has the capacity to refer the patients for appropriate counseling and other appropriate ancillary services.

"(iii) In any case in which the practitioner is not in a group practice, the total number of such patients of the practitioner at any one time will not exceed the applicable number. For purposes of this clause, the applicable number is 30, except that the Secretary may by regulation change such total number.

"(iv) In any case in which the practitioner is in a group practice, the total number of such patients of the group practice at any one time will not exceed the applicable number. For purposes of this clause, the applicable number is 30, except that the Secretary may by regulation change such total number, and the Secretary for such purposes may by regulation establish different categories on the basis of the number of practitioners in a group practice and establish for the various categories different numerical limitations on the number of such patients that the group practice may have.

"(C) For purposes of subparagraph, the conditions specified in this subparagraph with respect to narcotic drugs in schedule III, IV, or V or combinations of such drugs are as follows:

*The bill next describes the drugs that can be used for treatment of "narcotic" issues. Among the most important of those drugs is buprenorphine, one of the most widely used drugs for the treatment of opioid addiction. Buprenorphine is a Schedule III drug under the CSA, making it a legal treatment for opioid addiction.*

**Source:** Public Law 106-310.

### Opioid Use among Veterans (2013)

*One of the populations for which opioid abuse and addiction is most serious includes veterans of military service, who have been injured in combat or other conflict-related incidents. Many of these individuals seek help from the U.S. Veterans Administration (VA) for these pain issues. But some critics have argued that the VA relies too heavily on the use of opioids for treating these men and women, rather than addressing the root problems of a veteran's pain issues. In October 2013, the Subcommittee on Health of the Committee on Veterans' Affairs of the U.S. House of Representatives held hearings on this issue. Some comments from those hearings are reprinted here. (Ellipses indicate the omission of original text.)*

Rep. Jeff Miller (R-FL): . . . when these veterans reach out and entrust the VA to relieve their pain, the treatment they often receive is the systemwide default of prescribing prescription painkillers. CBS News has recently reported that based on VA data, over the past 11 years, the number of patients treated by the VA is up 29 percent, while the narcotic prescriptions written by VA doctors and nurse practitioners are up 259 percent.

Look, veterans depend upon VA to uphold its mission of restoring the health of those who have borne battle. But instead of helping them manage their battles with pain, VA has opted instead to use a treatment that has the power to destroy rather than to restore their lives.

VA can and must change course and act now to reduce their reliance on the use of prescription drugs. The veterans and their loved ones must be listened to, must be followed up with closely, and supported with a treatment that can best help them regain happy and healthy lives. Anything less is unacceptable.

Heather McDonald, wife of Specialist Scott McDonald (deceased): On April 30, 2011, [Scott] began seeking the treatment from the VA for back pain and mental illness. The Chalmers P. Wylie Ambulatory Care Center in Columbus, Ohio immediately starting prescribing medications. Beginning with Ibuprofen, Neurontin, and Meloxicam, and graduating to Vicodin, Klonopin, Celexa, Zoloft, Valium, and Percocet. This is where the roller coaster began.

My husband was taking up to 15 pills a day within the first six months of treatment. Every time Scott came home from an appointment, he had different medications, different dosages, different directions on how to take them. And progressively over the course of a year and a half of starting his treatment, the medications had changed so many times by adding and changing that Scott began changing. We researched many of the drugs that he was prescribed online and saw the dangerous interactions that they cause. Yet my husband was conditioned to follow orders. And he did so.

On September 12, 2012, Scott attended another of his scheduled appointments. This is when they added Percocet. This was a much different medication than he was used to taking, and which they prescribed him not to exceed 500 milligrams of Acetaminophen. Again, my husband followed orders.

Approximately 01:00 hours on the 13th of September, I arrived home from my job. I found Scott disoriented and very lethargic. I woke him and asked him if he was okay. He told me he was fine and that he just took what the doctors told him to take. At approximately 07:30 I found my husband cold and unresponsive. At 35 years old this father of two was gone.

\* \* \*

When our men and women signed that contract they gave their bodies to their country. And I ask now, as the people that have the power and the ability to make these changes happen, to force regulations to change on behalf of all of the veterans out there that have died. And for their families, I beg you to reopen this issue and reevaluate the distribution of narcotics to our men and women when they come home.

**Source:** "Between Peril and Promise: Facing the Dangers of VA's Skyrocketing Use of Prescription Painkillers to Treat Veterans." Hearing before the Subcommittee on Health of the Committee on Veterans' Affairs. U.S. House of Representatives. 113th Congress, First Session. Thursday, October 10, 2013.

### An Act to Prevent Opiate Abuse by Strengthening the Controlled Substances Prescription Monitoring Program (2016)

*One of the first states to adopt legislation dealing specifically with the current opioid epidemic was Maine. In 2016, the state legislature passed and the governor signed an act with this title designed to establish a mechanism by which the state's opioid crisis could be approached. (The act was actually an update of earlier legislation on this issue.) The citation that follows contains the primary elements of that bill, now part of the state's Chapter 488 of its Public Laws. (Ellipses indicate the omission of text from the original document.)*

Be it enacted by the People of the State of Maine as follows:

Sec. 1. 22 MRSA §7246, sub-§§1-A, 1-B and 1-C are enacted to read:

. . .

*[The first section of the act provides definitions of terms and other administrative issues mentioned in the current bill and existing legislation.]*

### § 2210. Requirements regarding prescription of opioid medication

1.  **Limits on opioid medication prescribing.** Except as provided in subsection 2, an individual licensed under this chapter whose scope of practice includes prescribing opioid medication may not prescribe:

    A.  To a patient any combination of opioid medication in an aggregate amount in excess of 100 morphine milligram equivalents of opioid medication per day;

    B.  To a patient who, on the effective date of this section, has an active prescription for opioid medication in excess of 100 morphine milligram equivalents of an opioid medication per day, an opioid medication in an amount that would cause that patient's total amount of opioid medication to exceed 300 morphine milligram equivalents of opioid medication per day; except that, on or after July 1, 2017, the aggregate amount of opioid medication prescribed may not be in excess of 100 morphine milligram equivalents of opioid medication per day;

    C.  On or after January 1, 2017, within a 30-day period, more than a 30-day supply of an opioid medication to a patient under treatment for chronic pain. "Chronic pain" has the same meaning as in Title 22, section 7246, subsection 1-C; or

D. On or after January 1, 2017, within a 7-day period, more than a 7-day supply of an opioid medication to a patient under treatment for acute pain. "Acute pain" has the same meaning as in Title 22, section 7246, subsection 1-A.

2. Exceptions. An individual licensed under this chapter whose scope of practice includes prescribing opioid medication is exempt from the limits on opioid medication prescribing established in subsection 1 only:

A. When prescribing opioid medication to a patient for:

(1) Pain associated with active and aftercare cancer treatment;

(2) Palliative care, as defined in Title 22, section 1726, subsection 1, paragraph A, in conjunction with a serious illness, as defined in Title 22, section 1726, subsection 1, paragraph B;

(3) End-of-life and hospice care;

(4) Medication-assisted treatment for substance use disorder; or

(5) Other circumstances determined in rule by the Department of Health and Human Services pursuant to Title 22, section 7254, subsection 2; and

B. When directly ordering or administering a benzodiazepine or opioid medication to a person in an emergency room setting, an inpatient hospital setting, a long-term care facility or a residential care facility.

As used in this paragraph, "administer" has the same meaning as in Title 22, section 7246, subsection 1-B.

3. **Electronic prescribing**. An individual licensed under this chapter whose scope of practice includes prescribing opioid

medication and who has the capability to electronically prescribe shall prescribe all opioid medication electronically by July 1, 2017. An individual who does not have the capability to electronically prescribe must request a waiver from this requirement from the Commissioner of Health and Human Services stating the reasons for the lack of capability, the availability of broadband infrastructure and a plan for developing the ability to electronically prescribe opioid medication. The commissioner may grant a waiver for circumstances in which exceptions are appropriate, including prescribing outside of the individual's usual place of business and technological failures.

4. **Continuing education**. By December 31, 2017, an individual licensed under this chapter must successfully complete 3 hours of continuing education every 2 years on the prescription of opioid medication as a condition of prescribing opioid medication. The board shall adopt rules to implement this subsection. Rules adopted pursuant to this subsection are routine technical rules as defined in Title 5, chapter 375, subchapter 2-A.

5. **Penalties**. An individual who violates this section commits a civil violation for which a fine of $250 per violation, not to exceed $5,000 per calendar year, may be adjudged. The Department of Health and Human Services is responsible for the enforcement of this section.

**Source:** Public Law 488. State of Maine. https://legislature .maine.gov/legis/bills/bills_127th/chapters/PUBLIC488.asp.

### An Act Concerning Involuntary Commitment to Treatment for Substance Use Disorders (2016)

*A legal controversy that has arisen as a result of the current opioid epidemic is whether or not a person can be committed, with or without his or her consent, for abuse of or addiction to an opioid drug. Some states already have laws that permit involuntary commitment for some types of mental disorders, and legislators in these and other states are asking whether such policies should be extended to substance abusers. New Jersey is one such state that was considering such a bill in 2016. The following selection presents the major features of that bill. (Ellipses indicate the omission of text from the original document.)*

AN ACT concerning involuntary commitment to treatment for substance use disorders, supplementing chapter 4 of Title 30 of the Revised Statutes, and amending P.L.1991, c.270 and 4 P.L.1987, c.116. . . .

17 3. (New section) The standards and procedures set forth in [this bill] shall apply to an adult involuntarily committed to treatment for a substance use disorder pursuant to [this bill] and an adult voluntarily admitted for treatment for a substance use disorder pursuant to [this bill] from a screening service to a residential substance use disorders treatment facility. . . .

4. (New section) The commissioner shall adopt rules and regulations pursuant to the "Administrative Procedure Act," 33 P.L.1968, c.410 (C.52:14B-1 et seq.) regarding a screening service and its staff that effectuate the following purposes and procedures:

a. A screening service shall serve as the facility wherein a person believed to be in need of involuntary commitment to treatment for a substance use disorder pursuant to [this bill] undergoes an assessment to determine what substance use disorder services are appropriate for the person and where those services may be most appropriately provided.

The screening service may provide emergency and consensual treatment to the person receiving the assessment, and may transport the person or detain the person up to 24 hours for the purposes of providing the treatment and conducting the assessment.

b. When a person is assessed by a mental health screener, and involuntary commitment to treatment for a substance use disorder seems necessary, the screener shall provide, on a screening document prescribed by the division, information regarding the person's history and available alternative facilities and services that are deemed inappropriate for the person. When appropriate and available, and as permitted by law, the screener shall make reasonable efforts to gather information from the person's family or significant others for the purposes of preparing the screening document. If a psychiatrist, in consideration of this document and in conjunction with the psychiatrist's own complete assessment, concludes that the person is in need of commitment to treatment for a substance use disorder, the psychiatrist shall complete the screening certificate. The screening certificate shall be completed by a psychiatrist, except in those circumstances where the division's contract with the screening service provides that another physician may complete the certificate.

Upon completion of the screening certificate, screening service staff shall determine, in consultation with the psychiatrist or another physician, as appropriate, the appropriate treatment of the person, taking into account the person's prior history of hospitalization and treatment and the person's current condition.

If a person has been admitted three times or has been an inpatient for 30 days at a residential substance use disorders treatment facility during the preceding 12 months, consideration shall be given to placing the person in a residential substance use disorders treatment facility.

The person shall be admitted to the appropriate facility as soon as possible. Screening service staff are authorized to transport the person or arrange for transportation of the person to the appropriate facility.

*The bill runs an additional 15 pages in which all aspects of a possible involuntary commitment are discussed and described.*

**Source:** Assembly, No. 1099. State of New Jersey. http://www .njleg.state.nj.us/2016/Bills/A1500/1099_I1.PDF.

### Remarks by President Trump on Combating Drug Demand and the Opioid Crisis (2017)

*Early in his first term in office, President Donald Trump addressed an issue about which he had spoken during the presidential campaign: the opioid crisis. In a speech delivered on October 26, 2017, he reiterated his concerns about the crisis and outlined his forthcoming efforts to deal with the issue. The speech focused on some general principles but did not provide specific actions that he might recommend for the crisis. A sense of what those actions might be was forthcoming, however, in the report of the President's Commission on Combating Drug Addiction and the Opioid Crisis, discussed in the next entry. The core of President Trump's remarks are provided here. (The presence of ellipses indicates the omission of text from the original address.)*

Beyond the shocking death toll, the terrible measure of the opioid crisis includes the families ripped apart and, for many communities, a generation of lost potential and opportunity.

This epidemic is a national health emergency, unlike many of us we've seen and what we've seen in our lifetimes. Nobody has seen anything like what's going on now.

As Americans, we cannot allow this to continue. It is time to liberate our communities from this scourge of drug addiction. Never been this way. We can be the generation that ends the opioid epidemic. We can do it. (Applause.) We can do it.

That is why, effective today, my administration is officially declaring the opioid crisis a national public health emergency under federal law, and why I am directing all executive agencies to use every appropriate emergency authority to fight the opioid crisis. This marks a critical step in confronting the extraordinary challenge that we face.

As part of this emergency response, we will announce a new policy to overcome a restrictive 1970s-era rule that prevents states from providing care at certain treatment facilities with more than 16 beds for those suffering from drug addiction.

A number of states have reached out to us asking for relief, and you should expect to see approvals that will unlock treatment for people in need. And those approvals will come very, very fast. Not like in the past—very, very quickly.

Ending the epidemic will require mobilization of government, local communities, and private organizations. It will require the resolve of our entire country.

*[Trump alludes to the presidential commission at this point and mentions that its report is forthcoming. He then mentions specific actions that the administration has already taken to deal with the opioid crisis.]*

The Centers for Disease Control and Prevention has launched a prescription awareness campaign to put faces on the danger of opioid abuse.

I want to acknowledge CVS Caremark for announcing last month that it will limit certain first-time opioid prescriptions to seven-day supplies, among other important reforms. And I encourage other companies to do their part to help to stop this epidemic.

The FDA is now requiring drug companies that manufacture prescription opioids to provide more training to prescribers and to help prevent abuse and addiction, and has requested that one especially high-risk opioid be withdrawn from the market immediately. We are requiring that a specific opioid, which is truly evil, be taken off the market immediately.

The U.S. Postal Service and the Department of Homeland Security are strengthening the inspection of packages coming into our country to hold back the flood of cheap and deadly fentanyl, a synthetic opioid manufactured in China and 50 times stronger than heroin.

And in two weeks, I will be in China with President Xi, and I will mention this as a top priority. And he will do something about it.

I am also pleased to report that for the first time, the Department of Justice has indicated [indicted] major Chinese drug traffickers for distributing—and they have really put very, very strong clamps on them. They've indicted them, the drug traffickers, for distributing fentanyl in the United States. So, Jeff, thank you very much. Good job.

And they've been indicted and we're not going to forget about them, believe me. They are doing tremendous harm to our country. The Justice Department is aggressively and, really, valiantly pursuing those who illegally prescribe and traffic in opioids, both in our communities and on the Internet.

And I will be looking at the potential of the federal government bringing major lawsuits against bad actors. What they have and what they're doing to our people is unheard of. We will be bringing some very major lawsuits against people and against companies that are hurting our people. And that will start taking place pretty soon.

We're also supporting first responders' and medical professionals' access to the tools they need to prevent deaths through life-saving overdose medications.

At my direction, the National Institute of Health, headed up by Francis Collins, has taken the first steps of an ambitious public-private partnership with pharmaceutical companies to develop non-addictive painkillers and new treatments for addiction and overdose. So important.

I will be pushing the concept of non-addictive painkillers very, very hard. We have to come up with that solution. We give away billions and billions of dollars a year, and we're going to be spending lots of money on coming up with a non-addictive solution.

We will be asking Dr. Collins and the NIH for substantial resources in the fight against drug addiction. One of the things our administration will be doing is a massive advertising campaign to get people, especially children, not to want to take drugs in the first place because they will see the devastation and the ruination it causes to people and people's lives.

. . .

We are already distributing nearly $1 billion in grants for addiction prevention and treatment, and over $50 million dollars to support law enforcement programs that assist those facing prison and facing addiction.

We have also launched an $81 million partnership to research better pain management techniques for our incredible veterans.

**Source:** "Remarks by President Trump on Combatting Drug Demand and the Opioid Crisis." 2017. https://www.whitehouse .gov/briefings-statements/remarks-president-trump-combatt ing-drug-demand-opioid-crisis/. Accessed on March 20, 2018.

### The President's Commission on Combating Drug Addiction and the Opioid Crisis (2017)

*On March 29, 2017, President Donald Trump issued Executive Order No. 13784, establishing a committee to study the issue of drug abuse and addiction, in general, and the nation's current opioid crisis, in particular. The committee's final report was due on June 27, 2017, but it was unable to meet this deadline. The first draft of the final report was issued, instead, on November 1, 2017. The committee issued a total of 56 specific recommendations for ways of achieving the president's stated objectives in issuing the executive order. The recommendations were classified into about a dozen categories and subcategories, including federal funding and programs; opioid addiction prevention (prescribing guidelines, regulations, and education; PDMP enhancements; supply reduction and enforcement strategies); opioid addiction treatment, overdose reversal, and recovery; and research and development. Among those recommendations are the following. (Ellipses indicate the omission of parts of the original text.)*

1. The Commission urges Congress and the Administration to block grant federal funding for opioid-related and SUD-related activities to the states, where the battle is happening every day. . . .

4. The Commission recommends that Department of Education (DOE) collaborate with states on student assessment

programs such as Screening, Brief Intervention and Referral to Treatment (SBIRT). SBIRT is a program that uses a screening tool by trained staff to identify at-risk youth who may need treatment. This should be deployed for adolescents in middle school, high school and college levels. . . .

6. The Commission recommends HHS [Department of Health and Human Services], the Department of Labor (DOL), VA/DOD [Veterans Administration], FDA [Food and Drug Administration], and ONDCP [Office of National Drug Control Policy] work with stakeholders to develop model statutes, regulations, and policies that ensure informed patient consent prior to an opioid prescription for chronic pain. Patients need to understand the risks, benefits and alternatives to taking opioids. This is not the standard today. . . .

7. The Commission recommends that HHS coordinate the development of a national curriculum and standard of care for opioid prescribers. An updated set of guidelines for prescription pain medications should be established by an expert committee composed of various specialty practices to supplement the CDC guideline that are specifically targeted to primary care physicians. . . .

17. The Commission recommends community-based stakeholders utilize Take Back Day to inform the public about drug screening and treatment services. The Commission encourages more hospitals/clinics and retail pharmacies to become year-round authorized collectors and explore the use of drug deactivation bags. . . .

19. The Commission recommends CMS review and modify rate-setting policies that discourage the use of non-opioid treatments for pain, such as certain bundled payments that make alternative treatment options cost prohibitive for hospitals and doctors, particularly those options for treating immediate post-surgical pain. . . .

23. The Commission recommends the enhancement of federal sentencing penalties for the trafficking of fentanyl and fentanyl analogues. . . .

33. The Commission recommends HHS/CMS, the Indian Health Service (IHS), Tricare, the DEA, and the VA remove reimbursement and policy barriers to SUD [substance use disorders] treatment, including those, such as patient limits, that limit access to any forms of FDA-approved medication-assisted treatment (MAT), counseling, inpatient/residential treatment, and other treatment modalities, particularly fail-first protocols and frequent prior authorizations. All primary care providers employed by the above-mentioned health systems should screen for alcohol and drug use and, directly or through referral, provide treatment within 24 to 48 hours. . . .

38. The Commission recommends DOJ broadly establish federal drug courts within the federal district court system in all 93 federal judicial districts. States, local units of government, and Indian tribal governments should apply for drug court grants established by 34 U.S.C. § 10611. Individuals with an SUD who violate probation terms with substance use should be diverted into drug court, rather than prison . . .

39. The Commission recommends the Federal Government partner with appropriate hospital and recovery organizations to expand the use of recovery coaches, especially in hard-hit areas. Insurance companies, federal health systems, and state payers should expand programs for hospital and primary case-based SUD treatment and referral services. Recovery coach programs have been extraordinarily effective in states that have them to help direct patients in crisis to appropriate treatment. Addiction and recovery specialists can also work with patients through technology and telemedicine, to expand their reach to underserved areas. . . .

41. The Commission recommends that federal agencies revise regulations and reimbursement policies to allow for SUD treatment via telemedicine. . . .

43. The Commission recommends the National Highway Traffic Safety Administration (NHTSA) review its National Emergency Medical Services (EMS) Scope of Practice Model with respect to naloxone, and disseminate best practices for states that may need statutory or regulatory changes to allow Emergency Medical Technicians (EMT) to administer naloxone, including higher doses to account for the rising number of fentanyl overdoses.

44. The Commission recommends HHS implement naloxone co-prescribing pilot programs to confirm initial research and identify best practices. ONDCP should, in coordination with HHS, disseminate a summary of existing research on co-prescribing to stakeholders. . . .

52. The Commission recommends federal agencies, including HHS (National Institutes of Health, CDC, CMS, FDA, and the Substance Abuse and Mental Health Services Administration), DOJ, the Department of Defense (DOD), the VA, and ONDCP, should engage in a comprehensive review of existing research programs and establish goals for pain management and addiction research (both prevention and treatment).

53. The Commission recommends Congress and the Federal Government provide additional resources to the National Institute on Drug Abuse (NIDA), the National Institute of Mental Health (NIMH), and National Institute on Alcohol Abuse and Alcoholism (NIAAA) to fund the research areas cited above. NIDA should continue research in concert with the pharmaceutical industry to develop and test innovative medications for SUDs and OUDs, including long-acting injectables, more potent opioid antagonists to reverse overdose, drugs used for detoxification, and opioid vaccines.

**Source:** The President's Commission on Combating Drug Addiction and the Opioid Crisis. 2017. https://www.white house.gov/sites/whitehouse.gov/files/images/Meeting%20 Draft%20of%20Final%20Report%20-%20November%20 1%2C%202017.pdf. For the president's executive order creating the commission, see https://www.federalregister.gov/documents/ 2017/04/03/2017-06716/establishing-the-presidents-com mission-on-combating-drug-addiction-and-the-opioid-crisis.

## Introduction

The story of opioids in human civilization dates back well over two millennia. That story can be found in a large number of books, articles, reports, and Internet web pages. This bibliography provides a list of only some of the most important works historically, as well as some of the most recent print and electronic publications on the topic.

Some resources are available in more than one format, usually as articles and as Internet reproductions of those articles. In such cases, information about both formats is provided. The reader is reminded that this list of resources is not meant to be exhaustive but is provided as a source of references with which one might continue one's research on the topic. The reader is also encouraged to review the reference lists for Chapters 1 and 2, which contain a number of other valuable resources, most of which are not duplicated in this bibliography.

## Books

Adams, Susan M., et al. 2017. *First, Do No Harm: Marshaling Clinician Leadership to Counter the Opioid Epidemic.* National Academy of Medicine. Washington, DC: National Academy of Medicine. https://nam.edu/wp-content/

A heroin addict injects the drug into his arm. Addicts must use the drug several times a day to fend off symptoms of withdrawal. They may inject the drug into their arms, legs, or even between their toes. (powerofforever/ iStockphoto.com)

uploads/2017/09/First-Do-No-Harm-Marshaling-Clinician-Leadership-to-Counter-the-Opioid-Epidemic.pdf. Accessed on January 9, 2018.

This book is written to discuss the role of clinicians in dealing with the opioid crisis. It contains chapters on the magnitude of the opioid crisis, characteristics of those who abuse opioids, factors that have driven the epidemic, effective pain management techniques, and ways in which clinicians can help to counter the opioid epidemic.

Booth, Martin. 1999. *Opium: A History*. New York: St. Martin's Griffin.

This book is one of the very best and most complete references on the history of opium, dating to the earliest periods of human civilization to the end of the 20th century.

Chouvy, Pierre-Arnaud. 2010. *Opium: Uncovering the Politics of the Poppy*. Cambridge, MA: Harvard University Press.

The author provides a very broad discussion of the role of the poppy and opium throughout human history, from its earliest appearances in ancient civilizations to its modern-day applications. The emphasis of the book is on the social and political settings in which the poppy plant has been cultivated and used.

Davenport-Hines, Richard P. T. 2001. *The Pursuit of Oblivion: A Global History of Narcotics, 1500–2000*. London: Weidenfeld and Nicolson.

This book provides an excellent general overview of the status of narcotic drugs around the world over a period of five centuries, with consideration of social attitudes, demography, legal status, and related issues.

Dikötter, Frank, Lars Laamann, and Zhou Xun. 2004. *Narcotic Culture: A History of Drugs in China*. Publishers: London: Hurst & Company; Chicago: University of Chicago Press.

This book opens with a chapter on the global spread of psychoactive substances between 1600 and 1900 before focusing on the opium wars, the place of opium in Chinese society, and the recent history of opium use and regulation in China up to about 1950.

Fareed, Ayman. 2014. *Opioid Use Disorders and Their Treatment*. New York: Nova Science Publishers.

> This book provides an excellent introduction to the problem of opioid use disorders. Chapters deal with topics such as diagnosing OUDs (opioid use disorders), opioid craving and noncraving medications, stress and OUD, pain and OUD, treatment of opioid withdrawal, and buprenorphine maintenance treatment.

"Fentanyl: A Briefing Guide for First Responders." 2017. Washington, DC: Department of Justice, Drug Enforcement Administration. https://www.dea.gov/druginfo/Fentanyl_Brief ingGuideforFirstResponders_June2017.pdf. Accessed on January 10, 2018.

> This government publication provides an overview of information about fentanyl and its analogs, along with specific suggestions for first-responders who have to deal with overdose issues. Chapters deal with topics such as a history of fentanyl, the nature of fentanyl and its analogs, common illicit forms of fentanyl and other related opioids, and recommendations for first-responders.

Flannery, Michael A. 2017. *Civil War Pharmacy: A History*. Carbondale: Southern Illinois University Press.

> The publisher claims that this book is "the first comprehensive examination of pharmaceutical practice and drug provision during the Civil War." The book provides a very detailed account of the drugs that were used during the war, the rules and regulations under which they were used, and their immediate and long-term effects on those engaged in the war.

Foreman, Judy. 2017. *The Global Pain Crisis*. New York: Oxford University Press.

This book may be of interest because it includes some topics that are less often included in general books on the opioid crisis, such as the status of the epidemic in other countries of the world and complementary and alternative methods for treating opioid dependence and addiction.

Foxcroft, Louise. 2017. *The Making of Addiction: The "Use and Abuse" of Opium in Nineteenth-Century Britain*. London; New York: Routledge/Taylor & Francis Group.

This book considers all aspects of the rise of opium use and abuse during the 19th century in Great Britain. It consists of chapters on Thomas De Quincey and the experience of addiction, the double-edged sword of opium, opium addiction in mid- to late-Victorian fiction, the Chinese influence, poisonous drugs and the medical profession in the nineteenth century, addiction as a disease, and late nineteenth-century theories of addiction.

Goldberg, Daniel S. 2017. *Bioethics of Pain Management: Beyond Opioids*. New York: Routledge.

This book focuses on the nature of pain, with a relatively modest section devoted to the use of opioids to treat pain. Chapters deal with the current state of pain in the United States, the history of pain, opioids and pain policy, and evidence-based pain policy recommendations.

Greek, Joe. 2018. *Coping with Opioid Abuse*. New York: Rosen YA.

This book is intended as an introduction to the current opioid crisis for readers in the age range of 12–17.

Hanes, William Travis, and Frank Sanello. 2007. *The Opium Wars: The Addiction of One Empire and the Corruption of Another*. Naperville, IL: Sourcebooks.

This book provides a comprehensive and very readable account of the events leading up to the opium wars, their history, and consequences resulting from the conflicts.

Hart, Carl L., and Charles J. Ksir. 2018. *Drugs, Society, and Human Behavior*, 16th edition. New York: McGraw-Hill Education.

> This is the latest edition of a highly respected text on a range of licit and illicit drugs, the way they work in the human body, and their role in the everyday lives of humans. Chapter 13 deals specifically with opioids, while other chapters deal with more general topics, such as the prevention and treatment of drug dependence and addiction.

Hendrickson, Hollie. 2016. *Prescription for Pain Management: 10 State Strategies*. National Conference of State Legislatures. Denver, CO: National Conference of State Legislatures.

> This book reviews policies and practices in 10 states for dealing with pain management and opioid-related issues. The book's special virtue is a very large number of in-text links that allow one to follow up on some specific aspect of the topic under discussion.

Katel, Peter. 2016. *Opioid Crisis: Can Recent Reforms Curb the Epidemic?* Washington, DC: CQ Press. http://library.cqpress .com/cqresearcher/document.php?id=cqresrre2016100700. Accessed on November 26, 2017.

> This book provides an excellent overview of the current opioid crisis, with sections on the history of opioid abuse and addiction; how the current crisis developed in the United States; a chronology of important events in the abuse of opioid through the ages; and some specific information on the way the crisis is affecting individuals, governmental bodies, and the nation as a whole. More than 100 resources are listed in the book.

McAnally, Heath B. 2018. *Opioid Dependence: A Clinical and Epidemiologic Approach*. Cham, Switzerland: Springer.

> One of the best, most complete, and most up-to-date books on the opioid crisis, this work provides detailed

information on virtually every aspect of the situation from a technical perspective, much of which can be understood by the average reader.

Ng, Richard. 2017. *Pain Doctor's Dilemma: Prescribing Opioids in an Era of Overdose*. Bloomington, IN: Liferich Publishing.
The author was sentenced to 87 months in prison for prescribing opioids for an undercover agent for other than medical reasons. In this book, he describes that experience and explains the practical and ethical issues pain doctors face today because of the opioid epidemic.

Perritano, John. 2017. *Opioids: Heroin, Oxycontin, and Pain-killers*. Broomall, PA: Mason Crest.
This book is a good general introduction to the opioid crisis for readers in the age range of 8–12 years.

Pierce, Simon. 2017. *Prescription Drugs: Opioids That Kill*. New York: Lucent Press.
This book is intended for readers between 7th and 10th grades. It includes chapters on the history of modern medicine, the rise of prescription drug abuse, the consequences of addiction, recovery from addiction, and the fight against prescription drug abuse.

Porter, Ruth, and Maeve O'Connor, eds. 2008. *Substance P in the Nervous System*. Ciba Foundation Symposium. Hoboken, NJ: John Wiley & Sons.
The 18 chapters in this book cover all aspects of the role of substance P in the brain known to the time of publication.

Quinones, Sam. 2015. *Dreamland: The True Tale of America's Opiate Epidemic*. New York: Bloomsbury Press.
The author provides a popular description of the process by which heroin and other opiate addictions have come to be the nation's "most serious drug problem" in

the 21st century. His approach includes a very personal story of the opioid epidemic in one specific rural region of Texas.

Rotchford, J. Kimber. 2017. *Opioids in Chronic Pain Management: A Guide for Patients.* Port Townsend, WA: Olympic Medical Services.

This book is designed for the layperson who wants to know more about pain management. The book discusses options that are available for pain management, the process of developing a program to deal with pain, and ways of assessing and revising the effectiveness of that program.

Shattuck, Gary G. 2017. *Green Mountain Opium Eaters: A History of Early Addiction in Vermont.* Charleston, SC: The History Press.

The author provides a fascinating reconstruction of the half-century of history during which opium became the "drug of choice" among residents of one of the most remote regions in the United States. The epidemic became so bad that one medical authority of the time called the problem "the crying evil of the day."

Stolberg, Victor B. 2016. *Painkillers: History, Science, and Issues.* Santa Barbara, CA: Greenwood Press.

This book provides an excellent general introduction for young adults on the topics of pain management and opioids. It contains sections on the general nature of painkillers; a brief history of painkillers; how painkillers work; effects and applications; risks, misuse, and overdose; production, distribution, and regulation; the social dimensions of pain killers, and the future of painkillers.

## Articles

Beletsky, Leo, and Corey S. Davis. 2017. "Today's Fentanyl Crisis: Prohibition's Iron Law, Revisited." *The International Journal on Drug Policy*. 46: 156–159. http://www.ijdp.org/ article/S0955-3959(17)30154-8/fulltext. Accessed on January 10, 2018.

   The "Iron Law" mentioned in the title of this article was first coined by marijuana advocate Richard Cowan in 1986. It posits that the greater efforts exerted on drug control by law enforcement, the more potent the prohibited drug and/or its analogs become. The authors argue that the law applies to the increasing potency of heroin and fentanyl and its analogs during the current opioid crisis.

Beletsky, Leo, Josiah D. Rich, and Alexander Y. Walley. 2012. "Prevention of Fatal Opioid Overdose." *JAMA*. 308(18): 1863–1864.

   The authors point out that federal efforts for dealing with the opioid abuse issue have focused almost entirely on monitoring and securing the drug supply. They suggest that attention should also be paid to the use of naloxone, an antagonist to opioids, which can prevent death if supplied early enough in the respiratory failure experienced by a patient.

Birch, Edward A. 1889. "The Use of Indian Hemp in the Treatment of Chronic Chloral and Chronic Opium Poisoning." *The Lancet*. 133(3422): 625–627. http://www.onlinepot.org/medi cal/Dr_Tods_PDFs/s3_2.pdf. Accessed on January 14, 2018.

   This (obviously outdated) article describes a physician's experience in treating chronic pain with cannabis. He reports that he was "satisfied of its immense value" and especially "the *immediate* action of the drug."

Boehnke, Kevin F., Evangelos Litinas, and Daniel J. Clauw. 2016. "Medical Cannabis Use Is Associated with Decreased

Opiate Medication Use in a Retrospective Cross-Sectional Survey of Patients with Chronic Pain." *Journal of Pain.* 17(6): 739–744.

The purpose of this research was to learn whether individuals with chronic pain had begun to substitute marijuana for opioids for the treatment of that pain. In this study, 64 percent of subjects did follow this route.

Brady, Joanne E., et al. 2015. "Emergency Department Utilization and Subsequent Prescription Drug Overdose Death." *Annals of Epidemiology.* 25(8): 613–619.e2. https://www.ncbi .nlm.nih.gov/pmc/articles/PMC4675463/pdf/nihms740868 .pdf. Accessed on January 13, 2018.

The purpose of this study was to determine what relationship, if any, exists between emergency department (ED) visits for drug overdose and later deaths from overdose. The researchers found that the number of ED visits is a good predictor of risk for death and recommend that prevention programs be developed for frequent ED overdose visits.

Butler, Stephen F., Emily C. McNaughton, and Ryan A. Black. 2015. "Tapentadol Abuse Potential: A Postmarketing Evaluation Using a Sample of Individuals Evaluated for Substance Abuse Treatment." *Pain Medicine.* 16(1): 119–130.

Tapentadol is a relatively new opioid analgesic of considerable interest to the medical profession because it is a powerful painkiller but is much less subject to nonmedical use than are most other opioids. This study was designed to measure the extent the compound was used illicitly compared to oxymorphone, hydromorphone, hydrocodone, morphine, fentanyl, oxycodone, tramadol, and buprenorphine. Researchers found that the expected claims for the high effectiveness and low abuse potential for the compound were confirmed. Also see the companion study on the same compound at Emily C. McNaughton, et al. 2015. "Assessing Abuse Potential of New Analgesic

Medications Following Market Release: An Evaluation of Internet Discussion of Tapentadol Abuse." *Pain Medicine.* 16(1): 131–140.

Chakravarthy, Bharath, Shyam Shah, and Shahram Lotfipour. 2012. "Vital Signs: Prescription Drug Monitoring Programs and Other Interventions to Combat Prescription Opioid Abuse." *Western Journal of Emergency Medicine.* 13(5): 422–425. https://escholarship.org/uc/item/4zz8q955. Accessed on January 9, 2018.

> The authors use data from the CDC *Morbidity and Mortality Weekly Report* to assess the efficacy of state programs for prescription drug monitoring in preventing injury and death from the nonmedical use of prescription drugs such as opioids and find that states with strong programs of this kind tend to be more effective in reducing injury and death from prescription drug overdose.

Cole, Jon B., and Lewis S. Nelson. 2017. "Controversies and Carfentanil: We Have Much to Learn about the Present State of Opioid Poisoning." *The American Journal of Emergency Medicine.* 35(11): 1743–1745.

> The authors focus on the dangers posed by an increasingly popular analog of fentanyl, carfentanil.

David, Jonathan M., et al. 2014. "Using Poison Center Exposure Calls to Predict Prescription Opioid Abuse and Misuse-Related Emergency Department Visits." *Pharmacoepidemiology and Drug Safety.* 23(1): 18–25.

> The authors use data from the Researched Abuse, Diversion and Addiction-Related Surveillance System poison center program and from the Drug Abuse Warning Network to determine the effectiveness of poison centers as early-warning systems for possible prescription drug abuse. They find that poison centers can play an essential role in this method of diagnosis.

Fels, Helena, et al. 2017. "Two Fatalities Associated with Synthetic Opioids: AH-7921 and MT-45." *Forensic Science International.* 277: e30–e35.

This article reports in detail on the deaths of two individuals who died from overdoses of the substances named in the title. The two are, as yet, not particularly popular but do hold the potential for adding to issues relating to the opioid crisis in general. For more detailed information about these drugs, see reports by the European Monitoring Centre for Drugs and Drug Addiction at http://www.emcdda.europa.eu/attachements.cfm/att_222584_EN_AH-7921.pdf and http://www.emcdda.europa.eu/system/files/publications/810/TDAS14007ENN_477731.pdf.

Hartung, Daniel, et al. 2014. "Extended-Release Naltrexone for Alcohol and Opioid Dependence: A Meta-Analysis of Healthcare Utilization Studies." *Journal of Substance Abuse Treatment.* 47(2): 113–121. https://www.ncbi.nlm.nih.gov/pmc/articles/PMC4110954/pdf/nihms603325.pdf. Accessed on January 15, 2018.

This study compared the cost of injectable naltrexone to the oral form of the drug. Although the cost of about $1,000 a month for the injectable form was much higher than that for the oral form (about $2 per day), the overall health care savings were greater with the former. For a good summary of this research, see http://oregonstate.edu/ua/ncs/archives/2014/may/extended-release-medication-offers-significant-promise-treating-alcohol-opioid-dep. For an estimate of the cost of the oral form of the drug, see "Determining What Your Naltrexone Cost Will Be," in the Internet section.

Herry, C., et al. 2013. "Reducing Abuse of Orally Administered Prescription Opioids Using Formulation Technologies." *Journal of Drug Delivery Science and Technology.* 23(2): 103–110.

The authors review some of the methods that are now available for producing drugs in formats that make them less likely to be used for nonmedical purposes, while retaining their legitimate access for patients for whom they are intended.

Hikin, Laura, et al. 2018. "Multiple Fatalities in the North of England Associated with Synthetic Fentanyl Analogue Exposure: Detection and Quantitation. A Case Series from Early 2017." *Forensic Science International.* 282(1): 179–183.
    The authors discuss their work in connection with the discovery of 25 deaths associated with fentanyl analogs, substances for which no deaths had previously been reported in the United Kingdom.

Hwang, Catherine S., et al. 2015. "Prescription Drug Abuse." *JAMA Internal Medicine.* 175(2): 302–304.
    The authors report on a survey of 420 primary physicians in the United States concerning their attitudes about prescription drug abuse. The primary findings were that 90 percent of respondents thought that prescription drug abuse was a "big" or "moderate" problem in their communities; 85 percent said that opioids were misused in clinical practice; and 45 percent said they were less likely to prescribe opioids than they were in the previous year.

Ihongbe, Timothy O., and Saba W. Masho. 2016. "Prevalence, Correlates and Patterns of Heroin Use among Young Adults in the United States." *Addictive Behaviors.* 63: 74–81.
    This article provides a good overall picture of the status of heroin addiction among young adults in the United States, including the factors mentioned in the title of the report.

Kerensky, Todd, and Alexander Y. Walley. 2017. "Opioid Overdose Prevention and Naloxone Rescue Kits: What We Know and What We Don't Know." *Addiction Science & Clinical Practice.* 12: 4. https://doi.org/10.1186/s13722-016-0068-3. https://

ascpjournal.biomedcentral.com/articles/10.1186/s13722-016-0068-3. Accessed on January 10, 2018.

The authors take note that the value of naloxone kits in treating opioid overdoses has now been clearly confirmed. They mention a number of questions that remain about their use, however, such as the following: Who should receive naloxone kits and education? Should naloxone be offered to individuals who are already receiving other opioid therapies? How should we compare the risks and benefits of using naloxone? And how should naloxone be administered and at what dose?

Koneru, Anupama, Sreemantula Satyanarayana, and Shaik Rizwan. 2009. "Endogenous Opioids: Their Physiological Role and Receptors." *Global Journal of Pharmacology.* 3(3): 149–153. https://pdfs.semanticscholar.org/e83a/851842f363f7e7f561c5ca465df9578d6bbc.pdf. Accessed on January 13, 2018.

This article provides a somewhat technical and advanced introduction to the endogenous opioid system in the brain and the role of opioid receptors.

Krausz, Michael R., and Kerry L. Jang. 2018. "North American Opioid Crisis: Decline and Fall of the War on Drugs." *The Lancet Psychiatry.* 5(1): 6–8.

The authors argue that the "war on drugs" that has gone on in the United States for nearly a half century has been a failure in reducing the nation's drug problem and, more to the present time, the mind-set that calls drug use a "crime" has deterred opioid abusers from seeking the treatment they need to stay alive.

Kuramoto, Janet, et al. 2012. "Suicidal Ideation and Suicide Attempt across Stages of Nonmedical Prescription Opioid Use and Presence of Prescription Opioid Disorders among U.S. Adults." *Journal of Studies on Alcohol and Drugs.* 73(2): 178–184.

Researchers found that people who had once abused prescription drugs and then quit were at greater risk for suicidal thoughts and actions than were those who had never used such drugs and those who were addicted to the drugs.

Lankenau, Stephen E., et al. 2012. "Initiation into Prescription Opioid Misuse amongst Young Injection Drug Users." *The International Journal on Drug Policy.* 23(1): 37–44.
This article reports on a study attempting to determine the factors that lead to intravenous drug users' initiation into prescription drug abuse. Researchers found that the main factor was easy access to drugs used by parents, family, and friends and that prescription drug abuse was often the first step in transitioning to other forms of drug abuse, especially involving the use of heroin.

Leoìn, Casey, et al. 2018. "Changes in Public Order after the Opening of an Overdose Monitoring Facility for People Who Inject Drugs." *International Journal of Drug Policy.* 53: 90–95.
These researchers were interested in the question as to what would happen to a community in which a new harm reduction program, Supportive Place for Observation and Treatment, was created by Boston Care for the Homeless Program. They discovered a decrease of about 28 percent in the number of oversedated individuals on the streets in the area.

Lucyk, Scott N., and Lewis S. Nelson. 2017. "Novel Synthetic Opioids: An Opioid Epidemic within an Opioid Epidemic." *Annals of Emergency Medicine.* 69(1): 91–93.
This article summarizes recent research on new kinds of synthetic opioids and the problems they face for emergency department physicians and other health care workers.

Majeed, Muhammad Hassan, Ali Ahsan Ali, and Donna M. Sudak. 2018. "Mindfulness-Based Interventions for Chronic Pain: Evidence and Applications." *Asian Journal of Psychiatry.* 32: 79–83.
The authors suggest that mindfulness-based interventions have demonstrated "consistent moderate success" in the

treatment of chronic pain disorders. The benefits of such treatments are low risk and better outcomes when comorbidities such as anxiety or depression are present in the patient.

Manchikanti, Laxmaiah, et al. 2017. "Responsible, Safe, and Effective Prescription of Opioids for Chronic Non-Cancer Pain: American Society of Interventional Pain Physicians (ASIPP) Guidelines." *Pain Physician.* 20(2S): S3–S92. http://www.painphysicianjournal.com/current/pdf?article= NDIwMg%3D%3D&journal=103. Accessed on January 12, 2018.

This detailed and comprehensive document makes 22 recommendations for "best practice" prescribing of opioids and monitoring their use.

Mastropietro, David J., and Hossein Omidian. 2014. "Abuse-Deterrent Formulations: Part 1—Development of a Formulation-Based Classification System." *Expert Opinion on Drug Metabolism & Toxicology.* 11(2): 193–204.

Mastropietro, David J., and Hossein Omidian. 2015. "Abuse-Deterrent Formulations: Part 2—Commercial Products and Proprietary Technologies." *Expert Opinion on Drug Metabolism & Toxicology.* 16(3): 305–323.

These two articles provide a comprehensive review of the variety of formulations that have been and are being developed as a way of making it more difficult to use opioids and other prescription drugs for nonmedical purposes.

McQueen, Karen, and Jodie Murphy-Oikonen. 2016. "Neonatal Abstinence Syndrome." *New England Journal of Medicine.* 375(25): 2468–2479.

This excellent article provides a comprehensive overview of NAS, including the history of its discovery, epidemiology, terminology, clinical features and outcomes, prevention, identification of infants at risk, and management.

Merlin, M. D. 2003. "Archaeological Evidence for the Tradition of Psychoactive Plant Use in the Old World." *Economic Botany.* 57(3): 295–323. https://ia801605.us.archive .org/23/items/Merlin2003AncientPsychoactivePlantUse/ Merlin_2003_Ancient_Psychoactive_Plant_Use.pdf. Accessed on January 12, 2018.

> This article covers several psychoactive substances but has an excellent section on the early history of opium in human civilizations.

Misailidi, Nektaria, et al. 2018. "Fentanyls Continue to Replace Heroin in the Drug Arena: The Cases of Ocfentanil and Carfentanil." *Forensic Toxicology.* 36(1): 12–32.

> This article describes the role of two relatively new fentanyl analogs in the current opioid crisis.

Misailidi, Nektaria, et al. 2018. "Furanylfentanyl: Another Fentanyl Analogue, Another Hazard for Public Health." *Forensic Toxicology.* 36(1): 1–11.

> The authors describe one of the newest fentanyl analogs, its history, mode and location of production, distribution, its legal status, and effects on the human brain.

Netherland, Julie, and Helena B. Hansen. 2016. "The War on Drugs That Wasn't: Wasted Whiteness, 'Dirty Doctors,' and Race in Media Coverage of Prescription Opioid Misuse." *Culture, Medicine, and Psychiatry: An International Journal of Cross-Cultural Health Research.* 40(4): 664–686.

> The authors report on a study comparing the way the heroin crisis among black and brown Americans largely in urban areas and largely white, rural, and suburban opioid misuse has been treated by the media. The story they present, they conclude, "is reminiscent of the legal distinction between crack cocaine and powder cocaine of the 1980s and 1990s."

Oei, J. Lee. 2018. "Adult Consequences of Prenatal Drug Exposure." *Internal Medicine Journal.* 48(1): 25–31.

The author reviews the issue of neonatal abstinence syndrome in the nation today and asks what is known about the long-term effects of this condition on individuals who experienced that problem. He concludes that "vulnerability to health and neurocognitive issues are pervasive and long-lasting as are lifestyle issues."

Pasquale, Margaret K., et al. 2014. "Cost Drivers of Prescription Opioid Abuse in Commercial and Medicare Populations." *Pain Practice.* 14(3): E116—E125.

The prescription drug abuse epidemic has had serious consequences not only in the field of health care, social issues, personal well-being, and politics but also in the field of economics. This study explores some of the factors in the prescription drug abuse epidemic that have affected health care costs for both the general population and those enrolled in the Medicare program.

Pergolizzi, Joseph V., Jr., et al. 2018. "Going Beyond Prescription Pain Relievers to Understand the Opioid Epidemic: The Role of Illicit Fentanyl, New Psychoactive Substances, and Street Heroin." *Postgraduate Medicine.* 130(1): 1–8.

The authors point out that the current opioid epidemic now goes far beyond the abuse of prescription opioids to include a range of other illicit opioids. The purpose of this article is "to consider the roles of all substances that contribute to the opioid epidemic in America."

Philpot, Lindsey M., et al. 2017. "Controlled Substance Agreements for Opioids in a Primary Care Practice." *Journal of Pharmaceutical Policy and Practice.* 10: 29. doi:10.1186/ s40545-017-0119-5. https://www.ncbi.nlm.nih.gov/pmc/

articles/PMC5596855/pdf/40545_2017_Article_119.pdf. Accessed on January 14, 2018.

The authors describe a program, controlled substance agreements, by which individuals who have been prescribed opioids for chronic pain agree to participate in follow-up counseling and education about opioid safety, appropriate dosing, and tapering off use.

Prekupec, Matthew P., Peter A. Mansky, and Michael J. Baumann. 2017. "Misuse of Novel Synthetic Opioids: A Deadly New Trend." *Journal of Addiction Medicine.* 11(4): 256–265. https://www.ncbi.nlm.nih.gov/pmc/articles/PMC5537029/pdf/adm-11-256.pdf. Accessed on January 11, 2018.

The authors provide an excellent and complete overview of current problems associated with illicitly manufactured fentanyl. It includes data on epidemiology of use, pharmacology and toxicology, intoxication and management, forensic detection, legal and regulatory issues, and other related emerging threats.

Raffa, R. B., et al. 2018. "The Fentanyl Family: A Distinguished Medical History Tainted by Abuse." *Journal of Clinical Pharmacy and Therapeutics.* 43(1): 154–158.

This article reviews the history of fentanyl and its analogs, going back to the 1950s. It discusses the beneficial features of the drugs and explains how the family has lost some of its allure because of its role in the current opioid epidemic.

Raffaeli, Genny, et al. 2017. "Neonatal Abstinence Syndrome: Update on Diagnostic and Therapeutic Strategies." *Pharmacotherapy: The Journal of Human Pharmacology and Drug Therapy.* 37(7): 814–823.

The authors provide an update on the most common and most effective methods for the diagnosis and treatment of NAS.

Reiman, Amanda, Mark Welty, and Perry Solomon. 2017. "Cannabis as a Substitute for Opioid-Based Pain Medication: Patient Self-Report." *Cannabis and Cannabinoid Research.* 2(1): 160–166. http://online.liebertpub.com/doi/pdf/10.1089/can .2017.0012. Accessed on January 14, 2018.

The authors explored the issue as to whether cannabis can be used as an adjunct to or a substitute for prescription opioids for the treatment of chronic pain. They said that respondents "overwhelmingly reported that cannabis provided relief on par with their other medications, but without the unwanted side effects. Ninety-seven percent of the sample 'strongly agreed/agreed' that they are able to decrease the amount of opiates they consume when they also use cannabis, and 81% 'strongly agreed/agreed' that taking cannabis by itself was more effective at treating their condition than taking cannabis with opioids."

Schuckit, Marc A. 2016. "Treatment of Opioid-Use Disorders." *New England Journal of Medicine.* 375: 357–368. http:// www.nejm.org/doi/full/10.1056/NEJMra1604339#t=article. Accessed on January 15, 2018.

This article reviews the variety of approaches that are available for treating opioid use disorder, along with suggestions for rehabilitation and maintenance.

Soelberg, Cobin D., et al. 2017. "The US Opioid Crisis: Current Federal and State Legal Issues." *Anesthesia and Analgesia.* 125(5): 1675–1681.

This article provides a good, general overview of the major legal issues relating to the opioid crisis as of late 2017.

Soledad Cepeda, M., et al. 2013. "Opioid Shopping Behavior: How Often, How Soon, Which Drugs, and What Payment Method." *The Journal of Clinical Pharmacology.* 53(1): 112–117.

The purpose of this research study was to determine the characteristic features displayed by so-called doctor shoppers who attempt to purchase prescription drugs from a variety of sources.

Terplan, Mishka. 2017. "Women and the Opioid Crisis: Historical Context and Public Health Solutions." *Fertility and Sterility.* 108(2): 195–199.

The author compares the effect of the current opioid crisis on women to a similar situation in the early 20th century. She suggests that practitioners consider the special issues involved in treating women with opioid issues compared to the general population.

Tolia, Veeral N., et al. 2015. "Increasing Incidence of the Neonatal Abstinence Syndrome in U.S. Neonatal ICUs." *New England Journal of Medicine.* 372: 2118–2126. http://www.nejm.org/doi/citedby/10.1056/NEJMsa1500439#t=citedby/ Accessed on January 11, 2018.

This article provides some of the most complete and most up-to-date statistics on the demographics of NAS in the United States as of 2015.

Walsh, Sharon L., and Shanna Babalonis. 2017. "The Abuse Potential of Prescription Opioids in Humans—Closing in on the First Century of Research." *Current Topics in Behavioral Neurosciences.* 34: 33–58.

This article provides an unusually detailed description of attempts to develop an analgesic for chronic pain throughout the 20th century, an excellent reference for the history of opioids in the United States during that period of time.

Weisberg, D., and C. Stannard. 2013. "Lost in Translation? Learning from the Opioid Epidemic in the USA." *Anaesthesia.* 68(12): 1215–1219. http://onlinelibrary.wiley.com/doi/10.1111/anae.12503/epdf. Accessed on January 9, 2018.

The authors compare the prescription drug abuse epidemic in the United States with similar problems in the United Kingdom and suggest that there are lessons to be learned in the United Kingdom based on the experience in the United States.

Wickramatilake, Shalini. 2017. "How States Are Tackling the Opioid Crisis." *Public Health Reports*. 132(2): 171–179.
The authors report on a nationwide review of policies and practices of state health agencies in dealing with the opioid crisis. They conclude that, in general, the states have demonstrated a "robust response" to the crisis.

Wright, Eric R., et al. 2014. "The Iatrogenic Epidemic of Prescription Drug Abuse: County-Level Determinants of Opioid Availability and Abuse." *Drug and Alcohol Dependence*. 138: 209–215.
This study explores the question as to the relationship between the availability of opioids in a geographical region and the amount of prescription drug abuse and finds that such a relationship exists. Counties with a larger concentration of pharmacists and dentists tend to have a greater number of illicit prescription drug users, thus supporting an iatrogenic (i.e., caused by medical treatment itself) basis for prescription drug abuse.

Wu, Jasmanda, and Juhaeri Juhaeri. 2016. "The US Food and Drug Administration's Risk Evaluation and Mitigation Strategy (REMS) Program—Current Status and Future Direction." *Clinical Therapeutics*. 38(12): 2526–2532.
The authors provide a good general overview of the current REMS program of the FDA that includes the case history of a specific (non-opioid) drug, dronedarone. They also discuss some future possibilities for the program. The article is useful because of the numerous links to other articles dealing with the REMS program.

## Reports

Austin, Gregory A. 1978. "Perspectives on the History of Psychoactive Substance Use." Rockville, MD: National Institute

on Drug Abuse. https://babel.hathitrust.org/cgi/pt?id=uc1.32
106001081378;view=1up;seq=7. Accessed on January 8, 2018.
This research report contains chapters on the use and misuse of drugs such as tobacco, cocaine, opioids, and stimulants at various times in history dating back two millennia
to the present day and in different countries, such as Great
Britain, Jamaica, China, and the United States.

"Database of Statutes, Regulations, & Other Policies for Pain
Management." 2017. Pain & Policies Study Group. http://
www.painpolicy.wisc.edu/database-statutes-regulations-other-
policies-pain-management. Accessed on January 8, 2018.
This website summarizes recommendations by professional organizations for laws and policies relating to the
opioid epidemic, along with a detailed review of existing
laws and regulations in all 47 states where they exist and
the District of Columbia. (The three states without such
legislation were Illinois, Montana, and South Dakota.)

"Facing Addiction in America: The Surgeon General's Report on
Alcohol, Drugs, and Health." 2016. U.S. Department of Health
and Human Services. https://addiction.surgeongeneral.gov/
surgeon-generals-report.pdf. Accessed on November 24, 2017.
This comprehensive report summarizes the status of drug
use problems in the United States as of the mid-2010s.
Chapters of the report deal with issues such as a general
introduction to the problem and an overview of the report; the neurobiology of substance use, misuse, and
addiction; prevention programs and policies; early intervention, treatment, and management of substance abuse
disorders; recovery and paths to wellness; health care systems and substance abuse disorders; and a vision for the
future and public health aspects of the problem.

"Federal Guidelines for Opioid Treatment Programs." 2015.
Rockville, MD: Substance Abuse and Mental Health Ser-
vices Administration. HHS Publication No. (SMA) PEP15-
FEDGUIDEOTP. https://store.samhsa.gov/shin/content//PE

P15-FEDGUIDEOTP/PEP15-FEDGUIDEOTP.pdf. Accessed on January 8, 2018.

This document is an updated version of an earlier edition from 2007. It provides detailed recommendations for every aspect of opioid treatment programs, such as facility management, telemedicine services, risk management, community relations, pregnant and postpartum patients, neonatal abstinence syndrome, clinical assessment, testing and screening for drug use, recordkeeping and documentation, and pharmacotherapy.

Hersman, Deborah A. P. 2017. "How the Prescription Drug Crisis Is Impacting American Employers." National Safety Council. http://www.nsc.org/NewsDocuments/2017/Media-Briefing-National-Employer-Drug-Survey-Results.pdf. Accessed on January 13, 2018.

This PowerPoint presentation summarizes the results of a survey commissioned by the National Safety Council to discover "U.S. employers' perceptions of and experiences with prescription drugs, and processes and policies for dealing with it." The survey discovered a number of interesting points, such as that more than 70 percent of employers report having been impacted by the current opioid epidemic, only 19 percent feel competent to deal with such issues in the workplace, 76 percent are not providing training to help supervisors identify possible drug abusers, and 41 percent of employers who have required drug testing do not include opioids in their testing panel. For detailed information about the survey itself, see "Prescription Drug Misuse Impacts More Than 70% of U.S. Workplaces." 2017. National Safety Council. http://www.nsc.org/Connect/NSCNewsReleases/Lists/Posts/Post.aspx?ID=182. Accessed on January 13, 2018.

National Academies of Sciences, Engineering, and Medicine. 2017. *Pain Management and the Opioid Epidemic: Balancing Societal and Individual Benefits and Risks of Prescription*

*Opioid Use.* Washington, DC: The National Academies Press. doi:10.17226/24781. https://www.nap.edu/download/24781. Accessed on January 9, 2018.

This report is a response to a request by the Food and Drug Administration to

- update the state of the science on pain research, care, and education since publication of the 2011 Institute of Medicine (IOM) report *Relieving Pain in America: A Blueprint for Transforming Prevention, Care, Education, and Research,* including the evolving role of opioids in pain management;
- characterize the epidemiology of the opioid epidemic and the evidence on strategies for addressing it;
- identify actions the FDA and other organizations can take to respond to the epidemic, with a particular focus on the FDA's development of a formal method for incorporating individual and societal considerations into its risk-benefit framework for opioid approval and monitoring; and
- identify research questions that need to be addressed to assist the FDA in implementing this framework. (From the report's Summary, page 1)

O'Connor, Sean. 2017. "Fentanyl: China's Deadly Export to the United States." Washington, DC: U.S.-China Economic and Security Review Commission.

The author describes in some detail how drug manufacturers in China are able to export fentanyl and its analogs to the United States through a "chain of forwarding systems, mislabeling narcotic shipments, and modifying chemicals so they are not controlled in the United States."

O'Donnell, Julie K., R. Matthew Gladden, and Puja Seth. 2017. "Trends in Deaths Involving Heroin and Synthetic Opioids Excluding Methadone, and Law Enforcement Drug Product Reports, by Census Region—United States, 2006–2015." *Morbidity and Mortality Weekly Report.* 66(34): 897–903.

https://www.cdc.gov/mmwr/volumes/66/wr/mm6634a2.htm.
Accessed on January 12, 2018.

This report contains some of the most recent data available on death rates from all opioid-related substance (except methadone) from 2006 to 2015.

"Prescribing Policies: States Confront Opioid Overdose Epidemic." 2017. National Conference of State Legislatures. Denver, CO: National Conference of State Legislatures. http://www.ncsl.org/Portals/1/Documents/Health/prescribingOpioids_final01-web.pdf. Accessed on November 26, 2017.

This report provides an excellent summary of the various types of prevention and treatment programs that individual states have developed for dealing with the opioid epidemic.

"A Prescription for Action." 2016. National Association of Counties and the National League of Cities. n.p. http://opioidaction.org/report/. Accessed on January 8, 2018.

This report analyzes the effect of the current opioid crisis on cities and counties, explains how it is different from earlier drug epidemics, and lays out a series of recommendations for ways in which governmental agencies at all levels can begin to deal with the crisis.

"Progress Report on the Joint Statement of Action to Address the Opioid Crisis in Canada (December 2016 to February 2017)." 2017. Health Canada. http://www.ccsa.ca/Resource%20Library/CCSA-Addressing-Opioid-Crisis-in-Canada-Summary-Report-2017-en.pdf. Accessed on January 9, 2018.

Although this book has said little about the opioid crisis in countries other than the United States, such a crisis exists in many other nations of the world. This recent publication summarizes efforts being made in Canada to deal with that country's opioid epidemic.

Reddy, Uma M., et al. 2017. "Opioid Use in Pregnancy, Neonatal Abstinence Syndrome, and Childhood Outcomes: Executive Summary of a Joint Workshop by the Eunice Kennedy Shriver National Institute of Child Health and Human Development, American College of Obstetricians and Gynecologists, American Academy of Pediatrics, Society for Maternal-Fetal Medicine, Centers for Disease." *Obstetrics and Gynecology.* 130(1): 10–28. http://journals.lww.com/greenjournal/fulltext/ 2017/07000/Opioid_Use_in_Pregnancy,_Neonatal_ Abstinence.4.aspx. Accessed on January 11, 2018.

This article provides a report of a conference convened to "address numerous knowledge gaps and to review the evidence for the screening and management of opioid use in pregnancy and neonatal abstinence syndrome." The five major issues addressed at the conference were optimal screening programs for opioid use in pregnancy; complications of pregnancy associated with opioid use; appropriate treatments for pregnant women with opioid use disorders; the best approaches for detecting, treating, and managing newborns with NAS; and the long-term effects of prenatal opioid exposure on children.

Sacco, Lisa N., and Erin Bagalman. 2017. "The Opioid Epidemic and Federal Efforts to Address It: Frequently Asked Questions." Congressional Research Service. https://fas.org/ sgp/crs/misc/R44987.pdf. Accessed on January 8, 2018.

This report lists some commonly asked questions about the opioid epidemic and answers to those questions in five general areas: overview of opioid abuse, overview of opioid supply, select federal agencies and programs that address opioid abuse, recent legislation, and opioid abuse and state policies.

"A Second Chance: Overdose Prevention, Naloxone, and Human Rights in the United States." 2017. Human Rights Watch. http://fileserver.idpc.net/library/usnaloxone0417_web .pdf. Accessed on November 26, 2017.

Human Rights Watch is interested in issues of opioid abuse because individuals who are opioid abusers or addicts deserve to receive the best possible medical care for their condition. The organization strongly recommends the use of naloxone for opioid overdoses and presents its views in this report. The major part of the report focuses on the advantages of using naloxone for opioid issues.

"The 2018–2023 World Outlook for Opioids." 2017. Warsaw, Poland. Healthcare Market Research Reports.

This report provides information on the outlook for the opioids epidemic for more than 190 countries around the world.

"The Underestimated Cost of the Opioid Crisis." 2017. The Council of Economic Advisors. https://www.whitehouse.gov/ sites/whitehouse.gov/files/images/The%20Underestimated% 20Cost%20of%20the%20Opioid%20Crisis.pdf. Accessed on January 9, 2018.

This report begins with the assumption that previous reports on the economic costs of the opioid epidemic "greatly understate it by undervaluing the most important component of the loss—fatalities resulting from overdoses." It then offers a new analysis of the situation and suggests that the crisis is about $504.0 billion in 2015, about six times the other most recent study of this type.

Weiss, Audrey J., et al. 2017. "Opioid-Related Inpatient Stays and Emergency Department Visits by State, 2009–2014." Statistic Brief #219. Healthcare Cost and Utilization Project. https://www.hcup-us.ahrq.gov/reports/statbriefs/sb219-Opioid-Hospital-Stays-ED-Visits-by-State.jsp. Accessed on January 13, 2018.

This report provides some of the most recent data available on visits to emergency departments in all 50 states and the District of Columbia between 2009 and 2014.

## Internet

Anson, Pat. 2016. "'Opioid Vaccine' Could Revolutionize Addiction Treatment." Pain News Networks. https://www.pain newsnetwork.org/stories/2016/11/29/opioid-vaccine-could-revo lutionize-addiction-treatment. Accessed on January 9, 2018.

This article provides a general overview of the search for an opioid vaccine, with the current status of that research effort. For a more detailed and technical description of progress in the field, see Raleigh, M. D., et al. 2017. "Safety and Efficacy of an Oxycodone Vaccine: Addressing Some of the Unique Considerations Posed by Opioid Abuse." *PLOS One.* https://doi.org/10.1371/journal.pone.0184876, http://journals.plos.org/plosone/article?id=10.1371/journal.pone.0184876. Accessed on January 9, 2018.

"Associated Medical Problems in Patients Who Are Opioid Addicted." 2005. Treatment Improvement Protocol (TIP) Series, No. 43, Chapter 10. Rockville, MD: Center for Substance Abuse Treatment. Substance Abuse and Mental Health Services Administration. https://www.ncbi.nlm.nih.gov/books/NBK64167/. Accessed on January 14, 2018.

This chapter reviews some of the issues involved in treating individuals with opioid dependence or addiction, who also have comorbidities such as diabetes, asthma, hypertension, severe dental problems, seizure disorders, chronic obstructive pulmonary disease, coronary artery disease, or other illnesses related to long-term heavy tobacco use.

Aswell, Tom. 2018. "Will Louisiana's Opioid Lawsuit Make a Difference? A Realistic Case for Big Pharmaceutical Companies to Emerge as Winners." *Louisiana Voice.* https://louisianavoice.com/2018/01/05/will-louisianas-opioid-lawsuit-make-a-difference-a-realistic-case-for-big-pharmaceutical-companies-to-emerge-as-winners/. Accessed on January 9, 2018.

The author takes a look at political factors involved in Louisiana's efforts to combat the opioid epidemic in the state by suing large pharmaceutical companies.

Beier, Michael. 2016. "Is Addiction a 'Brain Disease'?" Harvard Health Publishing. https://www.health.harvard.edu/blog/
is-addiction-a-brain-disease-201603119260. Accessed on January 16, 2018.

> Beier explains why he believes the answer to this question
> is *yes* and provides some useful links to others who think
> as he does. For a contrary view, see Satel (2016).

"A Brief Overview of Risk Evaluation & Mitigation Strategies." 2017. U.S. Food and Drug Administration. https://www
.fda.gov/downloads/AboutFDA/Transparency/Basics/
UCM328784.pdf. Accessed on January 12, 2018.

> In the Food and Drug Administration Amendments Act
> of 2007, the U.S. Congress gave the FDA authority to
> require manufacturers to provide evidence that new drugs
> provided greater benefit than any harm that might result
> from their use. REMS requirements have, since that time,
> become an essential feature of the FDA's monitoring of
> new drug products. This slide show provides a good general overview of the program.

"Call to Action and Issue Brief: Justice System Use of Prescription Drug Monitoring Programs—Addressing the Nation's
Prescription Drug and Opioid Abuse Epidemic." 2015. Global
Justice Information Sharing Initiative. https://it.ojp.gov/
gist/174/Call-to-Action-and-Issue-Brief—Justice-System-Use-
of-Prescription-Drug-Monitoring-Programs—Addressing-
the-Nations-Prescription-Drug-and-Opioid-Abuse-Epidemic.
Accessed on January 9, 2018.

> This brochure describes PDMPs (prescription drug monitoring programs) in place in the various states and outlines some of the reasons that law enforcement agencies
> need to be intimately involved in these programs. It also
> provides some specific suggestions as to how the integration of law enforcement activities with PDMPs can be
> accomplished most successfully.

Clayton, Chris. 2018. "Farm Groups Step Up to Tackle Opioid Crisis." https://www.dtnpf.com/agriculture/web/ag/perspectives/blogs/ag-policy-blog/blog-post/2018/01/03/farm-groups-step-tackle-opioid-2. Accessed on January 9, 2018.

This short article reviews ways in which two of the nation's largest farm groups, the American Farm Bureau Federation and the National Farmers' Union, have begun to take action against the opioid epidemic in rural areas. The article is useful because of the links it provides to other stories with more details about this situation.

"Combatting the Opioid Epidemic: A Review of Anti-Abuse Efforts in Medicare and Private Health Insurance Systems." 2017. Permanent Subcommittee on Investigations. Committee on Homeland Security and Governmental Affairs. https://www.gpo.gov/fdsys/pkg/CPRT-114SPRT23066/pdf/CPRT-114SPRT23066.pdf. Accessed on November 26, 2017.

This subcommittee meeting dealt with the types of programs and principles that have been developed for dealing with the nation's current opioid epidemic.

Conroy, Michael. 2017. "Special Schools Help Opioid-Addicted Teens Stay Clean." STAT. https://www.statnews.com/2017/04/25/schools-opioid-addicted-teens/. Accessed on January 15, 2018.

An estimated 1,100 teenagers begin misusing opioids every day in the United States. One of the many challenges faced by these young adults is remaining in an educational situation, such as high school. This article reviews a "recovery school," where students can continue their education while getting assistance in dealing with their substance abuse problems.

Dawson, George. 2017. "Why Buprenorphine Is No Panacea for Opioid Addiction—An Insider View." Real Psychiatry. http://

real-psychiatry.blogspot.com/2017/02/why-buprenorphine-is-no-panacea-for.html. Accessed on January 14, 2018.

Buprenorphine has many advocates as an effective drug for the treatment of opioid addicts. This author points out a number of problems with that form of treatment, however, such as the need for indefinite treatment, the street value of the drug, the small, "but significant," street value for addicts, and the lack of appropriate prescribing.

Derse, Arthur, and Diana Contino. 2016. *The Opioid Epidemic: New Policies, Treatments, and Non-Opioid Alternatives.* Cary, NC: Relias Learning. https://www.ahcmedia.com/products/86427-the-opioid-epidemic-new-policies-treatments-and-non-opioid-alternatives. Accessed on January 9, 2018.

This e-book is available only online and by purchase. It summarizes information of interest especially to practitioners in the field, such as the current state of the epidemic, best practices in hospital prescribing practices, options for non-opioid treatment of pain, and latest information on medication-assisted treatments for opioid addiction.

"Determining What Your Naltrexone Cost Will Be." 2018. Naltrexone HQ. http://naltrexonehq.com/naltrexone-cost/. Accessed on January 15, 2018.

This website provides an estimate of the cost of using the oral form of naltrexone and ways in which that cost may vary from person to person.

Drennan, Ian R., and Aaron Orkin. 2016. "Opioid Crisis: Prehospital Naloxone Administration for Opioid-Related Emergencies." *JEMS.* 41(3). http://www.jems.com/articles/print/volume-41/issue-3/special-focus-resuscitation-recommendations/prehospital-naloxone-administration-for-opioid-related-emergencies.html. Accessed on January 9, 2018.

The authors provide a well-documented description of the use of naloxone in the treatment of opioid overdoses, including an update of the 2015 American Heart Association guidelines for naloxone treatment.

Erickson, Amanda. 2017. "Opioid Abuse in the U.S. Is So Bad It's Lowering Life Expectancy. Why Hasn't the Epidemic Hit Other Countries?" *Washington Post.* https://www.washington post.com/news/worldviews/wp/2017/12/28/opioid-abuse-in-america-is-so-bad-its-lowering-our-life-expectancy-why-hasnt-the-epidemic-hit-other-countries/?utm_term= .f1eb16c82cdf. Accessed on January 10, 2018.

This article reviews one of the most troubling trends caused by the opioid epidemic: a reduction in the life expectancy of Americans in 2015 and 2016. The article is especially helpful because of links to related articles and hundreds of blog comments on the topic.

"Examining the Opioid Epidemic: Challenges and Opportunities." 2017. Committee on Finance. U. S. Senate. https://www .finance.senate.gov/hearings/examining-the-opioid-epidemic-challenges-and-opportunities. Accessed on November 26, 2017.

This hearing explored the nature of the U.S. opioid epidemic and the ways in which both individuals and the federal government are being and will continue to be impacted by the epidemic.

Gonzalez, Robbie. 2018. "Scientists Just Solved a Major Piece of the Opioid Puzzle." *Wired.* https://www.wired.com/story/scientists-just-solved-a-major-piece-of-the-opioid-puzzle/. Accessed on January 9, 2018.

The author explains, in clear language, a discovery made that is fundamental to understanding and perhaps treating opioid dependence and addiction. The article to which this review appears is Che, Tao, et al. 2018. "Structure of the Nanobody-Stabilized Active State of the Kappa Opioid Receptor." *Cell.* 172(1–2): 55–67. http://www.cell .com/cell/fulltext/S0092-8674(17)31491-5. Accessed on January 9, 2018.

Graedon Joe. "What Is the Other Side of the Opioid Crisis?" The People's Pharmacy. https://www.peoplespharmacy.com/2017/10/08/what-is-the-other-side-of-the-opioid-crisis/. Accessed on January 10, 2018.

This web page focuses on the way concerns about the opioid epidemic have affected individuals with chronic pain who depend on the drugs for their day-to-day survival. The article is followed by several strongly worded blog entries on the topic.

Gurman, Sadie. 2018. "Feds Employ Data-Driven Early Warning System in Opioid Fight." *Washington Post.* https://www.washingtonpost.com/national/armed-with-new-data-officials-target-drug-dealing-doctors/2018/01/01/75033c6c-ef01-11e7-95e3-eff284e71c8d_story.html?utm_term=.031e02b4ccb8. Accessed on January 12, 2018.

This article describes a new approach instituted by the federal government for identifying doctors who overprescribe or misprescribe opioids. The system makes use of data to locate health care workers who prescribe opioids at rates higher than should be expected, patients who travel unusually long distance to get a prescription, and individuals who have died within 60 days of receiving a prescription.

Gussow, Leon. 2017. "Fentanyl, Carfentanil and the Opioid Crisis: Where Do We Stand Now?" *The Poison Review.* http://www.thepoisonreview.com/2017/09/19/fentanyl-carfentanil-and-the-opioid-crisis-where-do-we-stand-now/. Accessed on January 10, 2018.

This blog provides an excellent discussion of the role of fentanyl and its analogs in the current opioid crisis. Of special interest are the blog comments on the topic, with responses from the author of the article.

"Help Reinforce Your Recovery." 2017. Vivitrol. https://www.vivitrol.com/. Accessed on January 15, 2018.

This information sheet is provided by the manufacturers of Vivitrol, an injectable form of naltrexone for opioid addiction.

"How Does the Opioid System Control Pain, Reward and Addictive Behavior?" 2007. European College of Neuropsychopharmacology. EurekaAlert. https://www.eurekalert .org/pub_releases/2007-10/econ-hdt101207.php. Accessed on January 13, 2018.

This article provides a good general introduction to the topic of endogenous opioids and their actions in the brain.

"Increase in Hepatitis C Infections Linked to Worsening Opioid Crisis." 2017. Centers for Disease Control and Prevention. https://www.cdc.gov/nchhstp/newsroom/2017/hepatitis-c-and-opioid-injection-press-release.html. Accessed on January 9, 2018.

This article takes note of the explosive growth in hepatitis C cases in the United States in recent years (up as much as 400 percent over the past decade among Americans aged 18–29) and explains how that trend is associated with opioid abuse.

"An Introduction to Extended-Release Injectable Naltrexone for the Treatment of People with Opioid Dependence." 2012. Substance Abuse and Mental Health Services Administration. https://www.integration.samhsa.gov/Intro_To_Injectable_ Naltrexone.pdf. Accessed on January 15, 2018.

This advisory statement provides detailed information for specialists in the field on all aspects of the use of injectable naltrexone for individuals with opioid dependence or addiction, including how it compares with other medication-assisted treatment options, and clinical strategies that may be used to select, initiate, and administer treatment.

Koh, Howard K. 2017. "JAMA Forum: Community-Based Prevention and Strategies for the Opioid Crisis." News@JAMA.

https://newsatjama.jama.com/2017/08/22/jama-forum-community-based-prevention-and-strategies-for-the-opioid-crisis/. Accessed on January 10, 2018.

> Koh reviews a number of community-based options for dealing with prevention of the opioid crisis. Of special value for the article is the number of links to other related articles on the topic.

Lee, Joshua D. 2013. "Extended-Release Naltrexone." Drug Court Practitioner Fact Sheet. https://www.ndci.org/wp-content/uploads/NDCI&SAMHSA-Naltrexone-FS%20(1)%20(1).pdf. Accessed on January 15, 2018.

> One of the common uses of naltrexone maintenance therapy for opioid abusers is for individuals in the criminal justice system: those who have been convicted of a crime or those released from jail or prisons. This publication reviews the evidence for this practice that the drug provides drug courts with "an effective tool to discourage program violations and promote successful outcomes for their participants."

Luthra, Shefali. 2016. "Hoping to Attack Opioid Epidemic at Its Source, State Medicaid Programs Are Limiting Prescriptions." STAT. https://www.statnews.com/2016/11/23/medicaid-opioid-limits/. Accessed on January 12, 2018.

> This article provides a very good summary of changes in state laws designed to reduce the number of opioid prescriptions being written by physicians, as a way of reducing release of those drugs to abusers. It contains a number of good links to articles dealing with more specific aspects of the issue.

Lynn, John. 2017. "ePrescribing and Combating the Opioid Crisis." Hospital EMR and HER. https://www.hospitalemrandehr.com/2017/12/15/eprescribing-and-combating-the-opioid-crisis/. Accessed on January 10, 2018.

> This video is focused on a discussion of the ways in which eprescribing of drugs can be used to help fight the opioid epidemic.

"Mandatory Guidelines for Urine Testing Updated to Include Four Semi-Synthetic Opioids." 2017 Substance Abuse and Mental Health Services Administration. https://www.samhsa.gov/newsroom/press-announcements/201709291000. Accessed on January 12, 2018.

This article reviews new federal requirements for the testing for four semisynthetic opioids: oxycodone, oxymorphone, hydrocodone, and hydromorphone. The article explains the rationale for testing and exceptions granted for positive results. The detailed regulation itself can be found at https://www.federalregister.gov/documents/2017/01/23/2017-00979/mandatory-guidelines-for-federal-workplace-drug-testing-programs.

Marechal, Iris. 2018. "The Opioid Crisis: A Consequence of U.S. Economic Decline?" Washington Center for Equitable Growth. http://equitablegrowth.org/equitablog/value-added/the-opioid-crisis-a-consequence-of-u-s-economic-decline/. Accessed on January 16, 2018.

Some experts have suggested that the opioid epidemic can be explained, at least in part, by the economic decline in the United States over the past decade. They refer to these deaths as "deaths of despair" because individuals have lost hope in their ability to survive under present economic conditions. This article presents arguments supporting this theory, as well as research that tends to make it less attractive.

"Naltrexone Implant for Preventing Opioid Addiction Relapse." 2017. Rehabs.com. https://luxury.rehabs.com/naltrexone-vivitrol/implant-for-opiate-addiction/#definition. Accessed on January 15, 2018.

Naltrexone is available in the United States in one of two forms: a pill or an injectable extended-release suspension. The drug is also available in Europe and Australia in another form: a subcutaneous implant. This article describes this method of naltrexone use, its advantages and disadvantages, and its cost in places where it is available.

"Opioid Overdose." 2017. Centers for Disease Control and Prevention. https://www.cdc.gov/drugoverdose/index.html. Accessed on January 9, 2018.

> This website provides an excellent general introduction to the current opioids overdose, including sections on factual information about opioids, ways in which states are trying to deal with the problem, information for health care providers, and data on the current crisis. This web page contains many useful links to related topics on the CDC website.

"Opioid Use Disorder: Diagnostic Criteria." 2013. American Psychiatric Association. https://pcssmat.org/wp-content/uploads/2014/02/5B-DSM-5-Opioid-Use-Disorder-Diagnostic-Criteria.pdf. Accessed on January 15, 2018.

> This publication is an extract from the *Diagnostic and Statistical Manual of Mental Disorders, Fifth Edition*, outlining the diagnostic criteria for the disorder, along with a detailed discussion of its characteristic features, methods of prevention, and approaches to treatment.

"Opioids: How They Trick the Brain to Make You Feel Good." 2015. *Vancouver Sun.* http://www.vancouversun.com/Opioid s+they+trick+brain+make+feel+good+with+video/9894363/story.html. Accessed on January 9, 2018.

> This article and accompanying video illustrate the changes that occur in the brain when the body ingests an opioid.

"Opioids: The Prescription Drug & Heroin Overdose Epidemic." 2017. U.S. Department of Health and Human Services. https://www.hhs.gov/opioids/index.html. Accessed on November 26, 2017.

> This website provides an excellent general introduction to the subject of the nation's current opioid epidemic, with sections on drugs and pain medications, prevention, treatment and recovery, overdose response, and health professional and law enforcement resources.

"Opioids in Palliative Care: Safe and Effective Prescribing of Strong Opioids for Pain in Palliative Care of Adults." 2012. NICE Clinical Guidelines, No. 140. Cardiff, UK: National Collaborating Centre for Cancer (UK).

> This publication summarizes current information on and recommendations for the use of opioid medications in palliative care, care of individuals with serious medical conditions, often those in the last stages of life. It discusses decisions as to which individuals may be candidates for opioid treatment, alternatives to opioids, and possible comorbidities and management of such adverse effects.

"The Physiological Mechanisms of Opioid Receptors." 2017. http://physiologicalmechanismsofopioids.weebly.com/. Accessed on January 9, 2018.

> This web page with its accompanying videos provides a more detailed and advanced description of changes that take place in the brain when it is exposed to opioids.

Pohle, Allison. 2016. "I'd Be in a Worse Situation—or Dead—if I Weren't Here." Boston.com. https://www.boston.com/news/local-news/2016/08/03/massachusetts-high-school-teens-addicted-heroin-stay-alive. Accessed on January 15, 2018.

> This long story about a recovery school in Massachusetts gives a vivid description of the experiences of teenagers who attend the school and attempt to deal with opioid addiction at the same time.

"Problem Behaviors Can Signal Risk in Prescribing Opioids to Teens." 2013. National Institute on Drug Abuse. http://www.drugabuse.gov/news-events/nida-notes/2013/07/problem-behaviors-can-signal-risk-in-prescribing-opioids-to-teens. Accessed on January 9, 2018.

> This article summarizes two research studies on the characteristics of adolescents who become prescription opioid drug abusers and the indications that these individuals may become more general substance abusers in the future.

"Profit Mining the Opioid Crisis: The Dark Underbelly of Lucrative Addiction Treatment Industry." 2018. Kaiser Health News. https://khn.org/morning-breakout/profit-mining-the-opioid-crisis-the-dark-underbelly-of-lucrative-addiction-treatment-industry/. Accessed on January 9, 2018.

> This article focuses on the rapid growth in "treatment" programs for opioids that has resulted in enormous profits for companies and individuals. Links to four *New York Times* article on the issue are included.

"Promote Safe Storage and Disposal of Opioids and All Medications." 2017. American Academy of Family Physicians. https://www.aafp.org/dam/AAFP/documents/patient_care/pain_management/safe-storage.pdf. Accessed on January 11, 2018.

> Storage and disposal of opioids are important issues in dealing with the current epidemic because the theft of those substances is one of the primary methods by which unauthorized users gain access to them. This publication provides some general guidelines for physicians in dealing with these issues. They are guidelines that will be of interest to nonspecialists also.

Raleigh, M. D., et al. 2017. "Safety and Efficacy of an Oxycodone Vaccine: Addressing Some of the Unique Considerations Posed by Opioid Abuse." *PLOS One*. https://doi.org/10.1371/journal.pone.0184876, http://journals.plos.org/plosone/article?id=10.1371/journal.pone.0184876. Accessed on January 9, 2018.

> This article provides a technical review of progress currently being made on the development of an opioid vaccine. For a simpler, general explanation, see Anson, Pat. 2016. "'Opioid Vaccine' Could Revolutionize Addiction Treatment." Pain News Networks. https://www.pain newsnetwork.org/stories/2016/11/29/opioid-vaccine-could-revolutionize-addiction-treatment. Accessed on January 9, 2018.

Rhyan, Corwin N. 2017. "Research Brief: The Potential Societal Benefit of Eliminating Opioid Overdoses, Deaths, and Substance Use Disorders Exceeds $95 Billion per Year." Center for Value in Health Care. https://altarum.org/sites/default/files/uploaded-publication-files/Research-Brief_Opioid-Epidemic-Economic-Burden.pdf. Accessed on January 13, 2018.

The author reports on a study attempting to determine the economic costs of the opioid crisis. He places a value of about $95 billion for these costs for 2016 with a predicted increase for 2017. Costs represent expenses related to productivity impacts; health care costs; and criminal justice, child and family assistance, and education.

Satel, Sally. 2016. "Is Addiction a Brain Disease?" The Conversation. https://theconversation.com/is-addiction-a-brain-disease-51248. Accessed on January 16, 2018.

The author reviews the debate as to whether or not addiction is a brain disease and lays out her own views that it is not. For a contrasting view of the question, see Beier (2016).

Shipley, Ahlishia. 2018. "Opioid Crisis Affects All Americans, Rural and Urban." U.S. Department of Agriculture. https://www.usda.gov/media/blog/2018/01/11/opioid-crisis-affects-all-americans-rural-and-urban. Accessed on January 16, 2018.

This article provides an overview of the opioid crisis in rural areas. It is especially helpful because of the numerous links it provides to other articles dealing with this issue.

Singer, Jeffrey A. 2018. "Stop Calling It an Opioid Crisis—It's a Heroin and Fentanyl Crisis." Cato Institute. https://www.cato.org/blog/stop-calling-it-opioid-crisis-its-heroin-fentanyl-crisis. Accessed on January 10, 2018.

The author provides evidence that the current "opioid crisis" is really one that results primarily from the abuse of heroin and fentanyl and its analogs. He claims that naming the epidemic correctly will help deal with the problem more readily.

Thomas, Ashley, and Tracy E. Weir. 2017. "'Breaking Bad' News: Sharing PHI during Opioid Crisis." Baker Donelson. https://www.bakerdonelson.com/breaking-bad-news-sharing-phi-during-opioid-crisis. Accessed on January 10, 2018.

This article is aimed primarily at attorneys but presents an interesting issue in the legal field: how does the occurrence of an opioid crisis affect federal laws about the sharing of one's personal health information?. The article reviews the recent clarifying comments from the Office of Civil Rights on this issue.

"What Are the State Governments Doing to Combat the Opioid Abuse Epidemic?" 2015. Subcommittee on Oversight and Investigations. Committee on Energy and Commerce. U.S. House of Representatives. https://www.gpo.gov/fdsys/pkg/CHRG-114hhrg96932/html/CHRG-114hhrg96932.htm. Accessed on November 26, 2017.

This congressional hearing focuses on ways in which various states are dealing with the nation's opioid epidemic.

# 7 Chronology

## Introduction

The use and misuse of opium and its derivatives have been a part of human civilization almost from the beginning of recorded history. Some of the most important events in that long history are listed in this chapter. For some early dates, only estimates (ca.) are available.

**Earliest times**    Scholars have long debated the earliest date at which the use of opium has been mentioned. According to one source, that date may be as early as about 6000 BCE (Richard Rudgley, 2000. *The Lost Civilizations of the Stone Age*. New York: Simon & Schuster, 2000, 138). Other authorities claim much later dates, perhaps the most common of which is about 3400 BCE. During this period, Babylonian farmers appear to have been growing the crop. Its possible use for psychoactive purposes is reflected in the name given to the plant around that time, hul gil, or "the joy plant."

**ca. 2100 BCE**    A stone tablet from Sumeria dating to this period contains instructions for the use of opium and other

Activists rally outside the New York City Police Department headquarters during a protest denouncing the city's "inadequate and wrongheaded response" to the overdose crisis. The group is calling for a more public health–focused approach and wants the $70 million allocated to the city and NYPD's "Healing NYC" program to be redirected to the Department of Health and Mental Hygiene. (Drew Angerer/Getty Images)

products in what is now regarded as the world's oldest written medical prescription.

**ca. 1500 BCE**   A statue from the Minoan civilization of the period shows a goddess wearing a crown with three removable capsules that appear to be poppy flowers. The statue's closed eyes suggest to some authorities a state of trance that might be attributed to the use of opium.

**ca. 1300 BCE**   By this period, knowledge of the cultivation and use of opium had spread from Mesopotamia to Egypt. Archaeological evidence suggests that the plant was grown in large fields around the city of Thebes. One of the minor components of the opium seed, *thebaine*, is supposedly named after the city where it was so popular. During this period, the poppy seed was thought to have magical properties, and its use was restricted to priests, magicians, and warriors.

**ca. 1100 BCE**   Craftsmen on the island of Cyprus appear to have invented a sharp knife designed specifically for harvesting opium seeds. The knives are virtually identical to similar instruments used in some cultures today for the same purpose.

**ca. 460 BCE**   The great Greek physician Hippocrates writes about the medical uses of opium. He suggests the plant can be used to treat certain types of medical problems, such as women's diseases and diarrhea. He dismisses the concept, however, that these effects are the result of some type of magical property of the plant.

**ca. 330 BCE**   Alexander the Great brings knowledge of the opium plant from the Middle East to Persia and India. He reputedly used the plant on his own troops to dull the pain experienced as a result of their long marches, increasing the period of time that they could remain in battle or in traveling. He apparently also used extracts of the poppy seed to dull the pain of wounded soldiers.

**ca. 200 CE**   The Greek physician Claudius Galenus (also Aelius Galenus), generally known just as Galen, lists a number of medical uses for opium, including "resists poison and venomous bites, cures chronic headache, vertigo, deafness, epilepsy, apoplexy, dimness of sight, loss of voice, asthma, coughs of all kinds, spitting of blood, tightness of breath, colic, the lilac poison, jaundice, hardness of the spleen stone, urinary complaints, fever, dropsies, leprosies, the trouble to which women are subject, melancholy and all pestilences."

**ca. 5th to 8th century** CE   Many authorities claim that the poppy plant and opium were introduced into China by Arabian traders at some point during this period. However, evidence exists that the Chinese already knew about the plant and its medical benefits by this time. The Chinese physician Hua To, for example, describes his use of opium to treat patients during the period of the Three Kingdoms (220–264 CE).

**ca. 1000** CE   In his most famous work, *al-Qānūn fī al-Tibb* (*The Canon of Medicine*), the Persian scholar Avicenna describes the many properties of opium, including its use as an analgesic, a hypnotic, an antitussive, a gastrointestinal remedy, and a poison and for the treatment of cognitive disorders, respiratory conditions, depression, neuromuscular disturbance, and sexual dysfunction. *The Canon* remains one of the most influential of all medical works over the next seven centuries.

**ca. 1000** CE   Writings from India indicate that opium was known and used in the country, although limited to the nobility and armed forces. In the latter case, the drug was thought to help soldiers fight more strongly and with greater courage.

**ca. 1200**   The use of opium for medical treatments, as in cases of diarrhea and sexual dysfunction, is mentioned in important medical books of the time, such as the *Shodal Gadanigrah, Sharangdhar Samahita*, and *Dhanvantri Nighantu*. The drug was also used for other purposes, such as a sign of hospitality and a symbol of wealth and power.

**ca. 1300**   A strong bifurcation of attitudes about opium use develops in Western Europe. Largely under the influence of the Inquisition and teachings of the Roman Catholic Church, the use of opium for recreational purposes is strongly condemned as a remnant of devil worship imported to Europe from the Far East. The church also, however, does not restrict the use of opium products for strictly medical purposes. The overall effect of this mixed message is that the use of opium and its discussion in the extant literature are greatly reduced for a period of more than 200 years.

**ca. 1500**  The first mention of opium smoking is attributed to Portuguese sailors who ply the course between Europe and China. The practice was considered, however, to be "barbaric" by the Chinese.

**1527**  Interest in the use of opium as a medical product returns to Europe, largely as a result of the invention of laudanum by the Swiss physician Theophrastus von Hohenheim, more commonly known as *Paracelsus*. He devises a variety of concoctions in which opium is mixed with one or more of a variety of substances, including citrus juice, spices such as cinnamon and cariophilli, crushed pearls, amber, musk, derivatives of a cow intestine and/or stag's heart, and a small amount of gold to make either a liquid product or solid black pills known as *Stones of Immortality*. The primary therapeutic use of the products was relief from pain.

**1563**  A book by the influential Portuguese physician Garcia da Orta, *Colóquios dos simples e drogas he cousas medicinais da Índia* (*Conversations on the Simples, Drugs and Materia Medica of India*) includes a discussion of the medical applications of opium.

**1606**  Queen Elizabeth I of England arranges for English ships to collect opium from plantations in India to be brought back to England. The program is the first step in a somewhat complex program that develops in England whereby it pays for imports from China in opium, rather than silver, as the Chinese had preferred. The influx of opium into China marks the beginning of an epidemic of opium smoking that is to disrupt China for nearly two centuries.

**1624–1660**   At some point during this period, Dutch traders introduce to China the practice of smoking *madak*, a mixture of opium and tobacco. A large and profitable trade developed with the export of madak from the Dutch East Indies to Taiwan and coastal regions in China. Its availability in these areas contributed to the development of opium-smoking parlors, where the drug was consumed for recreational purposes.

**1676**   English physician Thomas Sydenham publishes *Medical Observations Concerning the History and Cure of Acute Diseases*, a book that includes a description of a new form of Paracelsus's laudanum. It is a simpler concoction of the drug, consisting primarily of two ounces of opium and one ounce of saffron dissolved in a pint of wine, to which might be added other spices to improve its flavor. He writes that "medicine would be a cripple without it" and that it could be used not only for "a means of procuring sleep or of allaying pain, or of checking diarrhoea," but for "many purposes besides."

**1729**   Chinese emperor Yung Chen issues an edict prohibiting the sale of opium and opium products and the operation of opium-smoking establishments. The ban does not apply to the use of opium for medical purposes. Subsequent rulers continue the ban on opium products primarily because it was regarded as a culturally degenerate practice.

**1750–1757**   The British East India Company seizes control of the Indian states of Bengal and Bihar, where the majority of opium produced in India is grown. Over time, the company develops and expands the exportation of opium to China, often through illegal activities (because its recreational use was still prohibited in the country).

**1750–1800**   The British East India Company gradually increases its control over the production and shipment of opium to China. The volume of exports increases fivefold between 1730 and 1767.

**1753**   In his classic work on taxonomy, *Genera Plantarum*, Swedish botanist Carl Linnaeus classifies opium as *Papaver* *somniferum*, a species in the genus *Papaver* and the family Papaveraceae. The classifier *somniferum* comes from the Latin for "sleep-inducing."

**1796**   Chinese emperor Kia King, concerned about the growing use and misuse of opium in the country, issues a new edict prohibiting the importation, growth, or use of the drug for any purpose whatsoever. The drug is essentially ruled to be illegal anywhere in the country. Shipments from India are largely unaffected, however, as opium is brought into China illegally through the Portuguese port of Macao.

**1800**   The British-chartered, Syrian-based Levant Company obtains a monopoly for the purchase of opium from Turkey, where some of the best-quality plants were grown. The product was then transshipped to England, parts of Europe, and the British colonies (including the United States), where problems with opium abuse became endemic. Opium misuse by parents for pacifying their babies and children becomes one of the major causes of death of young people in Great Britain.

**1803**   German chemist Friedrich Sertürner isolates morphine from opium. Morphine is the first plant alkaloid to have been isolated, and Sertürner's accomplishment soon inspires a wave of similar alkaloid research leading to the isolation of products such as atropine, caffeine, cocaine, and quinine over succeeding decades.

**1805**   A number of enterprising American businessmen, including Charles Cabot, John Cushing, and John Jacob Astor, develop operations for the shipment of opium from Turkey to China, through the port of Canton. British and American companies, therefore, are largely able to avoid the emperor's 1796 edict banning the importation of the drug.

**1816**   British poet Samuel Taylor Coleridge publishes his poem "Kubla Khan" (originally written in 1797). The work was inspired by an opium-induced dream about a fanciful kingdom of Xanadu, which he called "a stately pleasure-dome."

A number of Coleridge's contemporaries wrote similar paeans to the visions and emotions created by the use of opium for recreational purposes.

**1821**   English author Thomas De Quincey publishes perhaps the most famous of all literary works on opium, *Confessions of an Opium Eater.* He offers the observation that "whereas wine disorders the mental faculties, opium introduces amongst them the most exquisite order, legislation and harmony," in which "the diviner part of his nature is paramount."

**1827**   Merck company chooses morphine and aspirin as the two drugs it first begins producing in bulk quantities. Its success with these two drugs largely establishes Merck as one of the world's largest and most successful drug companies for well over a century.

**1833**   Opium trade between Great Britain and China is so great that the British government takes charge of the activity. At the time, the Chinese government continues to legislate and act against the importation and use of opium, while the British government tends to "look the other way" about use at home. Records indicate that the British import for domestic use a total of 22,000 pounds of the drug from Turkey and India in 1830.

**1839**   The dispute over the opium trade between Great Britain and China reaches a peak when court official Lin Tse-hsu is authorized by the emperor to take "whatever actions may be necessary" to end the importation of opium through the port of Canton. Lin's actions there include placing the foreign community in Canton under siege and appropriation of more than 20,000 chests of opium. Friction between the two nations reaches a peak, and war breaks out. The war, known as the First Opium War, lasts until 1842.

**1842**   The First Opium War ends with signing of the Nanking Treaty. Terms of the treaty include transfer of ownership of Hong Kong from China to Great Britain; the ports of Amoy,

Canton, Foochow, Ningpo, and Shankhai are opened to British ships; and limitations on Chinese taxes are imposed.

**1843**    Scottish physician Alexander Wood invents the hypodermic needle. Injection of morphine with the needle vastly increases the magnitude of the drug's effect and reduces the time for that effect to occur.

**1856**    Continuing friction between China and Great Britain following the First Opium War leads to the outbreak of hostilities again, resulting in the Second Opium War (also known as the Arrow War). The war lasts until 1860 when China surrenders and signs the Treaty of Tientsin. The treaty requires China to remove all restrictions on the use of opium and to open all of its ports to trade.

**1861–1865**    Morphine becomes the drug of choice for treating soldiers injured during the Civil War. The practice is so widespread that the use and abuse of morphine becomes known as the "army disease."

**ca. 1870**    The rise of patent medicines as treatment for a wide variety of diseases and illnesses begins in the United States. According to one survey, more than 50,000 patent medicines containing opium are available by 1900.

**1874**    English chemist Charles Romley Alder Wright produces a chemical derivative of morphine. His research is motivated by a desire to discover a compound that has all the medically beneficial qualities of morphine, without the risks of addiction associated with its use. He treats morphine with acetic acid, producing a compound known as diacetylmorphine, or heroin. The discovery obviously did not achieve its objective, although it did result in the formation of a new and later notable opioid.

**1875**    The San Francisco (California) Board of Supervisors adopts an ordinance making it illegal to "keep, or maintain, or visit, or in any way contribute to the support of such a place, house, or room, where opium is smoked." The ordinance is designed to provide some degree of control over opium smoking among the Chinese population, where as many as 30 percent are thought to be regular smokers. The ordinance is poorly enforced, as was the case in similar ordinances adopted shortly thereafter in other U.S. cities.

**1878**    The British Parliament adopts the Opium Act of 1878, limiting the sale of recreational opium to Indians and Chinese and prohibiting the sale at all to Burmese citizens.

**1887**    The U.S. Congress passes an act prohibiting the importation of opium by any Chinese, but not American, person. (Chinese individuals were prohibited from becoming citizens of the United States at the time.) The law is 24 Stat. L. 409.

**1890**    The U.S. Congress passes the first law regulating the use of opium for all citizens of the country. The law does not penalize the manufacture, sale, or use of the drug but does establish a tax of $10 per pound on "all opium manufactured in the United States for smoking purposes." The legislation appears to have had no effect on opium use in the country.

**1902**    Conquest of the Philippine islands by the United States in the Spanish-American War not only brought new land to American control but also introduced a challenging drug problem for the government. Historically, opium had been sold (but only to Chinese individuals) by a governmental monopoly. After the war, the U.S. government was faced with a challenge as to how it was to deal with opium smokers, eventually deciding to prohibit all use of the drug except for medical purposes.

**1902**    Physician C. B. Burr writes in the *Journal of the American Medical Association* about the problems of morphine addiction and its treatment. This article is one of the earliest commentaries on the addictive properties of morphine and heroin and their potential medical implications.

**1906**    The U.S. Congress passes one of the most significant public health acts in history, the Pure Food and Drug Law.

Motivated to a considerable extent about concerns over the sale and use of patent medicines, the act essentially banned the use of opium in most types of medication. The act had first been introduced in 1879 but failed to pass. It was reintroduced more than 200 times over the next 27 years before finally being passed in 1906.

**1909**   The first international conference on opium is held in Shanghai. The original purpose of the meeting is to consider ways of dealing with opium problems in China and the rest of Southeast Asia. The conference ultimately decides that the opium problem can be treated only from a worldwide perspective in which all nations consider ways in which they are involved in the opium trade. The conference adopts plans for an international treaty on the topic. (*See* **1912**.)

**1912**   The International Opium Convention is signed at The Hague, the Netherlands, by delegates from China, France, Germany, Italy, Japan, the Netherlands, Persia (Iran), Portugal, Russia, Siam (Thailand), the United Kingdom, and the United States. The treaty includes 25 articles in 6 chapters dealing with the control of all phases of opium trade, from growth and preparation to distribution and use. Although supposedly restricted to opium and morphine, the conference also adds cocaine and marijuana to drugs of concern to be covered by the treaty.

**1912**   Charles Edward Terry, then city chief of public health, proposes a system for monitoring opium use in the city. His plan calls for (1) pharmacists to report to Terry's office cases in which a person has been prescribed more than three grains of opium and (2) the city to establish a clinic for providing narcotics to individuals who are thus identified as being addicted to the drug. (Cocaine addiction is also included in the plan.) Terry's clinic is the first of its type in the United States. (*Also see* **1924** and **1925**.)

**1914**   In an effort to develop an orderly system for the control of opium use in the United States, Congress passes the Harrison Narcotics Act of 1914. The act establishes "a special tax on all persons who produce, import, manufacture, com-pound, deal in, dispense, sell, distribute, or give away opium or coca leaves, their salts, derivatives, or preparations." Anyone dealing with any aspect of the drug must also register for the purpose. The act is not clear about the medical uses of opium although courts later interpret the act to permit medical uses of the drug, provided it is not made available to opium users.

**1916** German chemists Martin Freund and Edmund Speyer synthesize oxycodone.

**1920** German chemists Carl Mannich and Helene Löwen-heim synthesize hydrocodone.

**1922** The U.S. Congress passes the Narcotic Drug Import and Export Act, a document that largely restates and reinforces bans on the importation of opium into the country. Cocaine is added to the list of prohibited drugs, which are, for the first time in U.S. history, referred to collectively as *narcotics*. The act also creates a Federal Narcotics Control Board, consisting of three cabinet members, to carry out provisions on the act. In the following year (1923), the board adopts a ban on importa-tion and sale of all narcotic drugs.

**1924** The Heroin Act of 1924 bans the manufacture, impor-tation, possession, and use of heroin for any reason whatsoever in the United States, including all medical applications.

**1924** The idea of special clinics designed to provide narcot-ics to drug addicts (*see* **1912**) becomes so popular that 34 such clinics in 12 states have been created. The largest such clinic (Atlanta) reports having 525 clients and the smallest (Meriden, Connecticut) 2.

**1924** Researchers at the German pharmaceutical company Knoll synthesize hydromorphone.

**1925** The U.S. Treasury Department closes the last remain-ing narcotics treatment clinic in Knoxville, Tennessee. The department's argument was that maintenance clinics were in-terfering with other efforts to cure addiction.

**1928**    American physician Charles E. Terry and his wife, Mildred Pellens, publish one of the most comprehensive studies on opium in U.S. history, *The Opium Problem*.

**1930/1932 (?)**    German chemist Otto Eisleb (or Eislib) synthesizes the first synthetic opioid, pethidine (Dolantin, Demerol). The compound's narcotic effects are later discovered by another Farben chemist, Otto Schaumann, in 1939. The drug was found to have about a tenth of the potency as morphine and, therefore, safe for general use. This belief was later shown to be incorrect, and the compound is later found to be addictive also.

**1936**    Representatives of a number of nations meet in Geneva to adopt the Convention for the Suppression of the Illicit Traffic in Dangerous Drugs, an effort to criminalize trafficking in illegal drugs. When the United States finds itself unable to support the final document, it loses any chance of being a strong partner in preventing the worldwide distribution of illegal drugs.

**1937**    In their search for a substance that could be used as a surgical anesthesia, two researchers at the firm of IG Farben, Max Bockmühl and Gustav Ehrhart, synthesize a compound that they call Hoechst 10820, or polamidon. The compound's name is later changed to *methadone*, a substance that has been used as an analgesic and treatment of narcotic addiction.

**1942**    The U.S. Congress passes the Opium Poppy Control Act of 1942, prohibiting the growing of opium poppies (*Papaver somniferum*) in the United States. The act is made necessary by the loss of poppy seed imports, used almost exclusively in food preparations, by the outbreak of World War II.

**1948**    The United Nations sponsors an international conference to update a treaty for the control of narcotic drugs signed in 1931. The document signed at the meeting is called the Protocol Bringing under International Control Drugs outside the Scope of the Convention of 13 July 1931 for Limiting the Manufacture and Regulating the Distribution of Narcotic Drugs.

It takes an important step in recognizing that a number of substances not previously defined formally as illegal substances—including a number of synthetic products—have effects similar to those of marijuana, cocaine, heroin, morphine, and other "traditional" drugs.

**1951** The U.S. Congress passes the Boggs Act of 1952, named after Louisiana congressman Hale Boggs. The act imposes severe penalties for drug convictions: a $2,000 fine (in all cases) and imprisonment for 2–5 years, for a first offense; 5–10 years, for a second offense; and 10–20 years for a third offense.

**1956** The Narcotics Control Act of 1956 amends the Boggs Act of 1951 (*see* **1951**), significantly increasing the penalty for the importation, sale, and use of opiates. A first offense may be punished with a fine of up to $20,000 and imprisonment of 2–10 years. For second and third offenses, the penalties rise to a fine of $20,000 (in both cases) and terms of imprisonment from 5 to 20 years and 10 to 40 years, respectively.

**1959** Belgian physician Paul Janssen synthesizes the opioid fentanyl. It was first used as an intravenous anesthetic in the mid-1990s and, by the middle of the 2010s, had become one of the most popular drugs used by opioid abusers and addicts.

**1961** A conference sponsored by the United Nations adopts the Single Convention on Narcotic Drugs, an effort to update and consolidate a number of previously adopted conventions, protocols, and agreements on the manufacture, distribution, and sale of illegal drugs, including the International Opium Convention of 1912; the Agreement Concerning the Manufacture of, Internal Trade in, and Use of Prepared Opium of 1925; the International Opium Convention of 1925; the Convention for Limiting the Manufacture and Regulating the Distribution of Narcotic Drugs of 1931; the Agreement for the Control of Opium Smoking in the Far East of 1931; the Protocol Amending the Agreements, Conventions and Protocols on Narcotic Drugs of 1912; 1925, 1931, 1936, and 1946; the Protocol Bringing under International Control Drugs outside the Scope of the Convention of 1931; and the Protocol for Limiting and Regulating the Cultivation of the Poppy Plant, the Production of, International and Wholesale Trade in, and Use of Opium of 1953.

**1970**   The Comprehensive Drug Abuse Prevention and Control Act (commonly known simply as the Controlled Substances Act) is adopted as an attempt to consolidate all drug-related laws passed up to this date. It also establishes a classification system for drugs that includes five categories, or "schedules." Opium, its derivatives, and related compounds are all placed in Schedule I. Drugs in this category meet the three criteria: the drug (1) has a high potential for abuse; (2) has no currently accepted medical use in treatment in the United States; and (3) lacks acceptable safety standards for use of the drug or other substance under medical supervision. For drugs in this category, it is illegal for any person to manufacture, distribute, or dispense, or possess with intent to manufacture, distribute, or dispense a controlled substance; or to create, distribute, or dispense, or possess with intent to distribute or dispense a counterfeit substance.

**1973**   As part of Reorganization Plan No. 2, President Richard M. Nixon establishes the Drug Enforcement Administration. The action is taken to deal with the "supply" part of the nation's drug problem, complementing the Controlled Substances Act of 1970, designed to control the "demand" side of the problem. The intent of the act was to bring all federal agencies responsible for the control of drug traffic in the country under a single office.

**1974**   The Narcotic Addict Treatment Act of 1974 amends the Controlled Substances Act of 1970 to provide, for the first time in American history, registration of physicians allowed to treat narcotic addicts with opiates and/or opioids. Also for the first time, it provides legal definitions and authorizations for *maintenance treatment* and *detoxification treatment* programs.

The act also created the National Institute on Drug Abuse (NIDA) whose purpose it was to conduct research on and make recommendations about drug-related issues.

**1986**   The U.S. Congress passes the Anti-Drug Abuse Act of 1986. The act consists of two major titles, one dealing with Anti-Drug Enforcement and the other with International Narcotics Control. The first title is divided into 21 subtitles dealing with a host of issues, perhaps the most important of which is Subtitle E: Controlled Substances Analogue Enforcement Act of 1986, which states that substances that are chemically and pharmacologically similar to substances listed in Schedule I or Schedule II of the Controlled Substances Act of 1970 (known as analogs of the listed drugs) are also classified as Schedule I drugs. As a consequence, all opiates, opioids, and other compounds related to them and/or to opium are also classified in the same schedule as is opium itself.

**1988**   The Anti-Drug Abuse Act of 1988 for the first time imposes penalties on users of illegal drugs. Prior to this time, penalties for illegal drug use were limited to producers and distributors of such substances. One provision of the act establishes the Office of National Drug Control Policy, with responsibility for developing policies for control of the nation's drug abuse problems.

**1994**   The Violent Crime Control and Law Enforcement Act of 1994 introduces the death penalty for anyone convicted of operating large-scale drug distribution programs, one of the first times the death penalty is permitted for crimes in which a death is not involved.

**2000**   The Drug Addiction Treatment Act of 2000 allows, for the first time, certain qualifying physicians to treat patients with opioid addictions in their private office or a clinical setting. They may also prescribe and dispense appropriate drugs for such treatments. The only drug that meets the conditions for such programs at the time is buprenorphine.

**2008**  The FDA approves release of tapendatol, the first narcotic analgesic acting on the central nervous system approved in almost three decades in the United States. Tapendatol has analgesic effects less than those of morphine but more than a number of other opioids. It is listed as a schedule II drug and becomes commercially available in 2009.

**2010**  The FDA approves the release of a reformulated version of the popular drug OxyContin that makes it more difficult to inhale or inject, thus reducing the risk of the drug's being used for nonmedical purposes. The drug manufacturer, Purdue Pharma, discontinues shipping the original OxyContin formulation to pharmacies.

**2010**  The number of prescriptions written for opioid analgesics reaches 209.5 million, a nearly 300 percent increase over the number written only 20 years before in 1991 (75.5 million).

**2014**  Reflecting concerns about its use for nonmedical purposes, the DEA reschedules the drug hydrocodone from Schedule III to Schedule II in the national Schedules of Controlled Substances.

**2016**  President Barack Obama signs the Comprehensive Addiction and Recovery Act of 2016, making a number of changes and additions to the whole range of drug addiction, ranging from prevention programs to recovery options for drug abusers and addicts. Among the provisions of the act are improved access to overdose treatment, more liberal approaches to private physician treatment of drug addiction, extending of treatment options to nurse practitioners and physicians' assistants, and state demonstration grants for experimental approaches to the prevention and treatment of drug abuse and addiction.

**2017**  President Donald Trump declares the nation's opioid abuse and addiction problems a "national health emergency, unlike many of us we've seen."

**2017**   Researchers at the Albany Medical College and Albert Einstein College of Medicine report that a combination of over-the-counter pain medications is as effective in treating severe pain as is a standard dose of opioids.

**2017**   NIDA reports that more than 64,000 Americans died of opioid overdoses in 2016, the most recent year for which data are available. The number represents an increase of 280 percent over totals for 2002.

# Glossary

An understanding of the nature of opioids and related issues usually depends on mastering a number of new and unfamiliar concepts. This glossary provides definitions for some of the important words used in this book, as well as other terms one may encounter on additional reading or research about opioids.

**addiction** A long-lasting and typically recurring psychological and/or physiological need for one or more substances, such as alcohol, tobacco, or opioids, that generally results in permanent or long-lasting changes in the neurochemistry of the brain.

**agonist** A chemical that binds to a receptor, usually in the central nervous system, and activates that receptor. Agonists may be classified as **full agonists**, which block a receptor site completely, and **partial agonists**, which block a receptor less completely.

**analgesic** A drug capable of relieving pain. Opioids are one type of widely used analgesics.

**analog** (also **analogue**) A chemical compound similar in structure to some other chemical compound.

**antagonist** A chemical that binds to a receptor, usually in the central nervous system, and then blocks the action of that receptor.

**buprenorphine**    A semisynthetic narcotic analgesic that acts as a partial opioid agonist, thereby relieving the symptoms of opioid withdrawal such as agitation, nausea, and insomnia.

**central nervous system (CNS)**    The brain and spinal cord.

**chemical dependence**    A condition that develops when one's body undergoes changes that result in a continual physiological need for a particular drug or other substance.

**chronic**    Any condition that persists over long periods of time.

**dependence**    A condition in which an individual develops a fixation on or craving for a drug that is not necessarily so severe as to be classified as an addiction but that may, nonetheless, require professional help to overcome.

**detoxification**    The process by which an individual is aided in the process of withdrawing from drug abuse or addiction.

**dopamine**    A neurotransmitter whose action is responsible for a number of mental states, including pleasure, feelings of emotion, physical movements, and motivation to take action.

**drug**    A chemical used in the diagnosis, cure, mitigation, treatment, or prevention of disease or to bring about an alternation in one's mental or emotional state.

**drug diversion**    The process during which a legal drug, such as a prescription opioid, is transferred to another person for whom it was not originally prescribed or intended.

**enabling**    The act of supporting or contributing to the destructive behavior of a substance abuser, sometimes based on the enabler's best intentions of helping that person.

**endogenous**    Produced naturally within the body.

**euphoria**    A sense of happiness, ease, pleasure, joy, and/or well-being.

**exogenous**    Produced outside the body.

**full agonist**    *See* **agonist**.

**intervention** An event in which a group of individuals confront a substance abuser with the demand for specific action by that person to begin dealing with his or her addiction.

**laudanum** A tincture of opium, that is, opium powder dissolved in alcohol.

**ligand** A molecule or ion that binds to a (usually) larger molecule to form a new unified structure. When an opioid bonds to a receptor site, it results in the formation of a ligand that consists of the receptor site and the opioid molecule.

**maintenance** A stage of drug treatment and recovery during which a person is given opioid drugs to assist him or her through the period of withdrawing from opioid abuse or addiction. The three opioid maintenance drugs approved for use in the United States by the U.S. Food and Drug Administration are methadone, buprenorphine, and naltrexone.

**MAT** *See* **medication-assisted therapy**.

**medication-assisted therapy** The use of medications, in combination with counseling and behavioral therapies, to provide a "whole-patient" approach to the treatment of opioid and other substance use disorders.

**methadone** An opioid agonist that affects receptors in the same way that opioids do. It is often used in the treatment of opioid abuse or addiction.

**morbidity** Illness.

**mortality** Death.

**multiple drug use** A situation in which an individual abuses or becomes addicted to more than one psychotropic drug at the same time. Experts currently believe that the vast majority of opioid abuse, addiction, and overdose cases involve multiple drug use.

**naloxone** A synthetic opioid antagonist that blocks opioid uptake and is most commonly used in cases of opioid overdose. Its best known commercial name is Narcan.

**naltrexone**    A synthetic opioid antagonist that blocks heroin uptake and is, therefore, used primarily in the treatment of heroin addiction, especially during recovery phases of treatment.

**Narcan.** *See* **naloxone.**

**narcotic**    Any drug that, in small doses, produces insensitivity to pain, dulls the senses, and induces deep sleep but in larger doses may result in numbness, convulsions, and coma. The term has historically been used to refer to opium, opiates, and opioids.

**neurotransmitter**    A chemical that carries a nerve impulse between two neurons.

**opiate**    Any drug or other substance derived from or chemically related to opium.

**opiate/opioid receptor**    A molecule or portion of a molecule that recognizes and binds to the opium molecule and other molecules similar in structure to it. The three most common types of opioid receptors are called delta (δ), kappa (κ), and mu (μ) receptors.

**opioid**    Any substance, natural or synthetic, related to opium in its chemical structure and pharmacological effects.

**opium**    An addictive narcotic extracted from the seeds of the opium poppy, *Papaver somniferum.*

**overdose**    (verb) To take an excessive, risky, and potentially fatal quantity of a harmful substance.

**partial agonist**    *See* **agonist**.

**precursor chemical**    A chemical used to make some other substance, for example, the raw materials used to make illicit drugs.

**prescription drug**    A drug that can be purchased only with a medical prescription provided by a registered medical provider, such as a physician or a physician's assistant.

**psychotropic**    Having an effect on the mind.

**relapse**    The return of a condition, such as addiction to or dependency on a drug, which had formerly been successfully overcome.

**Schedule (drug)**    A category into which the federal government classifies certain drugs based on their potential medical use and their possibility of illicit recreational applications.

**semisynthetic opioids**    Opioids whose molecules consist partially of natural opium extracts and partly of synthetic additions. Some common semisynthetic opioids are oxycodone, oxymorphone, and hydrocodone.

**serotonin**    A neurotransmitter associated with a number of mental and emotional functions, including appetite, learning, memory, mood, muscular contraction, and sleep. A number of drugs reduce or increase the amount of serotonin available in the brain, thereby moderating one or more of these actions.

**synaptic gap**    The space between two neurons.

**tolerance**    Developing immunity to the effects caused by a substance such that one requires a larger amount of the substance over time to achieve the same results obtained from smaller amounts earlier on in its use.

**withdrawal**    The process by which an individual is able to stop using a harmful drug.

abstinence treatment approach, 106–107

Academy of Integrative Pain Management (AIPM), 171–173

acetylation, 195

acetylsalicylic acid, 195

Act Concerning Involuntary Commitment to Treatment for Substance Use Disorders, 2016, 263–265

Act to Prevent Opiate Abuse by Strengthening the Controlled Substances Prescription Monitoring Program, 2016, 260–263

addiction, 167
versus. dependence, 44
opioid, 43–44
opium, 22–23
treatment of, 106–114
in women versus men, 23

Addiction, Recovery, and Coping (ARC) (A-B Tech event), 144

Addiction Research Center, 203

Advocates for Opioid Recovery (AOR), 174–176

agonist/antagonist theory, addiction treatment and, 107–111

agonists, described, 108

AIPM. *See* Academy of Integrative Pain Management

*al-Bayan fi al-human* (*Important Measurements of the Human Body*) (Ibn Sallum), 12

Alcoholics Anonymous 12-step program, 106–107

Alexander the Great, 12–13

Allergan, 78, 181

multistate legislation of
opiates, 92–93
Muslim opium use, 11–12

Nalone, 110, 190
naloxone, 110, 190
naltrexone, 110
Narcan, 110, 190
Narcanti, 110, 190
narceine, 24
Narcon, 110
Narcotan, 190
Narcotic Control Act of
1956, 34
Narcotic Drug Import and
Export Act of 1922, 33
narcotics, availability of,
grades 8, 10, and 12,
241–243
narcotine, 24
National Alliance for Model
State Drug Laws, 182
National Alliance of
Advocates for
Buprenorphine
Treatment (NAABT),
199–201
National Association of
Attorneys General, 182
National Association of State
Controlled Substances
Authorities (NASCSA),
201–202
National Council on
Alcoholism, 178

National District Attorneys
Association, 182
National Family Partnership,
182
National Governors
Association, 182
National Health Council,
177
National Institute on
Drug Abuse (NIDA),
202–205
National Sheriffs'
Association, 182
"Neat, Plausible, and
Generally Wrong: A
Response to the CDC
Recommendations for
Chronic Opioid Use"
(Martin, Potee, and
Lazris), 85
neonatal abstinence
syndrome (NAS),
68–71
treatment of, 110–111
*nepenthes,* 9
neurotransmitters, 42
*New England Journal of
Medicine,* 76, 158
New York Medical Society on
Alcoholism (NYMSA),
178–179
Nixon, Richard M., 203
Northeastern University,
182
noscapine, 24

## About the Author

**David E. Newton** holds an associate's degree in science from Grand Rapids (Michigan) Junior College, a BA in chemistry (with high distinction), an MA in education from the University of Michigan, and an EdD in science education from Harvard University. He is the author of more than 400 textbooks, encyclopedias, resource books, research manuals, laboratory manuals, trade books, and other educational materials. He taught mathematics, chemistry, and physical science in Grand Rapids, Michigan, for 13 years; was professor of chemistry and physics at Salem State College in Massachusetts for 15 years; and was adjunct professor in the College of Professional Studies at the University of San Francisco for 10 years.

The author's previous books for ABC-CLIO include *Global Warming* (1993), *Gay and Lesbian Rights* (1994, 2009), *The Ozone Dilemma* (1995), *Violence and the Mass Media* (1996), *Environmental Justice* (1996, 2009), *Encyclopedia of Cryptology* (1997), *Social Issues in Science and Technology: An Encyclopedia* (1999), *DNA Technology* (2009, 2016), *Sexual Health* (2010), *The Animal Experimentation Debate* (2013), *Marijuana* (2013, 2017), *World Energy Crisis* (2013), *Steroids and Doping in Sports* (2014, 2018), *GMO Food* (2014), *Science and Political Controversy* (2014), *Wind Energy* (2015), *Fracking* (2015), *Solar Energy* (2015), *Youth Substance Abuse* (2016), *Global Water Crisis* (2016), *Youth Drug Abuse* (2016), *Same-Sex Marriage* (2011, 2016), *Sex and Gender* (2017), and *Sexually Transmitted Diseases* (2018). His other recent books include *Physics: Oryx Frontiers of Science Series* (2000), *Sick!* (four volumes) (2000);

*Science, Technology, and Society: The Impact of Science in the 19th Century* (two volumes, 2001); *Encyclopedia of Fire* (2002); *Molecular Nanotechnology: Oryx Frontiers of Science Series* (2002); *Encyclopedia of Water* (2003); *Encyclopedia of Air* (2004); *The New Chemistry* (six volumes, 2007); *Nuclear Power* (2005); *Stem Cell Research* (2006); *Latinos in the Sciences, Math, and Professions* (2007); and *DNA Evidence and Forensic Science* (2008). He has also been an updating and consulting editor on a number of books and reference works, including *Chemical Compounds* (2005); *Chemical Elements* (2006); *Encyclopedia of Endangered Species* (2006); *World of Mathematics* (2006); *World of Chemistry* (2006); *World of Health* (2006); *UXL Encyclopedia of Science* (2007); *Alternative Medicine* (2008); *Grzimek's Animal Life Encyclopedia* (2009); *Community Health* (2009); *Genetic Medicine* (2009); *The Gale Encyclopedia of Medicine* (2010–2011); *The Gale Encyclopedia of Alternative Medicine* (2013); *Discoveries in Modern Science: Exploration, Invention, and Technology* (2013–2014); and *Science in Context* (2013–2014).